The Selected Writings of James Weldon Johnson

The Selected Writings of James Weldon Johnson

VOLUME I

THE *NEW YORK AGE* EDITORIALS (1914–1923)

Edited by   Sondra Kathryn Wilson

New York Oxford   Oxford University Press   1995

Oxford University Press

Oxford   New York
Athens   Auckland   Bangkok   Bombay
Calcutta   Capetown   Dar es Salaam   Delhi
Florence   Hong Kong   Istanbul   Karachi
Kuala Lumpur   Madras   Madrid   Melbourne
Mexico City   Nairobi   Paris   Singapore
Taipei   Tokyo   Toronto

and associated companies in
Berlin   Ibadan

Published by Oxford University Press, Inc.,
200 Madison Avenue, New York, New York 10016

Library of Congress Cataloging-in-Publication Data
Johnson, James Weldon, 1871–1938.
[Selections. 1995]
The selected writings of James Weldon Johnson
edited by Sondra Kathryn Wilson.
p. cm.   Includes bibliographical references and index.
Contents: v. 1. The New York Age editorials (1914–1923)
v. 2. Social, political, and literary essays.
ISBN 0–19–507644–3 (v. 1)
1. Afro-Americans—Politics and government.
2. Afro-Americans—Intellectual life.
3. Afro-Americans—History.
I. Wilson, Sondra K.   II. Title.
PS3519.O2625A6   1995   814'.52—dc20
94–31400

Printed in the United States of America
on acid free paper

9 8 7 6 5 4 3 2 1

To

O. Jewel Sims Okala

Keeper of the

James Weldon Johnson tradition

and

Laura Clemmons Powell

Honor Spingarn Tranum

With very special thanks to Henry Louis Gates, Jr.

and the staff of the W. E. B. Du Bois Institute, Harvard University

Contents

THREE

New York Age Literary Editorials

James Weldon Johnson
(June 17, 1871–June 26, 1938)

A Chronology

1871   Born to James and Helen Louise Dillet Johnson on June 17 in Jacksonville, Florida.

1884   Makes trip to New York City.

1886   Meets Frederick Douglass in Jacksonville.

1887   Graduates from Stanton School, Jacksonville; enters Atlanta University Preparatory Division.

1890   Graduates from Atlanta University Preparatory Division. Enters Atlanta University's freshman class.

1891   Teaches school in Henry County, Georgia, during the summer following his freshman year.

1892   Wins Atlanta University Oratory Prize for "The Best Methods of Removing the Disabilities of Caste from the Negro."

1893   Meets Paul Laurence Dunbar at the Chicago World's Fair.

1894   Receives B.A. degree with honors from Atlanta University. Delivers valedictory speech "The Destiny of the Human Race." Tours New England with the Atlanta University Quartet for three months. Is appointed principal of Stanton School in Jacksonville, Florida, the largest African-American public school in the state.

1895   Founds the *Daily American*, an afternoon daily serving Jacksonville's black population.

1896   Expands Stanton School to high school status, making it the first public high school for blacks in the state of Florida.

1898   Becomes the first African-American to be admitted to the Florida bar.

1900   Writes the lyrics to "Lift Every Voice and Sing" with music by his brother J. Rosamond Johnson. Meets his future wife, Grace Nail, in New York.

1901   Elected president of the Florida State Teachers Association. Nearly lynched in a Jacksonville park. This near lynching made him realize that he could not advance in the South.

1902   Resigns as principal of Stanton School. Moves to New York to form musical trio—Cole and the Johnson Brothers. As part of this trio he writes over 200 popular songs, many of which are used in Broadway productions.

1903   Attends graduate school at Columbia University, where he studies with Brander Matthews, professor of dramatic literature.

1904   Writes two songs for Theodore Roosevelt's presidential campaign. Becomes a member of the National Business League, an organization founded by Booker T. Washington. Receives honorary degree from Atlanta University. During this time he meets W. E. B. Du Bois, then a professor at Atlanta University.

1905   Cole and the Johnson Brothers go on European tour. Becomes president of the Colored Republican Club in New York City.

1906   Accepts membership in the American Society of International Law. Is appointed U.S. consul to Venezuela by President Roosevelt.

1909   Is promoted to U.S. consul to Nicaragua.

1910   Marries Grace Elizabeth Nail, daughter of well-known Harlem businessman John Bennett Nail, on February 3, in New York City.

1912   Publishes anonymously *The Autobiography of an Ex-Colored Man,* probably the earliest first-person narrative in fiction written by an African-American.

1913   Resigns from the consular service on account of race prejudice and party politics.

1914   Accepts position at the *New York Age* as contributing editor. Becomes a founding member of The American Society of Composers, Authors, and Publishers (ASCAP). Joins Sigma Pi Phi fraternity and Phi Beta Sigma fraternity.

1915   Becomes member of the NAACP. Puts into English the libretto of *Goyescas,* the Spanish grand opera, which is produced at the Metropolitan Opera House.

1916   Attends the NAACP Conference in Amenia, New York, at the estate of J. E. Spingarn. Delivers speech "A Working Programme for the Future." Joins the staff of the NAACP in the position of field secretary.

1917   Publishes volume *Fifty Years and Other Poems.* Publishes poem *Saint Peter Relates an Incident of the Resurrection Day.* With W. E. B. Du

Bois, leads over 12,000 marchers down New York's Fifth Avenue to protest lynchings and riots. Becomes acting secretary of the NAACP. Supports U.S. entry into World War I and fights against the atrocities perpetrated against black soldiers. Meets Walter White in Atlanta and persuades him to join the staff of the NAACP. Attends conference of the Intercollegiate Socialist Society in Bellport, New York; gives talk on the contribution of the Negro to American culture. With W. E. B. Du Bois, becomes charter member of the Civic Club, a liberal club that grew to be a strong influence in the life of Negro New Yorkers.

1918   Is responsible for an unprecedented increase in NAACP membership in one year, particularly in the South, making the NAACP a national power.

1919   Prepares the first statistical analysis of lynching. Participates in converting the National Civil Liberties Bureau, a permanent organization, to the American Civil Liberties Union.

1920   NAACP board of directors name him secretary, making him the first African-American to serve in that position. Based on his earlier investigation of the American Occupation of Haiti, he publishes four articles on "Self-Determining Haiti" in the *Nation.*

1922   Publishes *The Book of American Negro Poetry.*

1924   Assists several writers of the Harlem Renaissance.

1925   Receives NAACP's Spingarn Medal. Co-authors with J. Rosamond Johnson *The Book of American Negro Spirituals.*

1926   Co-authors with J. Rosamond Johnson *The Second Book of American Negro Spirituals.* Purchases an old farm in the Massachusetts Berkshires and builds a summer cottage called "Five Acres."

1927   During the height of the Harlem Renaissance, *The Autobiography of an Ex-Coloured Man* is reprinted. (The spelling *coloured* was used to attract British sales of the book.) *God's Trombones* is published.

1928   Receives Harmon Award for *God's Trombones.* Receives D. Litt. from Howard University and Talledega College.

1929   Takes a leave of absence from the NAACP. Attends the Third Japanese Biennial Conference on Pacific Relations. Receives Julius Rosenwald Fellowship to write *Black Manhattan.*

1930   Publishes *Black Manhattan.* Publishes *Saint Peter Relates an Incident* in a small private edition. Resigns as secretary of the NAACP on December 17.

1931   Publishes the revised and enlarged edition of *The Book of American Negro Poetry*. NAACP honors him by hosting a testimonial dinner in New York City attended by over 300 guests. Is appointed vice president and board member of the NAACP. Accepts Fisk University appointment as the Adam K. Spence Professor of Creative Literature.

1933   Publishes autobiography *Along This Way*. Attends the Second NAACP Amenia Conference.

1934   Is appointed visiting professor, fall semester, at New York University, becoming the first African-American to hold such a position at the institution. Receives the Du Bois Prize for *Black Manhattan* for the best book of prose written by an African-American during a three-year period. Publishes *Negro Americans, What Now?*

1935   Publishes *Saint Peter Relates an Incident: Selected Poems*.

1938   Dies as the result of an automobile accident in Wiscasset, Maine, nine days after his 67th birthday on June 26. Funeral held at the Salem Methodist Church in Harlem on Thursday, June 30. Is cremated and interred in the Nail family plot in Green-Wood Cemetery in Brooklyn, New York.

The Selected Writings of James Weldon Johnson

Introduction

Frequently one gets the impression that James Weldon Johnson does not get his historical due regarding the quest for freedom in America. He often seems immobile and mired in the preforties period of the black struggle. The *New York Age* editorials by Johnson presented in this volume will demonstrate the flaws of such a notion by shedding light on his centrality and historical significance in the African-American journey. Moreover, the editorials included here create a relevant and dynamic present by providing a unique opportunity for revivification of many of the unresolved conflicts. The real challenge of this volume is for readers to view James Weldon Johnson's ideas in light of the present African-American experience and discover for themselves that his insights are ageless.

During lectures, social engagements, and in general human contact, I am frequently asked how I became involved with the life of James Weldon Johnson. As a doctoral student at Columbia University during the early 1980s, I lived in a book-cluttered studio apartment on the university's campus. Propped in bed on several pillows one morning around 2 A.M. reading the newly released autobiography *Standing Fast* by the late civil rights leader Roy Wilkins, I was caught by Wilkins's characterization of James Weldon Johnson. Wilkins recalled his first encounter with Johnson during the NAACP Kansas City Conference of 1923. He wrote, "And it was my first chance to see the leaders of the NAACP—James Weldon Johnson, the poet, playwright, lawyer, diplomat, and gentleman. . . ."[1] Having distinguished himself in a myriad of careers, Johnson's life, I thought, was undoubtedly one of valiancy and triumph.

That Johnson's roles as literary artist and charismatic race leader stand in need of closer scrutiny is hardly questionable. His success as a literary artist is anchored in the oral traditions of his people. He realized that it was only out of these sources that the power—sometimes mythic, sometimes symbolic—came to withstand racism. The African-American tradition as conceived by Johnson was dependent on its ability to relate to the unique human situation facing oppressed people universally and black people specifically. To the extent that he did this it can be said he was successful.

He had been deeply affected by the majestic beauty of the Negro Spirituals and the artistic power of the old-time black church sermons that came out of the hearts and souls of a people in captivity—a people who reshaped a Christian cosmology to fit their spiritual needs and ultimately transformed American Protestantism along the way.[2] These people did not record their oral traditions, but Johnson's writings became an instrument for reproducing the black spirit. As literary artist, James Weldon Johnson created an important body of American literature based on the developing black ethos.

Johnson was one of the NAACP's most talented and sanguine tacticians during the 1920s. When he joined the staff of the NAACP in 1916, there were seventy-one branches. By 1919, there were 441 branches. According to NAACP Chairman of the Board J. E. Spingarn, Johnson's organizing skills were pivotal in making the NAACP a national power. Undoubtedly Johnson's success in building public opinion through education helped to make his selection as the first African-American to head the NAACP inevitable in 1920. NAACP Field Secretary Robert Bagnall wrote, "Found every branch I visited clamoring for the ratification of Johnson as Executive Secretary."[3]

In pondering the legacy of Johnson, I became beleaguered by the divergence between his important and numerous contributions and the undersized level of his recognition within American culture. This concern brought me to this present work. I have spent over ten years in careful study of the life and voluminous writings of James Weldon Johnson. As I worked, my conviction that his influence must be subsumed into mainstream twenty-first-century American thought grew stronger.

In this volume, however, my endeavor is far more modest than that. My aim here is to show that James Weldon Johnson was a "mass educator" for all Americans but, more specifically, for black Americans. As editor of the *New York Age*, he knew that the real movement against white oppression in America during the early part of the twentieth century would have to come from the oppressed themselves. The black press as a racial institution takes second place to the black church in terms of the number of people it reaches and its degree of influence. With this power comes a critically significant responsibility—to determine what information is needed to educate black America. Johnson's diversified background qualified him as one of the ablest persons of the day to take on such an important challenge. This position placed him in the forefront as a leading spokesperson for black America.

In focusing on Johnson as a mass educator, I hope to show that his writings served as a means of generating public opinion to build the early civil rights movement in America. In the pages of the *Age,* he assumed several secondary roles within the context of his primary role of mass educator. He was exemplary as an agitator, a philosopher, a literary critic, and a mentor to aspiring creative artists.[4] I have called Johnson's *Age* editorials a colossal rebuttal to the absurdity of American race prejudice. He used his power as a writer to present race prejudice as such a foolish and absurd thing that even those who practiced it should have been compelled to see that it was ridiculous.

My aim in presenting Johnson as a mass educator is supported by a model that I devised to explain his possible methods to influence, expose, attack, and interpret. Without this model, what I am trying to convey to the reader might prove elusive. This model consists of four critically significant concepts that reveal the prevailing themes of Johnson's editorials. They are:

1. *White America's contradictions.* By Johnson's trenchant focus on lynching and mob violence and other forms of race prejudice, Johnson skillfully revealed to his readers the contradictions between white America's actions and the aims of the United States Constitution. He articulated, too, that it was the "Negro" who believed that the Constitution meant exactly what it said. This led him to conclude that to a large extent blacks were being better Americans than many white citizens.

2. *Race pride.* Johnson's emphasis on the presentation and discussion of African-American heritage was paramount in advancing identity acquisition and ultimately race pride. Every activity of significance related to African-American life engaged his attention, and he in turn informed his readers.

3. *Strategies to combat white oppression.* Johnson understood that finding workable methods to alleviate white oppression required determination, skill, and effort. In the pages of the *Age,* he often examined several methods to help extirpate the race problem, and he subsequently focused on the method that he believed to be the most sound.

4. *Universality.* My use of the concept "universality" centers on Johnson's acknowledgment of the problems within the African-American community. In an editorial included in Chapter 9, "Ruffianism in Harlem" (April 29, 1915), we see him denounce Harlem hoodlumism. Johnson reminded his readers that the problems experienced within the African-American community were not unique to them. In varying degrees, the same problems existed within every group. We see Johnson substantiate this notion by using the universal to explain the particular, and he simultaneously uses the particular to explain the universal.

I have provided an Editor's Note to introduce each chapter in this volume, emphasizing its educative relevance based on the four concepts of the model: white America's contradictions, race pride, strategies to combat white oppression, and universality.

Beginning in 1914 and for nearly ten years, Johnson's weekly column for the *New York Age* appeared beneath the masthead "Views and Reviews." The *Age,* the oldest of the New York black papers, was one of the most influential newspapers in the country. Johnson was forty-three when he arrived at the *Age,* and he had already achieved wide recognition in a number of careers. Nevertheless, in each career, limitations had been placed on him on account of race. But now, for the first time, he could identify and articulate his positions on the contemporary issues related to black life. Working directly for the Black Cause, we see him record his strongest protest voice yet revealed.[5] Johnson articulated the function of his editorials in his second column. Black papers are not simply newspapers, he proclaimed. "They are race papers. They are organs of propaganda."[6] He also made it known in his early columns that he favored protest for justice tied to as much unyielding political and economic pressure that black people could muster.

In his weekly column, Johnson taught African-Americans what this nation's Constitution should mean for them within the continental boundaries of the United States of America. The editorials presented in this volume are indeed a reflection of that education. These writings are done in a precise, methodical, and calm manner. There are no examples of baseless accusations that might fuel the fire of racial hatred. On the one hand, he labored to reveal the mechanisms by which blacks were estranged from themselves through his interpretation of the impact of racism on their lives. On the other hand, he showed whites the scars that were inflicted by the chains of racism. It was these scars that make his writings irrefutable. These editorials are representative of a man in search of a reclamation or acquisition of humanity for his people. As a political, social, and cultural visionary, James Weldon Johnson understood that the United States could not achieve the promise of the Constitution until all of its people were free.

One | New York Age Social Editorials

7 | Race Prejudice and Discrimination

If the main cause of prejudice against the Negro is due to the feeling that he is mentally and intellectually an inferior, then this prejudice may be removed by his giving proof of possessing the same degree of these qualities as is possessed by the people among whom he lives.

James Weldon Johnson, "The Proof of Equality"
(April 8, 1915)

James Weldon Johnson proclaimed that, in the main, prejudice and discrimination against African-Americans were founded on white America's belief that brilliance and blackness were mutually exclusive. In these editorials, Johnson centered his belief on certain white academicians and others who laid a theoretical groundwork in their attempt to prove that blacks were mentally, morally, and physically inferior to whites. These claims were picked up by the movie industry, writers, and others that led to the transformation of minstrel characters into one of America's chief forms of entertainment. The minstrel stage, moving pictures, and books combined to produce a picture of all blacks as lazy, shiftless, unreliable, and incapable of moral and intellectual development. It was these images that became paradigmatic for whites in their thinking about blacks in America. These damaging portraits of blacks helped to gird the pervasive and perpetual legal system of racism, which caused blacks to look at life through the narrow prism of their relationship to society as second-class citizens. Johnson called this a *dwarfing experience.*

The use of stereotypical concepts as a barometer to judge the race was an organized effort, according to Johnson. "Our opponents are always thinking for us," he writes. "That is why we need to be always on the alert. That is why so much truth is expressed in the line, 'Eternal vigilance is the price of liberty.' "[1] To counter these awful claims, Johnson pointed to studies by African-American and Harvard-trained sociologist W. E. B. Du Bois and others. Johnson's concept of the race rearing a group of African-American writers and artists who could smash the old stereotypes is discussed in this section, however, in more detail in Chapter 13.

In these editorials, you will note Johnson's consistent attacks on statements and actions by pusillanimous whites, who could only maintain a semblance of superiority by trying to convince America and the world that blacks were mentally and morally inferior. He consistently underscored the folly of white America's concept of this nation as a civilized and Christian state of a great democracy.

Henry Ford's New Role

February 4, 1915

Last week we presented Henry Ford to our readers as a great captain of industry and a man of broad sympathies. In this role, Mr. Ford has attracted the attention and gained the approval of the world. It is a role in which he shines. His views on industrial questions have filled the newspapers.

We see this week that Mr. Ford is not free from that common human failing of not knowing when to stop talking. Misled, perhaps, by the attention given to his economic opinions, Mr. Ford has allowed some reporter to lure him into expressing for the public his views on religion, on a future existence, and other metaphysical subjects—and, incidentally, on the Negro.

The interview states that after Mr. Ford expressed his certainty of a hereafter—as if his certainty carried any weight on such a question—he went on to say:

> Maybe there will be a superman. If we came up from the lower animals as Darwin said, why shouldn't something come up from us?
>
> Take the Negro, for instance, he is a developing race. He may go up and up. We have a number in our plant, but not doing specialized work. The Negro's skull is all in one piece. He is made differently from a white man. We could train them, but they fit in at smaller tasks.

It can be seen that Mr. Ford is not so much at home in evolution and anthropology as he is in economics and industries.

We are glad to learn that he has some Negroes in his factories. He says they are not doing specialized work. If Mr. Ford will take the trouble to investigate he will find that these colored men in his factories are doing only the "smaller tasks" not because their "skulls are made in one piece," but because they are not being given a fair field. We say confidently to Mr. Ford that if he gives his colored workmen equal opportunity he will find that they can make anything.

We also feel inclined to suggest to Mr. Ford that, in [the] future, for the sake of his own reputation, he confine his newspaper interviews to economic and industrial questions.

Uncle Tom's Cabin and the Clansman

March 4, 1915

Ten or twelve days ago the New York dailies printed a despatch from Atlanta, Ga., which stated that a theatrical company was forbidden to play the usual version of "Uncle Tom's Cabin" in that city. The action was taken on account of a protest made by some local organization. However, the play was changed and given the Arcadian title of "Old Plantation Days," the offensive parts were expurgated, Simon Legree was transfigured into a sort of benevolent patriarch, Uncle Tom was made into a happy old darkey who greatly enjoyed being a slave and who ultimately died of too much good treatment, and so a performance was given that was no doubt a great success and offended nobody's sensibilities. All of which is very amusing.

A few days later the New York dailies printed a despatch from Washington which stated that "The Birth of a Nation," a moving picture play founded on Thomas Dixon's novel, "The Clansman," had been given its initial performance at the The White House.

"The Clansman" did us much injury as a book, but most of its readers were those already prejudiced against us. It did us more injury as a play, but a great deal of what it attempted to tell could not be represented on the stage. Made into a moving picture play it can do us incalculable harm. Every minute detail of the story is vividly portrayed before the eyes of the spectators. A big, degraded looking Negro is shown chasing a little golden-haired white girl for the purpose of outraging her; she, to escape him, goes to her death by hurling herself over a cliff. Can you imagine the effect of such a scene upon the millions who seldom read a book, who seldom witness a drama, but who constantly go to the "movies"?

This play was passed by the Board of Censors, and is scheduled to open in one of the New York theatres this week. Due to the efforts of Prof. Joel E. Spingarn, the Board of Censors was induced to demand a second exhibition, and, as a result, its former approval was withdrawn. But the Board has no legal authority, and the producers can proceed without its approval; [if] they do, it will be up to the police. Prof. Spingarn deserves great credit, even if the steps he has already taken do not result in stopping the play.

Some years ago the Irish in this section of the country broke up every performance of a farce comedy call "McFadden's Flats," because in it Irishmen were represented wearing green whiskers and raising pigs in the parlor. Not long ago they stopped the dramas being performed by the Irish players from Ireland, because some of the characters were objectionable. But here comes a stupendous moving picture play that seriously attempts to hold the American Negro up before the whole country as a degraded brute, and further, to make him the object of prejudice and hatred.

We, as law-abiding citizens, call upon the mayor and the police to see that the decision of the Board of Censors be sustained; that either the objectionable features be cut out or the production prohibited.

Let the 100,000 colored citizens of this city stand united and determined to see that this picture shall not be produced in such a manner as will misrepresent and vilify us as a race.

The Recent Ripper Case

March 25, 1915

In this city one evening last week a bright eyed little white girl five years of age, who had been sent on an errand, was attacked in the hallway of the apartment house where she lived by a fiend of the "ripper" class. The body of the child was horribly mutilated, she was almost completely disembowelled and her throat was slashed. The only clues found were a stick of lemon candy tightly clutched in the little victim's right hand and near her body a bloody piece of string to which clung a few strands of hair, presumably belonging to the perpetrator of the crime.

We recite this revolting deed only because it shows up a certain error. An error which by the kind of notoriety that has been given to it has come to be accepted as common truth.

Whenever the crime of rape has been committed by some degenerate Negro the news has always been given to the world in such a way as to foster and strengthen the impression that the blacks are by nature a race of sensual brutes.

In every book that seriously treats of the race question, the Negro's sensuality is dwelt upon. Some of these books go so far as to declare that the Negro is inferior in intellectual development because of the extreme strength of his sexual instinct.

Grant that the Negro is endowed with stronger sexual instinct and powers than the white race—and this is nothing to be ashamed of so long as those powers are controlled—still, let this be remembered, not yet had he sunk so low in abnormality and perversion as has the more advanced race.

Such a crime as the one cited above is so rare even among Negro degenerates of the lowest type as to be almost unknown, while among the lowest type of white degenerates it is of common occurrence.

In fact, the sex crimes committed by the dregs of the black race are almost wholesome when compared with the sex crimes committed by the dregs of the white race.

13

The New Era

April 1, 1915

Figures just given out by the United States Census Bureau at Washington mark the beginning of a new era for the colored race in this country.

The great bugboo has been the Negro's death rate. The figures show that in a decade he has not only reduced his death rate, but reduced it farther than the whites have reduced theirs. The decline in the death rate for colored was 3.4 and for whites 2.5 to the thousand population.

Fully as significant as the decline of the death rate was the increase in the ownership of homes. The Negroes in the South own 102,000, 3.14 per cent more homes than they did in 1900, and of these 30,449 are farm homes.

In the matter of home ownership, the cities making the best show are as follows:

In Petersburg, Va., 13 colored inhabitants to each owned home; in Danville, Va., 14; in Lynchburg, Va., and Wilmington, N.C. 15; in Ashville, N.C., 16; in Greensboro, N.C., Raleigh, N.C. and San Antonio, Texas, 17; in Nashville, Tenn., 18; in Montgomery, Ala., and Paducah, Ky., 20; in Charlotte, N.C., 21; in Birmingham, Ala., and Jacksonville, Fla., 22.

The cities making the poorest show are as follows:

In Norfolk, Va., 92 colored inhabitants to each owned home; in Baltimore, Md., 91; in Louisville, Ky., [and] in Savannah, Ga., 53; in Galveston, Texas, 48; and in Washington, D.C., 46.

The Proof of Equality

April 8, 1915

In the current number of "Everybody's Magazine," Dr. Booker T. Washington gives a sketch of Isaac Fisher. Mr. Fisher is the man who won the first prize of $500 which "Everybody's" offered for the best essay on the subject, "What We Know About Rum." His picture is published with the article, so no one can make the mistake of supposing that the winner was white.

This publication of Mr. Fisher's picture and the sketch about him is next in importance to his having won the prize, because it will, through the wide circulation of the magazine in which it is printed bring before thousands of white readers what will in many cases, be the startling fact that a Negro has brains that can accomplish the same things which are accomplished by brains located in the heads of white men. It will be establishing this fact with sufficient frequency and in sufficient variety that we shall undermine and overthrow the kind of prejudice which is our main handicap.

We say, "the kind of prejudice which is our main handicap," because there are various kinds of racial prejudice. They do not all exist for the same reason; or better, lack of reason. There are some forms of prejudice which are, at bottom, a compliment; as, for instance, one people might be prejudiced against another because certain superior qualities possessed by the latter. In some degree, this is true of the prejudice which exists against the Jews in certain countries. There was something of this in the prejudice against the Moors in Spain. We ourselves get an occasional hint of this form of prejudice; we see the the prosperity of colored farmers in North Carolina and Virginia causing certain whites to clamor for farm segregation.

But, in the main, prejudice against the Negro is founded in the feeling and belief that he is mentally and intellectually an inferior being.

It is sometimes stated that the main prejudice against the Negro is due solely to his color, but we have abundant proof that there is no great physical antipathy between the white and black races in this country—and there is less in other countries.

If the main cause of prejudice against the Negro is due to the feeling that he is mentally and intellectually an inferior, then this prejudice may be removed by his giving proof of possessing the same degree of these qualities as is possessed by the people among whom he lives. This, however, must be done not merely in isolated cases, but the proof must be given so frequently and in so many various ways as to create a general opinion.

So every Negro who accomplishes anything which demonstrates brain power and the ability of energizing with the brain picks a stone out of the wall of prejudice. Whether he works a farm so as to raise more than the average number of bales, or founds, and manages a successful business, or invents a new machine, or paints a great picture, or composes a great musical work, or writes a great book, he picks out his stone, be it large or small. Each time a Negro does something which was previously thought to be in the exclusive domain of things to be accomplished by white men's brains, he produces a shock that shakes the wall of prejudice, and a sufficient number of shocks will shake it down.

Of course, when this prejudice has been removed, another kind of prejudice may develop in its place, that is, the prejudice founded in a feeling of our inferiority may give place to a prejudice founded in the fear of competition, in the fear of ascendancy. This in a slight degree, is already taking place in some sections.

However, this would be a change for the better, because there can be no form of prejudice so odious, so humiliating and so harmful as that which is based on contempt.

15

A Trap

May 6, 1915

Word comes to us indirectly that the producers of "The Birth of a Nation" are showing their kindly feelings toward the Negro by offering to introduce into the first part of the picture some views of Hampton Institute. If this is true, the Dixon-Griffith combination is laying a reap in which, we are quite sure, the Hampton people will be too wise to walk.

If there was ever a case for the application of the old saw, "Beware of the Greeks bearing gifts," this is one. No good will toward the Negro need be expected or hoped for from Tom Dixon and his associates. There is absolutely nothing in their hearts but blind hatred for the race; and any protestation to the contrary is based on some hidden motive.

This "The Birth of a Nation" gang is evidently feeling the attacks made on their hell-inspired production; but it is not for Hampton to save them. If the picture can be killed, let it die, from first scene to last; for there isn't enough good in it to merit saving any part. The whole representation was conceived only in hatred for the North and contempt for the Negro; so let it die! Kill it!

The final effect of introducing views of Hampton Institute into the first part of the "Birth of a Nation" would be to have spectators feel at the end of the play that education for Negroes is a failure. In doing this the products would obtain the powerful endorsement of Hampton and thereby disarm criticism and repel attack, and still not change the main lessons taught by the play.

It is inconceivable that the Dixon-Griffith people after spending thousands of dollars to produce a picture whose sole purpose is to convince the North that it made a mistake in fighting to free the slaves, and to convince the nation that it must "keep the nigger down." It is inconceivable, we say, that these people would consider introducing into their picture views from a colored school in such a manner and to such an extent as to change the whole play into a propaganda of glorious uplift for the Negro. No such change of heart can be expected.

The offer to introduce these views, if it has been made, is nothing more than a trap. A trap, as we said, into which Dr. Frissell and the Hampton authorities will be too wise to walk.

A Weak Argument

June 10, 1915

Professor Yandell Henderson of the Yale Medical School is a pro-German. He recently had a controversy with Mr. G. M. Trevelyan, an English historian, in one of the daily papers. Mr. Trevelyan stated that the Germans were guilty of barbarities and atrocities which Anglo-Saxons could not find in their nature to commit. Professor Henderson, in reply, took up this point as follows:

> In commenting upon my statement Mr. G. M. Trevelyan (an English historian for whom I have the highest regard when his national prejudices or interests are not involved) in The Times next day intimated that America would be incapable of such a crime as Germany has committed toward Belgium and Austria toward Serbia. It is indeed inconceivable that as a nation we could commit such an act intentionally. But Mr. Travelyan doubtless knows that, whether it was a crime or a mistake or whatever the political motives involved, the imposition of Negro domination during the reconstruction period involved unspeakable horrors in some of the Southern States.

We predict the defeat of Professor Henderson if the debate is continued, for the simple reason that he fails to avail himself of the best arguments at hand. If he wanted to prove to Mr. Trevelyan that Anglo-Saxons can be as barbaric and cruel as Teutons why did he stop at citing the imposition of Negro domination upon some Southern states during reconstruction period? Why did he not put up a stronger argument by citing the more than two hundred years of inhuman slavery which Americans imposed upon Negroes? Or to be more recent, why did he not go into details about the sort of domination imposed by Americans upon Negroes since the reconstruction period?

We see no chance that Professor Henderson will win out in this controversy.

Some Recent Publications

June 17, 1915

We are indebted to Mr. Robert A. Pelham of the Census Bureau at Washington for a specially bound and embossed copy of the Bulletin, "Negroes in the United States." The general opinion is that statistics make very dry reading, but it is certain that a perusal of Bulletin 129 will prove not only interesting but inspiring to all intelligent colored Americans.

The book is a matter of additional pride because colored men were assigned to the work of compiling the data. Secretary Redfield is to be commended for this action. It is also gratifying to note that throughout, whenever we are referred to as a race, the word Negro is printed with a large "N." The Department of Commerce deserves credit for setting such a precedent.

But in reading a notice about the Bulletin in one of the Commerce Reports we find the Negro spelled with a small "n"; so we are inclined to think that the use of the large "N" in the Bulletin was due mainly to efforts made by the colored men engaged in compiling the work.

We thank Secretary Redfield for authorizing "N" in the Bulletin, and request that he have the order cover his entire Department.

We recommend a perusal of "Negroes in the United States" to all our readers, and reassure them that they will not find it dry. From the figures on "Mortality" and "Home Ownership" they will gain more solid encouragement than from the majority of books written in behalf of the race during the past ten years.

We congratulate Mr. Pelham and his colored associates on the work they have done and the service they have rendered.

"The Negro" is a new book by W. E. B. Du Bois. It is one of a series of nearly 100 volumes which constitutes the "Home University Library" is published under the direction of Prof. Gilbert Murrary, of Oxford, Mr. H. A. L. Fisher, of Sheffield University, Prof. J. Arthur Thompson, of Aberdeen, and Prof. W. T. Brewster, of Columbia University. Its purpose is to place into the hands of general readers a uniform set of books at a very moderate price and written by acknowledged authorities upon subjects of science, history, literature and art. In other words, to place the fundamentals of a university education within the reach of everybody. In consequence, these books have a wide sale and reach a large public; so we, as a race, are extremely fortunate in that a colored man, and one so ably fitted to do it, was chosen to write the volume on the Negro.

It is needless to say that the whole book is well written, but the first half is of surpassing interest and value. It is the first half which contains facts and information which will be found, perhaps, in no other one volume; at least, in no other one volume of this size. It would require months of weary reading and research for the individual seeker after information to dig out what is packed into these few pages.

The book ought to be generally read, for it contains more than mere information. It gathers and sets forth authentic data which forms the kind of historic background essential to race consciousness. We venture to say that every colored man or woman who will read this volume will be able to close the book and say, "I am not ashamed that I am a Negro."

Another book is not so recent, but which we have just had the opportunity to read is the life of the late Hon. Norris Wright Cuney by his daughter, Mrs. Maud Cuney Hare. The book is written in a clear and pleasing style and without heroics. Those who desire to know something about the life of a man who helped to make Negro history in this country and who wish to learn something about the political history of the Negro in Texas and the South will do well to read this book.

Watching the White Man Play

December 30, 1915

Most readers will have their sense of humor touched by a first reading of the following despatch from Annapolis; but if they will read it over thoughtfully they will find that it contains an element of pathos. Some readers may not be able to see the pathetic, because of the fact that at their closest point pathos and humor merge into each other, yet from that point there is a constant divergence until they are as far apart as the poles. For example, what is our first impulse when we see a man slip up on a banana peel or an icy pavement? Why to laugh, of course; but if he lies there still and unable to move on account of a broken arm or a fractured skull, all that is humorous in the situation immediately vanishes, and the tender emotions of the heart at once come into play.

So much for the psychology of the question; let us get to the Annapolis despatch:

> HAZING PARTY GETS HAZING.
>
> NEW WAITER AT NAVAL ACADEMY UPSETS SYSTEM.
>
> *Annapolis, Md., Dec. 21,*—In imitation of Naval Academy students, Negro waiters who serve the cadets recently established a system of hazing for new recruits to their ranks.
>
> Such a recruit arrived to-day from Virginia. The hazers got busy, but their subject objected. Three of the imitators were badly whipped and the others driven off with a pistol.

Certainly it is laughable to picture a band of hazers being turned upon the "hazee" and licked to a frazzle. A sight of the intended victim chasing his would-be persecutors around and around the chamber of horrors would surely bring from us roars of laughter. Where then does the pathetic element come in? The pathetic element can be discovered in the first paragraph of the quoted despatch, which reads as follows" "In imitation of Naval Academy students, Negro waiters who serve the cadets recently established a system of hazing for new recruits to their ranks." Now, if you are thoughtful, you will be struck by this question—"Can't the colored waiters at the Naval Academy find something better in which to imitate the cadets than the silly and oftimes brutal practice of hazing?"

Perhaps someone will think that the writer is a little hard on the waiters; the writer has no intention of being so; he makes due allowance for the fact that it is as natural for young colored fellows to indulge in pranks as it is for young white fellows. But that is not the point. The point is this, the relations between the colored waiters and the white cadets are such that the waiters have only small opportunity of observing the cadets applying themselves to their work; they see more of them during hours of relaxation and recreation; and so, the impression which the colored men gain of life at the Naval Academy is one of frivolity rather than hard, earnest work.

If such a relationship was limited to the Naval Academy, it would be a matter of no importance. But we have taken the Annapolis waiters only as a text. This relationship is very general. Thousands and thousands of our brightest young men, during their working hours, are engaged in watching the white man play; and in their leisure hours are engaged in giving an imitation of the white man at play. And there is where the pathos comes in.

A very large number of our most promising young men get their start in life through some occupation which throws them in contact with the white man when he is taking his pleasures. They see him dining and wining, dancing and gaming, lolling and loafing; most of them fail to understand that this generally means merely a brief relaxation for men who work like slaves; they have full opportunity to see how the white man spends his money, but none to see how he earns it; so, it is easy for them to gain the idea that life means pleasure.

Who has not witnessed the effects of this? Who has not often seen colored men who are employed in hotels or club houses or as valets spending from their few dollars in just the same manner as the men whom they serve spend from their hundreds of thousands or their millions? Isn't that a pathetic sight?

The employment which brings so many of us in contact with the white man at play is all right in itself; it is honest and often quite profitable; the danger lies in the great temptation to imitate him only in the things at which he plays. This temptation would be offset if there were equal opportunities to see him at work, to observe him in his factories and big business institutions, but there are not. In a word, we are, for the greater part, still in the position of working for the white man and not with him.

Nevertheless, as natural and alluring as it is for those who are thrown into this relationship to copy what is ephemeral rather than what is solid, they are not to be excused. They, and not only they, but the whole race, must realize that the most essential thing before us in this country is to learn the methods by which the white man accomplishes his work, and not the manner in which he takes his play.

Nature and Some Sociologists

January 6, 1916

Several weeks ago we commented upon an article on segregation written by Booker T. Washington and published after his death in "The New Republic." In the issue of "The New Republic" December 25, a man by the name of John Jay Lindley writes a letter in which he pointedly disagrees with the views that had been set forth by Dr. Washington. He makes an attempt to reason the matter out; and here is a sample of his reasoning:

> In the eyes of God all men are equal, but students of sociology know that there is a barrier which must forever exist between the whites and blacks, and which no time can remove. Certain laws in nature are as immutable as the seeds of time, and they cannot be changed. Silver is not gold, and while both metals can be made into beautiful creations, they must forever remain dissimilar. So it is with the white and the black race.

If Mr. Lindley made such an argument as that to a mule, he would be likely to get what he calls his brains kicked out; and yet, this is the sort of argument which, on account of its mouth-filling words, makes an impression on a great many human beings.

Here is a man virtually stating that God thinks all men are equal; but students of sociology know better. There is a class of sociological students who pretend to know more about the human race than God does, but we should like to know where any of them got the knowledge that "there is a barrier which must forever exist between the whites and blacks, and which no time can remove"? Mr. Lindley goes on to say that certain laws in nature are as immutable as the seeds of time, and they cannot be changed. What the "seeds of time" are, we do not know; but we take it that this statement will heighten and strengthen the "barrier" referred to in the first statement.

What is the barrier to which Mr. Lindley makes such oracular reference? Does he mean that there is an immutable law of nature which forbids white and black people living in the same block? If that were true it would be entirely unnecessary to enact city ordinances on the subject; it requires no legislative acts to keep terrapins from living up in the trees with the squirrels. Does he mean that there is a barrier fixed by nature which bars the black man from participating in the higher cultural life? The general progress of the whole race toward all that culture means, the marked advancement of so many thousands, and the possession of the highest culture by so many individuals absolutely disproves any such theory. Or does Mr. Lindley mean that there is a barrier fixed by nature between whites and blacks, such as there is between a higher and lower order of animals, which stands in the way of physical union between the races? Then we should like to have him account for the presence of the three or four million people of mixed blood in this country. Perhaps, our sociological friend's theory is that physical union between the races is possible, but is a violation of the laws of nature and in fact, a sort of crime of bestiality. This is a common theory and much preached by a certain class of "students of sociology." If this were true, the offspring of such a union would be monstrosities or degenerates. This we know is not so. Even the milder and quite familiar charge that the product of such a union is physically, mentally and morally inferior to both parent races, will not stand the most cursory study of the condition of people of mixed blood; to say nothing of the mention of such names as Dumas, Pushkin, Frederick Douglass and Booker T. Washington.

Now, the point we are driving at lies beyond the question of either segregation or amalgamation considered within their ordinary limits. We are driving at these pseudo-scientific theories which darkly hint at the existence of some mysterious, eternal bar-sinister which shuts the Negro off from the rest of humanity; a thing which no atomist or chemist or psychologist has yet been able to find. It has been demonstrated and is continually being demonstrated that a normal black man, given the same environment and opportunities, will develop physically, mentally and ethically the same as any other man. It has also been demonstrated and is continually being demonstrated that there is no natural physical aversion between the Negro and other races; in fact, just the opposite is true. And this is true not only of mere animal attraction, but also of the higher and purer affections. Many a white child has loved the broad bosom of its black mammy better than it did the arms of its own mother. Where, then, is this aversion established by nature and sanctioned by God? Prejudice against the Negro is a matter of training and education.

Still, in spite of their absurdity such theories as the one set forth by Mr. Lindley find many believers. Such a belief works a subtle injury to us which is more damaging than lynchings or other violent insults of prejudice, because its effect is to put us outside the human pale, to assign us to a place somewhere just this side of the most advanced apes.

Finally, let us say to Mr. Lindley and other such "students of sociology" that if colored people live together in the same sections or districts, they should do so for social or economic reasons or on account of their own preference, and not because they are forced by some legislative enactment. Especially do they object to being herded off in compliance with any law of nature-faking which attempts to rule them out of the human race?

Saluting the Flag

April 4, 1916

We recently received the following letter, written in a boyish hand:

615 Cherry St.
Des Moines, Ia.
March 20, 1916

Mr. James W. Johnson,
    Contributing Ed. New York Age, New York. Dear Sir: Please find enclosed clipping from the Evening Tribune of this city date of 18th instant. The incident is very peculiar, and I am anxious to have your comment upon same. Was the Juvenile Judge justified in his ruling? Should this boy be compelled to salute the flag? Are the boy's contentions justified by the facts in the case as cited by him?
                                                    Very truly, G.H. EDMUNDS.

The case referred to in the above letter has attracted some attention. Hubert Evans, a colored boy eleven years old, refused to salute the American flag in accordance with the rules of the public schools of Des Moines. He was taken before the judge of the Juvenile Court, who, after hearing the case, ordered the boy to go back to school and salute the flag.

The clipping sent by G. H. Edmunds gives an extended account of the hearing. It appears that both parents of the boy were present in court and upheld him in his position. It also appears that the parents and the boy belong to a "sanctified" sect known as the Sanctified Holy Church; and the mother is reported as saying the Holy Ghost told Hubert not to salute the flag. However, we pass over everything except the statements made by Hubert himself. The following two reasons were the ones given by him:

I won't salute the flag at school for I do not think it is right. It doesn't have God in it.

In the second place I haven't any country. It all belongs to the white man. If it wasn't for God, I would not be here. The white man doesn't count us.

Now, we shall take Hubert seriously. We shall assume that he knows the full weight and significance of his words; that he is actuated by conscientious scruples, and not merely led away by religious vagaries.

Carefully read the reasons stated above and we cannot but see that either one would be stronger, single and alone, than are the two of them coupled together. In fact, coupled together, they are contradictory.

In the first place, Hubert declines to salute the flag because "it doesn't have God in it"; and in the second place, he inadvertently has such bitter feelings. If it is God's fault that Hubert is in such a country as he feels this to be, we do not see how it would make saluting the flag any easier for him even if it did "have God in it" and the salutation were made a solemn religious ceremony. It would seem that his second reason would make him feel as bitter against God as he does against the country.

Many people make the mistake of supposing that every human act must be classified either as right or wrong. They do not realize that there is a class of acts which, in themselves, are neither right nor wrong. And, strange to say, it is over this neuter class that many of the fiercest human conflicts have been waged. In the whole human family there is no difference of opinion as to honest dealing and truth telling being right and thieving and lying being wrong. But people will differ seriously over the right or wrong involved in going to see a circus; and wars have been fought to settle questions equally as trivial. If it may be said that there is nothing of right in the mere act of saluting the flag of one's native land, it can be said with equal certainty that there is nothing wrong in it.

Hubert, in his second reason for not saluting the flag says, "I haven't any country. It all belongs to the white man." This statement would be more rational than the first, if it were true. But is it true? It is not. Three hundred years of labor and loyalty makes this country belong to the Negroes as much as it belongs to anybody else; and a good deal more than it belongs to many who are living under its flag. Of course, we have been wronged, we are still being wronged, many of our rights are still denied us, but the American Negro is not going to renounce his rights because some people in the country are opposed to his having them. No, he is going to work and fight until his every right is recognized and accorded. If he should lie down and say, "I haven't any country. It all belongs to the white man," he would not deserve a country.

Hubert seems to feel that the country is all wrong; that God is no where in it; Hubert is mistaken. Although many, sometimes a majority, of the people in this country are wrong, yet that abstract thing we call the Country is right, and is always making for the right. It was the spirit of righteousness that gave birth to this country, and that spirit, sooner or later, in spite of opposition, always makes its power felt. For two centuries there were enough people living under the American flag who were in favor of human bondage to make the country accept it, but at last the spirit of righteousness arose and swept the land like a flame, and slavery was destroyed. Finally, every other wrong against the Negro will be righted.

We say to Hubert that if God is anywhere, he is in the flag.

We realize that in the beginning we assumed more for this eleven-year-old boy than his slight shoulders should be made to bear. It is hardly to be doubted that the attitude which he has assumed is due more to the teachings of the "Sanctified Holy Church" than to anything else.

To our correspondent we say that we think the judge of the Juvenile Court was right in ordering Hubert to go back to school and conduct himself in accordance with the rules.

Between the Devil and the Deep Sea

September 27, 1917

The young men who have been working at the training camp for colored officers at Des Moines should have received their commissions on the fifteenth of this month. Instead, they have been required to re-enlist for a period of thirty days. The men in the white training camps who finished the work were commissioned on August 15.

The men at Des Moines have been held over for another month because, it is said, the colored drafted men whom they are to command have not yet been organized and sent to cantonments for training.

And colored men who have been drafted into the new national army have not yet been organized and sent to cantonments for training because the War Department has not yet been able to settle upon what policy will be adopted toward the colored conscripts.

The men at Des Moines showed their willingness to serve by the act of enlisting for the camp. The men who have been drafted stand ready to go. Secretary Baker is undoubtedly anxious to do the right thing. Where then is the trouble? There is a force at work that is holding colored men back from their rightful place in the army and the chance to serve the country.

What this force is does not puzzle us very much. It has been in evidence ever since the question of universal service was first broached in this country. It is nothing more or less than Southern prejudice.

If we were not so deeply concerned about seeing the Negro given his right to bear his part as a citizen in this struggle that the country is going through, the whole situation would be amusing. It would be amusing because it presents the most perfect illustration of those opposed to the Negro finding themselves placed in a position between the devil and the deep sea that could be imagined.

Here is the country involved in a tremendous war. A war that may strain its resources of both materials and men. And here are men influential in the Government and responsible to the country for the conduct of this war, who are opposed to making use of the services of a part of the population that has always helped to fight the nation's battles, and are ready today. We say, the situation is more amusing, it's ridiculous, it is absurd.

About 75,000 colored men were selected in the first draft, and none of them have yet been ordered into camp because the War Department does not know what to do with them. There is an element in the Government that is opposed to these men being trained with white troops; this feeling is prompted by prejudice. They are opposed to these men being trained alone; this feeling they pretend is prompted by fear. This end of the dilemma constitutes the devil.

And now for the deep sea. If they don't take these colored men and give them the right to bear arms and fight as equal citizens, they have got to send to the trenches, perhaps to die, a white man for each Negro they refuse.

When once the straight and simple path of justice is departed from, there is no telling where the road will lead.

Turn the Enemy's Flank!

April 19, 1917

It is up to the Negro just now to make a strategic move that will turn the enemy's flank. The same old element in the country which always opposes him has been making an attempt to arouse public sentiment against him by hanging a question mark on the loyalty of the race. As was to be expected, the attempt failed; and, on the Negro's most invulnerable spot. The country may have diverse opinions about him on many points, but as to his loyalty and bravery there is one overwhelming opinion. The record of the race through the whole history of the country has given such convincing proof of that loyalty and bravery that heretofore not even our bitterest enemies have thought it worth the effort to try to cast a cloud on them. And this attempt would never have been made had not the thought occurred to our enemies that present conditions offered an opportunity to couple us up with pro-Germanism.

The attempt to couple us up with pro-Germanism failed, but the effort is still being carried on by our enemies to exclude the race from all recognition and participation in the coming military activities. Certain Southern representatives in Congress are determined to shut the Negro out, and they are determined to do it at whatever cost to the Nation.

This very determination gives the Negro a chance to line up the liberal sentiment of the country on his side. It gives him a chance to open the eyes of the great North and West to the fact that Southern prejudice is not only against the best interest of the Negro but also against the common good of the country.

When this war has gone on for a while and the greater part of the nation realizes that thousands of brave and able men have been kept out of the ranks by race prejudice, while their services were badly needed; that ancient, Southern institution is going to receive a set back such as it has never had before.

The Hour of Opportunity

October 18, 1917

In one of last Sunday's papers, Frederic C. Howe, Commissioner of Immigration at Ellis Island, gave a very interesting interview on the probable movement of foreign-born persons to and from the United States after the war.

In Mr. Howe's opinion, a great tide from the United States back to Europe will set in. He states that on a most conservative estimate, at least two million people will return to Europe the first year after the war if they can secure accommodation. He bases this opinion on the following facts: first, a census taken by the railroad and steamship companies shows that more than a million of our foreign-born population are planning to return to Europe the moment peace is declared; second, a large number of employers in Western cities report that there seems to be a concerted movement on foot to induce Hungarians, Austrians, and other Central European peoples to return to their native lands; third, bankers in the coal and industrial regions report that Poles, Italians and Russians in very large numbers are saving money and making preparations to return.

A summary of Mr. Howe's explanation of this probable exodus is as follows: There are about fifteen million foreign-born persons in the United States. For more than three years these people have been almost entirely cut off from communication with their relatives and friends at home. The strong, human desire to see their relatives and friends and find out what condition they are in will be a compelling motive that will take many of these foreign-born people back. Then, there will be the quest for family property in the old countries. Some of them are, and many of them think they are, the sole heirs of family estates, and they are going back to claim them. Besides, there is the general expectation that there will be a breaking up of the great landed estates into small holdings which will make land cheap, and so Poles, Hungarians, Russians and Irish, too, are eager to get back and take advantage of the division.

Moreover, the European governments are laying and perfecting plans to encourage and stimulate this movement. This policy of the European governments is due to two causes: First, these governments found when the war broke out that every one of their citizens who had taken up residence in the United States was a man lost to the colors, unless he voluntarily joined them, and as none of these countries is by any means sure that this will be the last war, it does not want to be caught that way again. Second, these European countries are going to need every available able-bodied human being to help rebuild what has been destroyed. Already England has appointed a commission to provide ways and means for providing land for invalided and returned soldiers. This will mean the breaking up of large estates, many of which are to-day held as hunting preserves by the titled aristocracy. All of the countries of Europe will adopt more or less similar plans.

Perhaps the most striking change to result from this policy will be the change that will take place in Ireland. In 1840 Ireland had a population of more than eight million. In 1911 the population had dwindled to a little more than four million. That is, in a period of seventy years the population had decreased by half. This decrease was due in a large measure to migration to the United States. And the migration to the United States was due chiefly to land conditions in Ireland. If England establishes a liberal land policy, it is almost certain that hundreds of thousands of Irish people in this country will return to the Emerald Isle.

But why are all these mighty changes now taking place in Europe a matter of vital interest to the American Negro? It is because they are bringing about his economic emancipation.

In an article several weeks ago, I pointed out that the physical emancipation of the Negro by the Civil War and his enfranchisement by the Constitutional amendment still left him an economic slave. And his economic slavery was almost as bad as his physical slavery. We were four million people set free, without a dollar, without a foot of land, without even clothes, without education and without experience. We had placed in our hands a piece of paper called the ballot, and were told that we were citizens of the United States. Is there any wonder then that the piece of paper was snatched out of our hands, and we were made the victims of corruption?

In spite of emancipation and enfranchisement, we found ourselves in the position of absolute dependence upon the very people who had fought to keep us enslaved for the bare chance to live. Our bread was to be had at their mercy. This was but another form of slavery, and it was a form of slavery which, if not worse for the Negro, was at least advantageous to the employer class of the South. Because under the old form the owner had a certain amount of capital invested in the slave, and when the slave was sick or incapacitated, that capital was idle; and when the slave died, that capital was lost. (I do not think insurance was ever carried on slaves.) But under the new form, the employer class of the South got the use of the "slave" or tenant or peon or whatever we might term him without having any capital invested in him and without having even any responsibility for his welfare. These are the conditions under which the American Negro has struggled up for fifty years. The great miracle is that he has come up and not gone down.

When this government emancipated the slaves, it no doubt felt that it had taken the last step in democracy. The liberation of the slaves was no step in democracy at all, it was an act of common humanity. It was then up to this government to begin its steps in democracy. It did go as far as declaring the slaves to be citizens of the United States; but, as I pointed out recently, that was not far enough.

We need only look at the trend of thought and action in the European monarchies to-day in order to realize how far behind this great republic was fifty years ago. But, as I heard a well-informed lady remark in speaking on this subject a short while ago, the men at the head of this government fifty years ago didn't know any better. The ideas that are being generally discussed to-day never occurred to them. It never struck them to treat the right to property as less sacred than the right to life.

Here is Russia fully realizing that if she is to have a true democracy, the Russian peasant must be given a right to the land. So the great estates and tracts of idle land that have been held by the aristocracy and the government are to be divided among the hitherto pauperized Russian tenants. The new Russian government knows that to give these peasants a piece of paper with "ballot" and "citizenship" printed on it and leave them in their old economic condition will mean next to nothing. The other European countries realize that they cannot have stable governments after this war unless they follow much the same policy. Land for this purpose will be seized, if necessary.

Our government of fifty years ago did not hesitate to use human lives for the indirect purpose, at least, of freeing the slaves, but the thought that it would be just—and not only just, but wise and necessary—to divide up a part of the great Southern plantations among lately emancipated slaves and newly made citizens was at that time unthinkable.

If the slaves had been given a certain number of acres of land, with farm equipment, the land so deeded that it could neither be sold nor mortgaged, the Negro would have been able to maintain his citizenship in the South, and Southern history for the last half century would make better and brighter reading. To-day, such a course would be considered the obvious thing to do; fifty years ago it was too radical for serious consideration. Here we have one of the landmarks along the advance of democratic thought.

However in spite of the condition in which the Negro found himself after the Civil War, he has steadily fought for an economic footing and has, in a manner achieved it. It has been a long fight, a painful fight, and was being won only by the slowest degrees.

But here comes this great war that stopped foreign immigration, took immigrants out of the country, and bids fair to take out many more, and as a result, the Negro gets what should have been given him fifty years ago, his Economic Emancipation. But he does not get it as a gift, he gets it through the law of necessity; and that makes his hold upon it more secure.

Let the Negro get his feet firmly planted on the rock of economic security, let him have the chance to earn an adequate living independently, to gain his bread without accepting it as a favor from any man, and to do this in the civilized states of the North, states where he can rear his children to a fuller stature of manhood and womanhood, and no one need worry about the progress of the race.

And this is the chance that is coming to him out of the changes now taking place. He can't be kept out of it. And it is only just that he should not, for it is his heritage by right. It only rests upon the Negro to do his part.

This is indeed the hour of great opportunity.

Colored Officers in the Army

October 18, 1917

Six hundred and seventy-eight of the young men who were at the officers' training camp at Fort Des Moines have been commissioned. One hundred and sixty were commissioned as captains, three hundred and twenty as first lieutenants and one hundred and ninety-eight as second lieutenants. These new officers will command the 17th Division of the National Army.

Here we have a result better than could have been hoped for six or eight months ago. Nearly seven hundred commissioned officers in the army; one hundred and sixty of them captains. We knew we would be in the war; the question was, "will any of our men get the chance to become leaders?" Here we have nearly seven-hundred, the very best the race can furnish, young men from our colleges, from the progessions and from the business walks of life. We have in them the highest mental, physical and moral standard of the race, and we may confidently feel that they are going to give us reason to be proud of them.

There were many who felt that the establishment of the camp at Fort Des Moines was a mistake, but it can now be seen that the result could have been achieved in no other way; and it is a result worth achievement.

Pure Americans

November 8, 1917

A correspondent in the New York Sun is very much worked up over the proposition of calling out for military training the boys of 18, 19 and 20 years of age. He advances the argument that boys who have not reached the age which gives them say or voice in the Government should not be forced to do the fighting for their elders; and that no young man under 21 years should be compelled to enter training or active combat at this stage of the conflict.

He goes on to speak of the difficulty of transporting and the expense of maintaining any larger force than the Government already has in course of organization, and then says:

> Let us insist upon arrangements being made to force into the service the subjects of the Allies who are waxing fat in this country—they would be compelled to serve if at home; and a more proper proportion of the Negro race should be obliged to do service before we think of sacrificing the lives of too many pure American born boys.

This correspondent may be talking sense in the case of the subjects of the Allies who are "waxing fat in this country." But he makes a noise like an idiot when he talks of pure Americans in distinction to Negroes. There are many Negroes who have been a part of American soil and history for nearly three hundred years; the great bulk of them have been a part of American soil and history for more than a hundred years. The Negroes in this country are more truly American than two-thirds of the white population.

When this war broke out the nation was stunned to find itself split asunder by a number of hyphens; but the Negro stood together with the original stocks that landed at Plymouth and Jamestown as a part of the soil, the history, the traditions, the customs, the language, the religion of this country, and no other.

If this correspondent meant to say white Americans instead of pure Americans; well, that is a different story.

Experienced Men Wanted

November 8, 1917

An Age reader at Jacksonville, Florida, sends us a circular which is being distributed in connection with the army recruiting stations at Jacksonville, Tampa, Miami, Pensacola and Tallahassee, and which reads as follows:

NON-COMMISSIONED OFFICERS WANTED
WHITE MEN
MARRIED OR SINGLE
EXPERIENCED IN THE HANDLING OF COLORED MEN FOR

ENLISTMENT AS NON-COMMISSIONED OFFICERS IN THE SERVICE,
BATTALIONS, ENGINEER CORPS
NATIONAL ARMY.

"Experienced in the handling of colored men." That is about the most conspicuous example of grouping the Negro with the mule that has ever been brought to my attention. But aside from that, what kind of white non-commissioned officers does the War Department think it will get by allowing recruiting stations to advertise in the South for white men, "experienced in handling colored men?" Does the War Department have any idea of what it means in the South to have experience in handling Negroes? It generally means to have the qualifications of a slave driver, of a chain-gang guard, of an overseer of the roughest kind of labor. It means to be devoid of sympathetic understanding and human kindness. Of course, if it is absolutely necessary to have white non-commissioned officers over colored troops, the Department can find lots of white men in the South who would make intelligent and sympathetic officers; but it will not find these men by advertising there for white men who are "experienced in handling Negroes."

The War Department has adopted a policy of training Southern troops in the North and Northern troops in the South. In line with this policy, I would suggest, since the Department seems to deem it necessary that colored troops be commanded by white officers, that all white officers for colored troops be Northern men. It is true that the sort of Southern white man the Department would get by the above advertisement would have more "experience," but it would be experience of the wrong kind, it would be experience that would render him incapable of looking upon the men of his command as comrades in arms.

It is true that some of the finest and truest officers that the colored regiment of the regular army have are white men of Southern birth; but these men are entirely devoid of any "experience in handling Negroes" in the Southern sense. They went to West Point in their teens. Direct from West Point they went into the army and there have come to know the glorious traditions of the four crack colored regiments of the service, and to respect them and the men who made them. There is no plane of comparison between these officers and men taken out of civil life in the South and given command because of their "experience in handling Negroes."

Getting down to common sense and plain justice, since colored men must be in strictly colored regiments, all non-commissioned officers of these regiments should be colored men; more, all line officers of those regiments should be colored men; and there is no reason why, ultimately, all the field officers of those regiments should not be colored.

But if it is decreed that white men must officer colored regiments, then at least let them be Northern white, who have had no "experience."

"Why Should a Negro Fight?"

June 29, 1918

The above heading is the heading of an editorial in the Plainfield (N.J.) Courier-News of the 11th of this month. The Courier News editorial was called forth by a letter written by some colored person to the editor asking reasons why the Negro should fight to protect the country. Two Age readers in Plainfield sent us the article and asked us to reply to it.

The letter which was sent to the editor of the Courier-News reads as follows:

> Dear Sir: I am a buyer of your paper and I note in your column there are questions asked and answered. This is a question I should like you [to] answer. Why is it a Negro man should go to protect a country and public places when in it he can not even go in and drink a glass of ice cream soda nor even his female sex? E.R.

In the first place, this [is] a very lightweight letter. The person writing has picked out the weakest argument that could possibly be found. Of course, the denial of the privilege of drinking ice cream soda in certain places on account of race or color is a phase of the denial of full citizenship and common democracy; but it is trivial to single out as a reason why the Negro should not do his part in this great war. If the duty of the Negro to fight was really a question in the mind of the writer of the letter, it seems that he should have backed up his inquiry with such arguments as the lynching and burning alive of Negroes, without any effort on the part of authorities to punish the perpetrators of these crimes; the disfranchisement and "Jim Crowing" of the race, even of those who are bearing arms and wearing the uniform; the shutting out of Negroes from many of the fields of occupation; the criminally unfair division of the public school funds in many states; the absence of even handed justice in the courts of many of the states, and other arguments that would carry weight.

America is the American Negro's country. He has been here three hundred years; that is, about two hundred years longer than most of the white people. He is a citizen of this country, declared so by the Constitution. Many of the rights and privileges of citizenship are still denied him, but the plain course before him is to continue to perform all of the duties of citizenship while he continually presses his demands for all of the rights and privileges. Both efforts must go together; to perform the duties and not demand the rights would be pusillanimous; and to demand the rights and not perform the duties would be futile.

It is a fact that the Negro is denied his full rights as a citizen, and that

33

a good many people in the country are determined that he shall never have them; then the task before the Negro is to force the accordance of those rights, and that he cannot do by refusing to perform duties. In fact, the moment he ceases to perform the duties of citizenship he abdicates the right to claim the full rights of citizenship.

As regards the present war, the central idea behind Germany is force; if that idea wins, it will be worse for the American Negro and all the other groups belonging to submerged and oppressed peoples; so the American Negro should do all in his power to help defeat it.

Then, too, a German victory would mean the almost absolute destruction of France. France, the fountain of liberal ideas, the nation which more than any other in the world has freed itself from all kinds of prejudices, the nation which endeavors to practice as well as preach the brotherhood of man. The destruction of France would be the greatest blow to liberty that could now be dealt.

These are a few of the plain, logical reasons, based largely upon self interest; besides there are other and more altruistic reasons; we leave purely sentimental reasons out of consideration.

So much for the letter written to the Courier-News; now for the editorial written in answer to the letter. Here is the first sentence from it:

"A Negro should fight for this country because this nation freed him from the bonds of slavery."

Now if the editor of the Courier-News put up such an argument as that to a jackass he would get his brains kicked out. What was the slavery "from which this nation freed us?" It was slavery into which this nation put us and held us for two hundred and fifty years. Can a man throw you into prison without cause in order to place you under a debt of gratitude to him for taking you out? The editor of the Courier-News goes on to say:

> The Negro who tries to put himself on the level with white men socially is an enemy of the Negro race. The greatest men of that race have condemned those who are always finding fault because they cannot obtain service in hotels, restaurants and ice cream parlors patronized by the whites. It is the duty of these dissatisfied Negroes to open restaurants and ice cream parlors of their own and endeavor to conduct them better than any white man conducts his place of business.

We do not know from what part of the country the editor of the Courier-News hails, but his definition of "social equality" sounds very much as though it was made in Alabama or Mississippi. There is no more social equality in drinking ice cream soda in a public place than there is in riding in the same subway car. And where does this editor get his information that the greatest men of the race have condemned those who found fault because hotel and other public accommodations were refused to colored people?

His suggestion that Negroes should have their own hotels, theatres and other public places is impracticable. It would be impossible for the Negro or any other group in this country to duplicate the machinery of civilization. If a colored man is passing through Denver or Salt Lake City, is he to go without food and lodging because there are not enough Negroes in either of those cities to maintain a hotel or a restaurant? But even if the Negro could duplicate all of the machinery of civilization in the country and live his life separate and apart, would it be wise to have him do it? We are now trying to cut the hyphen out of our body politic, would it be wise to deliberately create another?

It is curious to note the amount of ego that goes with the attitude of the editor of the Courier-News on this question. He sits writing his little article shaming Negroes for wanting to associate with white people, not imagining for a moment that there are colored people who not only would not seek him for a social equal, but who probably might refuse to accept him as one. If he should be stopping at the Van-Astor hotel; and a colored man came in to register, the first thought to crop up in his mind would be, "Here is a Negro who wants to get into a hotel where I, a white man, and other white men are stopping," not knowing that what the Negro wants is something to eat and a place to sleep and that he is willing to pay for the best he can afford.

This ego is characteristic of all white people who talk like the editor of the Courier-News. They feel, when a Negro protests against discrimination and "Jim Crowism" that he is trying to get away from his race and associate with white people. When a self-respecting Negro so protests, the thought of merely associating with white people is the farthest from his mind; he is contending for a common democratic right which all other citizens of the country have, that of being accommodated in public places when he is clean, orderly and is able and willing to pay the price; or he is protesting against being forced to accept inferior service for the price of the best service, and he is especially resenting the badge of inferiority which being "Jim Crowed" places upon him.

This article of the Courier-News runs on for the length of a column, nearly all of it being a diatribe against Negroes who are seeking "social equality," meaning those who object to being "Jim Crowed" and shut out of theatres and hotels and restaurants and other public places where orderly conduct and the price are the only requisites exacted from other citizens. So it is not worth the while to quote any more of it.

We wish to say that there are many sound and solid reasons why the Negro should fight for his country, aside from the reasons that are altruistic and sentimental; but the editor of the Courier-News in using up a column of his more or less valuable space in answering the letter of E.R. failed to strike upon a single one.

The letter written to the Courier-News was lightweight, but the editor's article in answer to it did not weigh as much as the letter. His letter is entirely apart from the mark.

"Negro" with a Big "N."

August 17, 1918

One of our readers in Newark recently sent us some correspondence which he had with Mr. Ochs, owner of the New York Times, relative to the policy of that great paper in always printing the word "Negro" with a small "n." Our correspondent wrote to Mr. Ochs complaining of this policy of the Times and received the following letter in reply:

Dear Sir:

Mr. Ochs asked me to acknowledge your letter presenting arguments for spelling the word "Negro" with a capital letter.

The question has often been discussed. Generally the small letter is used in newspapers. From our point of view, the capitalization of the word would tend to accentuate a separateness of the colored portion of the population. That is just what we should avoid, is it not? Our view is that we should no more capitalize "negro" than "white." It would be calling special attention to the hue of a man's skin, accentuating a difference among Americans of different colors.

Yours very truly,

R.H. Graves,

Sunday Editor

It is hard to believe that this letter is from the Sunday Editor of the New York Times. We would not expect a letter of such weak reasoning from a backward child. In the first place, it brings a smile that hurts our face to think of the editorial staff of The Times delicately considering not to do anything that would "tend to accentuate a separateness of the colored portion of the population." In the second place, any ten year old boy ought to be able to see the fallacy of the grammatical reason that is usually given in support of using small "n" in "Negro." The argument is that the word "Negro" is an adjective, and adjectives are not written with capital letters.

This argument entirely ignores the fact that words in a living language have no fixed value or meaning. Many words are born and go through various changes in meaning; often they absolutely die; and sometimes they are reborn with still a different shade of meaning. For example, several centuries ago the word "wench" was a perfectly properly term to be applied to a woman, especially if she was a servant; but let any lady now apply the term to her cook, and she will have a fight on hand or the job of looking for another cook or both. There are also words that are born as outcasts, but finally acquire good standing in a language; the classic example in the American language is the word "blizzard."

This argument also ignores the fact that there are two kinds of grammar—grammatical grammar and logical grammar. Grammatical grammar rules that a singular subject must take a verb in the singular; but we may say, "The committee has decided thus and so." The use of a singular or plural verb depends upon whether we are thinking of the committee as a single body or as made up of several individuals.

Grammarians, who write the rules, are always trying to establish grammatical grammar, to give words a fixed and unchangeable status, but the people, who use the language, are constantly overriding the grammarians and establishing logical grammar; that is, giving to words the status and meaning which they have come to have through use.

We all know that philological research will show that the word "Negro" was originally an adjective meaning black. This is especially true of the Latin languages; for example in Spanish, un hombre negro means a black man, and un caballo negro means a black horse. But logical grammar and just a little plain, common sense tells us that when the word "Negro" is used not to qualify, but to denominate a race of people it is no longer an adjective, it is a proper name and should be written with a capital letter.

The Sunday Editor of The Times says: "Our view is that we should no more capitalize "negro" than "white." It would be calling special attention to the hue of a man's skin, accentuating a difference among Americans of different colors." It seems here that he has the whole thing backwards. When he writes the word "negro" with a small letter it is an adjective and means black. When he writes the word "Negro" with a capital letter it is not an adjective, it is a proper name and does not necessarily mean black. So there is less danger of calling special attention to the hue of a man's skin in writing "Negro" than in writing "negro."

The history and growth of the use of the word "negro" is somewhat curious. For a good many years the more advanced elements of the race objected to the term, and there are still many [who] object to it. We frankly admit that there are grounds for their objection. The growth of the use of the word is due mainly to two things: the fact that some years ago certain race leaders determined to redeem the word, and to the fact that it is a shorter word than "colored" and so fits better in the headlines. The headline writer can make a display in bigger type when he says, "NEGRO BURNED AT THE STAKE" than he could by saying, "COLORED MAN BURNED AT THE STAKE." The headline writer has, perhaps, done more to make the word general than anybody else.

Of course, there arises a question as to the wisdom of adopting a name that needed to be "redeemed." Why name a boy Benedict Arnold when he could be as easily named George Washington? Nor can it be helped but noticed that white people themselves, when they wish to speak softly to and about the race use the adjective "colored." The Sunday Editor of The Times does it in his letter. It must also be admitted that the term, "The negro" sets us off absolutely. So far as names go, at least, it would be much easier to go from "colored American" to "American citizen" than from "The Negro" to "American citizen." In fact, it may be said that so long as the race is exclusively known as "The Negro" it will not be a full participator in American democracy.

But the race leaders who adopted "Negro" to redeem it had their good reasons. We are separate people with needs different from the rest of the population; so the men who had to talk and write for the race felt the need of some concrete term; they could not be continually writing in adjectival phrases. Other race names were tried, "Afro-American," "Ethio-American," etc., but they were all found too clumsy. So "Negro" has come to be the race name used generally by the writers and newspaper men of the race; and whatever objections there may be to it, it is the best concrete term for the race that has yet been found.

But what's in a name? Our condition is the main thing to be changed; the name will take care of itself. However, we do insist that sticklers for grammatical grammar and others recognize that the word "Negro" when used to designate a race, is not an adjective, but a proper name, and should be written with a capital letter.

Army Qualifications

May 10, 1919

A board of United States army officers recently appointed to pass on the qualifications of a colored man who had served in the army over seas as an officer and had made application for retention in the regular army made the following recommendation upon his applications:

> The Board, therefore, recommends that he not be examined for appointment in the Regular Army.
>
> Reasons—Unqualified by reason of qualities inherent in the Negro race. An opinion of the Board based on the testimony of five white officers serving with the 368th Infantry, Negroes are deficient in moral fibre and force of character rendering them unfit as officers and leaders of men.

This serves to show how far the propaganda for discrediting the colored officer reaches. There are white men who were in the army and served over seas who are making it their business, no, more than that, their religion to spread the report that the colored officer was a failure. Now here comes an official board and makes the statement that not only this particular Negro, but no Negro is fit to be an officer in the United States army.

The Absurdity of It

July 5, 1919

We clip the following question from the pages of Judge:

> Why are many who smack their lips over food prepared by African cooks and served by African waiters so squeamish as to demand Jim Crow cars?

Judge might have added the fact of white babies in the arms of colored nurses, and even nursing at the breasts of colored women. And Judge might have added closer and more delicate relations, evidence of which may be found in any Southern town. We believe Judge is asking this question only to be asking it. We believe that Judge knows the answer; if it doesn't, we can give the answer for it, and in very short time and space.

The American Legion and the Negro

October 25, 1919

The question of Negro posts is rising up to plague the American Legion in the Southern States. Here is an organization of the veterans of the army which, according to current history, can be compared to only one other army the world has ever seen, to that army which set out with the purpose of freeing the Holy Land from the dominion of the hated infidel. The members of the American Legion belonged to the army which set out to make the world safe for democracy, yet in the Southern States they are saying that colored men who fought by their sides will not be allowed to join the organization on equal terms.

For himself this writer does not see that the Legion promises to be a factor for any great good; indeed, there are probabilities that its activities will be turned to trivial things; there is even danger, if its leadership is not of the wisest, that it may sometimes become an instrument for petty and partisan ideas.

The first effort made in the name of the Legion here in New York City was for a rather pretty object. The leaders set out to stop an opera company from producing German opera. A campaign was made in the theatre to stir up sentiment against allowing such a production. Wounded soldiers were taken before the Mayor to make stronger upon him the demand to forbid the performance. The result of this agitation was the getting together of a crowd around the theatre where the performance was finally given which might easily have developed into a dangerous mob had it not been for the effective work of the police. The leaders in this movement declared that they were not protesting against German opera, but against it being sung in the German language.As though it made any difference what language opera is sung in. So far as understanding the words go, an opera had just as well been sung in Choctaw as in any other language.

Nevertheless, the Legion is going to be formed, and it is going to exercise some influence in the country. Colored men who fought in the war have a perfect right to representation in the organization, and they should see to it that they get it. In every state in the country, South as well as North, colored veterans should form posts and apply for admission in the regular way. The national convention is to meet soon in Minneapolis, and colored men should be there to insist upon their right to membership and representation.

All of the country is not of one mind on this issue. Many of the white men in the Northern States believe that the Negro is entitled to full rights of membership and representation. However, if the Negro is not there to insist upon this for himself; the matter is likely to go by the board.

Colored men in the army have had to fight against greater odds than those involved in the question of equal recognition in the American Legion; so they should not hesitate to fight this battle. A firm light on this ground will serve to put before the American people in the clearest sort of light the whole question of injustice to the Negro.

Talking about Criminals

November 22, 1919

So much has been said and printed in big black type about crimes and criminals among Negroes that many people, no doubt, have come to regard crime and Negro as synonymous. This is especially true as to the crime of rape. The propaganda of connecting the crime of rape with the Negro has been carried on so long and with such effectiveness that the public at large has been made to look upon rape as a crime peculiarly common to the Negro race.

This has been done in spite of facts and figures which prove the contrary. Last spring the writer published in these columns figures which showed that the Negro is not only not more addicted but is less addicted to this crime than many of the other groups in this country. In fact, figures for New York City showed that he had a lower rape percentage than either the foreign-born or native-born whites; the exact figures being for foreign-born whites 1.08, for native-born whites, .08, and for Negroes .05.

This writer also made the statement that when the Negro is guilty of that crime, he is never guilty of it in the perverted and bestial forms so common among some other groups. Rape among Negroes is always a crime of lust and never a crime of bestiality or degeneracy.

Perhaps, this opinion which has been formed against the Negro can best be combatted by calling attention occasionally to crime as it is committed among other groups. The Buffalo newspaper published two weeks ago accounts of a most atrocious case of criminal assault which took place in that city. A white girl, fifteen years old, was assaulted on three different occasions in one night by a gang of eight white men, and left lying gagged and unconscious in a back yard. Such a crime as that would shock the lowest and most hardened Negro criminals.

The accused men have been arrested. They are all young men, their ages ranging from nineteen to twenty-seven. There has been no talk of mobs or lynching; which speaks well for the sense of law and order in the city of Buffalo.

Crushing Out Radicalism

November 29, 1919

"Crushing out radicalism" is now the favorite indoor and outdoor sport all over the country. It is being engaged in by the government, by the reactionary press, by various "legions" of this and that, and by certain individuals who have set themselves up as special guardians of the safety of the nation.

The principal rule of the game is: You may do anything you please, lawful or unlawful, so long as you do it in the name of crushing out radicalism.

So we see mobs, little ones and big ones, lynching men, whipping them, applying tar and feathers to them, ordering them out of town; doing it in the name of crushing out radicalism, in the name of upholding law and order. These mobs are acting as mobs always do, without any inquiry into the guilt of their victims; and more than that, they are acting with the approbation of a majority public opinion and with the silent sanction of legally constituted authority.

The remarkable thing about this whole anti-radical propaganda is that no one engaged in it seems to have any realization of its utter folly. Not one seems to know that never in the history of the world has it been possible to crush out radicalism which was based on truth; that radicalism based on truth has always grown stronger through attempts to crush it out; and that radicalism which was not based on truth died out of itself.

Let anyone with common sense read history, and what will he see standing out plainer than anything else? He will see how utterly futile were the efforts of the existing order in any age of the world to oppose the spread and the acceptance of radical thought which had truth and justice as its foundation stones. He will be struck with the stupidity, the absurdity, the asinine blunderings of those efforts. He will begin to feel amazed, if he is a humanitarian, and amused, if he is a cynic, at the thought that the existing order all through history goes on making the same mistakes over and over. He will absolutely agree with Bernard Shaw in saying that Hegel was right when he said that we learn from history that men never learn anything from history.

It is true that the leaders of the existing order have not learned anything from the fall of Babylon down to the present day. There is a simple explanation: the leaders of the existing order, by the very reason that they are the leaders of the existing order, constitute a class that is blind and static. By the very nature of their position they cannot act otherwise than they do.

In the light of history and common sense it would seem that those who maintain the existing order would not go mad and froth at the mouth when confronted by a radical change, but that they would investigate it and try and find out what truth and justice it contained. But following such a sensible line of conduct is not possible, for the reason that, up to the present development of society, those who maintain the existing order are also in possession of the wealth, the luxury, the leisure, the positions of preferment, the sincures and assured futures. Therefore they are opposed to any change right or wrong. They blindly fight all change, feeling that change of any kind will affect their possessions. This brings us up to the economic interpretation of history.

New ideas need never expect help from this class. Those who champion new ideas must realize that they shall ever have to fight for them in the arena. Those who champion new ideas are certain of victory, if the ideas they fight for are based on truth; for not in the whole history of the world has truth ever been more than temporarily vanquished.

The Obvious Thing to Do

November 29, 1919

The press a day or two ago carried a story which came up out of Louisiana. A story which sounded passing strange, but which was based on such obviously common sense action that the real strangeness comes in thinking of it as strange at all.

In Bogalusa, a town in Louisiana, they had trouble, serious trouble. As a result of this trouble, four men were killed and several others are wounded. The dead men are L. E. Williams, president of the local branch of the American Federation of Labor and editor of "The Press," a union labor newspaper; A. Bouchillon and Thomas Gaines, union carpenters; and A. J. O'Rourke, a leader in union labor circles. Among the wounded are Jules Leblanc, former army captain and member of the Loyalty League.

The trouble came about through a clash between the Loyalty League, comprising representatives of the Great Southern Lumber Company and other important business interests of Bogalusa on the one hand and members of the labor unions on the other. The Great Southern Lumber Company, so the the labor men assert, had locked out about 2,500 employees because they would not tear up their union cards.

The protests from the union labor men caused the Loyal League to get together some 500 armed members, who held up a train a half mile from the railroad station and searched it for "undesirables." After the search of the train failed to reveal anyone they could "run out" of town, the crowd started out to find Saul Dechus, a Negro, alleged to have been active in "disturbing the relations" between the races. They did not find him that night, but were dumbfounded the next day to see Dechus walking down the main street of the town, on either side of him an armed white man, one of them O'Rourke and the other a strong labor union man.

The Loyalty Leaguers made an attempt to take Dechus, charging that he had been trying to start race rioting. The white labor men stood by him. When the Leaguers were reinforced, the labor men retreated into a garage. The Leaguers stormed the garage in increasing strength, with the result as stated above.

Here was an instance of white working men and black working men standing together. It gives promise that the day will come when the white working men of the South will see and understand that their interests and the interests of the black working men of the South are identical.

The white working man of the South ought to be able to see that it is impossible for him to get what he is fighting for unless he joins hands with the colored man. And he ought to be able to see that it is the plan of those who keep him out of what he is fighting for to do it by keeping him and the Negro apart. When white and black working men get together in the South for their common economic advantage, there are going to be some mighty changes.

A comment worth making on this affair is that the New York "Tribune" headed the whole story as follows: "NEGRO CAUSES FATAL CLASH IN LOUISIANA." Anyone reading only the "Tribune's" heading would gain the impression that here was another clash instigated and initiated by Negroes. There was as much reason in the "Tribune's" heading as there would be in the statement that the murderer's victim caused the electrocution of the murderer.

Learning What Is in the Back of a Negro's Head

July 24, 1920

The editor of "The Commercial-Appeal," Memphis, Tennessee, has been having an interesting experience. A couple of weeks ago he attended a Sunday afternoon meeting of colored people at Clarksdale, Mississippi. The meeting was held in the courthouse yard and was attended by several thousand people. The editor of "The Commercial-Appeal" was so interested that he wrote a column and a half editorial in his paper on his impressions.

He was impressed by the fact that it was interesting to look at the Negroes from the stand. "They were earnest and sympathetic." He was also impressed by the fact that "all the Negroes had on clean clothes; they were considerate of one another; they were as orderly as if they were at church." These were all important things for "The Commercial-Appeal" editor to learn, but after all, they were impressions of externals. We regard of greater importance his impressions from the light he got on what the Negro is thinking, or, as he puts it, the things in the back of the Negro's head. On this point he says:

> We found out some of the things that are in the back of the Negro's head. If a white man addresses an audience of Negroes all the good effects of his speech will be lost when he calls them "darkeys" or "niggers." The average white man referring to the Negro as "darkey" or "nigger" does not mean to wound the Negro. We think the Negro is super-sensitive about it. But people are moved by notions, just as well as monumental facts, and if a notion is imbedded in the mind of a man then we should give it consideration either until it is removed or until the other man sees that it is not worth while.

44

The editor of "The Commercial" is undoubtedly among those who claim that the Southern white man knows the Negro best; yet, here he is, a man who has presumably lived all his life among Negroes and has just found out that when a white man addresses an audience of colored people "all the good effects of his speech will be lost" if he calls them "darkies" or "niggers." A Northern white man who had lived among colored people a week would know that much.

We have said before that the Southern white man deceived himself when he thinks that Southern white people know Negroes better than Northern white people do. Southern white people know the Negro from outside, and from the outside only. A New England white school teacher who has taught in a colored school in the South for three years knows more about the Negro from the inside, more about the bitterness and anguish of soul that the race so often passes through, about its hopes, its despairs and its aspirations than a Southern white woman learns in a lifetime.

Some of the other things that the editor of "The Commercial-Appeal" learned were what the Negro is thinking about double justice in the courts, what he is thinking about lynching, and what he is thinking about the "Jim Crow" car. He seemed to be impressed by the story of one colored man, who told how he had been obliged to ride 300 miles and stand up all the way, except for a few miles.

We are glad that the editor of so influential a newspaper as "The Commercial-Appeal" has come to realize that the important thing for the white people of the South is to learn what is in the back of the Negro's head. He himself has started late, but better late than never. We hope that his knowledge will increase and increase rapidly.

A Thorn in the KKK's Side

April 9, 1921

There comes to our desk a copy of "The Searchlight," published at Atlanta, Ga., and seemingly the official organ of the Ku Klux Klan. The editorial page of this particular issue of "The Searchlight" contains three double columns of editorial matter embracing five articles. In three of these articles the National Association for the Advancement of Colored People is referred to specifically in a manner which acknowledges that the KKK regards the NAACP as its bitterest and strongest enemy.

This is a good sign and it is in line with the truth that this writer has been trying to impress at every opportunity, the truth that the Negro in America will never get his full rights until those who wish to deny them to him are afraid to do it. Talk about appealing to the conscience, sense of justice and all that sort of thing sounds all right on certain occasions, but in practice the theory does not work. Our cause must be right and just in order to win ultimately but it will not win simply because it is right and just. Righteousness and justice must be backed up by power.

When the Negro in America gains sufficient power, through the coordination of all the elements of strength in the race to make his enemies afraid to ignore or infringe upon his rights, then and not until then will he be allowed the enjoyment of those rights.

How Opinion Is Created

March 4, 1922

We have often said in these columns that many colored people have the vague idea that the opposition which the Negro meets in the United States is something floating around in the air which they bump up against frequently and which incommodes or handicaps them. The opposition which we meet as a race is not that sort of thing at all. It is something which has been thought out and worked out. The Negro must realize that he can meet this opposition only through the same methods by thinking out and working out his plans.

This business of thinking out and working out opposition to the Negroes goes on daily. We are not merely up against opposition which was created fifty years ago, much of which has been overcome but we are up against opposition which is being created each day. Our opponents are always thinking for us. That is why we need to be always on the alert. That is why so much truth is expressed in the line, "Eternal vigilance is the price of liberty."

An example of this was given at the National Conference of Bar Associations which met last week in Washington. This conference was made up of the various state organizations of the American Bar Association. At this conference a resolution was adopted requiring future members of the bar to have at least two years college education in addition to their regular law school work. After considerable discussion and opposition, this resolution was adopted.

Now, among other resolutions, was one proposed by W. H. Ellis of Florida. A resolution which provided that the respective state bar associations be empowered to establish their own regulations and qualifications for admission to the bar. Here was a resolution which looked innocent enough on its face, but it was loaded, loaded for Negro aspirants to the bar. It simply meant that Southern state bar associations would make regulations that would look fair enough, but which could be used to prevent colored lawyers being admitted to practice.

We are glad to note that the resolution was defeated.

An Exploded Tradition

March 4, 1922

Traditions are very slowly built up but more slowly destroyed. It is curious to observe how a tradition which has been long founded persists in spite of facts which prove it to be false. There are several traditions of this latter kind which cling to the Negro. One of them is that he has more superstitious fears than anybody else in this country; that he is terribly afraid of graveyards and ghosts and all the other supernatural phenomena.

The Negro himself has helped to foster and support this tradition. A great many of his best stories and some of his songs are all about hair-raising episodes in graveyards and about running from ghosts. So it is natural that white people would swallow this tradition whole. It would take a Freudian analysis to explain why the Negro has so many stories about running. The colored soldiers before the War and during the War were responsible for some of the most humorous of all the war stories and a great part of these Negro stories were concerned with running away in fear.

Now, the fact of the matter is that the Negro soldier told these stories but none of them ran at any time.

This tradition about the superstitious fears of the Negro figured in an episode in Los Angeles in connection with the murder of William D. Taylor, the motion picture director. The episode was at the same time serious and amusing.

One of the most important witnesses in the case is Henry Peavey who was employed in Taylor's household before and at the time of the murder. The murder, as is known, is still an unsolved mystery and everybody who had any close relations with the murdered man has been put through the most rigid examinations by the police and District Attorney.

It seems to have occurred to several reporters on the Los Angeles "Examiner," the Hearst publication in Los Angeles, a few days ago, that if they took the proper means they could get some valuable information out of Peavey. Accordingly, they set the stage with considerable ingenuity, as they thought, to bring forth the desired information.

Two men drove up to where Peavey was living and asked him to come out. He said to them that he was not doing any talking to newspaper reporters. The men then declared to him that they were not newspaper re-

47

porters but officials of the law and that they had come to go over certain of Peavey's statements with him. They suggested that he go with them to the office of the "Examiner" to answer these questions. He was kept in the office of the "Examiner" several hours. Peavey stated that the "Examiner" men several times referred to a spiritualist who would arrange for a conference between him, Peavey, and Taylor's spirit. After nightfall they put Peavey into an automobile and drove out to the cemetery. One of the reporters remarked, "Gee! Goodness! It makes me nervous to drive into a cemetery at night. How do you feel, Henry?"

Peavey said that he replied, "It don't bother me." The party then drove up to the vault where Taylor was buried. The lights on the car were suddenly turned out. The party got out and walked over to the vault. As they did so a man walked out from behind the vault made up like a ghost. The reporters then exclaimed, "Look! Look! Look! There's Taylor." The "ghost," according to Peavey's story, commenced to make funny noises, dropped down and caught him around the feet and commenced groaning. The reporters kept trying to have Peavey make some sort of confession to the "ghost," but Peavey's response was far from being a confession. He said to the men "What in the hell are you guys trying to make out of me a fool?" This exclamation ended the seance.

Peavey reported to District Attorney Woolwine. Mr. Woolwine characterized the action of the "Examiner's" reporters as "presumptuous, dangerous and dastardly." He denounced the alleged abductors of Peavey as "conscienceless blackguards."

And so it is seen that this episode is at once serious and amusing—serious because it is a case of abduction, which is a crime, and amusing because these reporters based their faith and expended their good money for auto hire and other expenses on the old exploded tradition that the sight of a ghost would so terrorize a Negro that it would make him tell both things that he knew and did not know about the murder mystery.

The Absurdity of American Prejudice

September 9, 1922

We are all familiar with the fact that Americans who have color prejudice are quite willing to swallow it if the object of their prejudice can be proven to be anything except an American Negro, and so there are many instances of prejudice being laid aside when it was thought or known that the colored person concerned was a Cuban, or a South American. or an East Indian, or even a native African. Many an American white man, who holds color prejudice as a religion, has foresworn the faith by believing or pretending to believe that the colored person who slept under the same hotel roof with him, or rode in the same Pullman car, or ate in the same dining room, was something other than an American Negro.

The most amusing incident of this kind is reported in a dispatch from Deauville, France, published in an issue of *The New York World* last week. On the closing night of the Casino at this famous French watering place, the King of Spain was present. The King of Spain is a jolly monarch and he is said to have passed the greater part of the evening dancing with the Dolly sisters, well-known on the American stage. Near the King's table was a table occupied by Winkfield, the American jockey, who a few days before had won the Grand Prize of Deauville, of one hundred thousand francs, by riding the winning horse. Mr. Winkfield was entertaining a friend at supper.

Perhaps the name Winkfield does not mean much to many of my readers, yet there are some of them who will remember that when colored jockeys were in their heyday in the United States, Winkfield was one of the greatest of them. Since the almost complete ruling of colored jockeys off the American tracks, Winkfield has been riding in Europe.

The *World* reports that when "certain Americans" noted the presence of Mr. Winkfield and his friend, they promptly registered a protest with the management of the Casino. "Whereupon," the dispatch states, "the Maitre d'hotel with infinite tact, told the Americans that Winkfield was the Prince of Kapurthala, son of the Punjab Maharaja of that ilk." Promptly those who had wished that the dusky visitors be given the gate expressed an earnest desire to be presented to the Prince. Winkfield was advised and gracious but grinning, "held a minor court for the rest of the evening."

If there is anything more irrational than American race prejudice, we would like to know what it is.

Let Them Come

February 10, 1923

Reports from the South indicate that the migration of colored people to the North is on a steady increase. Mr. Phil H. Brown of the Department of Labor and Mr. Shelby J. Davidson of Washington are both quoted in a despatch from Washington as saying that the activities of the Ku Klux Klan are adding strength and speed to this movement. If this is the cause of the movement, it is a bad one and ought to be stopped, but nevertheless the movement, itself, is bound to be beneficial.

We repeat, Let Them Come. The only time in his history in this country that the Negro has been able to exercise a power which forced the South to retreat from its traditional position was when during the great war the Negro left that section in large numbers. When the tide of migration during the war was at its height the South was ready to make any concessions regarding the treatment of colored people. If the movement could have kept up at the same rate for two or three years longer many things would have been voluntarily yielded which must now be fought for. However, if the conditions which now favor the new migratory movement of Negroes from the South to the North keeps up, the same opportunities for better racial adjustment will come again.

The Immigration bill approved this week by the House Immigration Committee increases the chances of still more favorable conditions for migration. As to admissions of immigrants, the new bill provides a limitation to two per cent of the number of foreign born individuals of any nationality resident in the United States. The present restriction is three per cent. Under the new law it is estimated that the total number of immigrants entering the United States in any one year will not exceed 168,837. Admissions under the existing law total 358,023 yearly. If this new bill goes into effect it will mean that the efforts of the great capitalistic industries to flood the country with cheap labor will not be effective and thereby these lucrative fields of labor will be open for Negroes.

We repeat what we said last week: That colored citizens in all northern and western communities to which Negro migrants are likely to come should make organized preparation now to receive them; to aid them; to give them directions and do everything possible to help them become adjusted to their new surroundings. This should be done not only for the benefit of the new-comer, but also for the protection and in the best interests of those who are already here.

A Forgotten Friend

February 10, 1923

The newspapers last week announced the death of Mrs. Eva A. Ingersol, who died in her home at 53 Grammercy Park at the age of eighty-three. This brings to mind a name which only a generation ago was one of the best known names in the United States, Robert G. Ingersol.

The majority of people who remember Ingersol at all remember him as one of the most popular orators that ever spoke from an American platform. But there was another side to Ingersol with which not many of his countrymen, perhaps, are familiar. He was a great lover of freedom. More particularly still the colored people of the United States ought to know and remember that Robert G. Ingersol was one of the greatest defenders the Negro in the United States ever had, one who was never afraid to come to his defense.

An incident is related which occurred before the Civil War. It was when Frederick Douglass was making anti-slavery speeches in the Middle west that he spoke one night in a town where after the meeting he found that there was no place where he would be allowed to sleep. Robert Ingersol took Frederick Douglass to his home and gave him a bed.

So far as this writer can remember, Ingersol was the first American whose voice commanded the ear of the nation to denounce lynching. It was after the burning of Sam Hose that Ingersol indicated American civilization with a vehemence that could not be surpassed. There are also records of many incidents of kindness and assistance from him to ambitious young colored men.

Robert G. Ingersol, like Thomas Paine, will on account of his religious beliefs, or rather unbeliefs, perhaps never be accorded his proper place as a great American. Nevertheless he was such. It would be well for the colored people of the United States at least to remember Ingersol as something more than an infidel.

The New Exodus

March 3, 1923

The new exodus of Negroes from the South is assuming proportions that are causing great alarm among the white people of that section. The principal newspapers of Georgia are discussing the question pro and con. Some of them are endeavoring to belittle the whole movement. *The Atlanta Constitution* is inclined to attach small importance to it and to attribute the movement, such as it is, more to economic than to other reasons.

A number of prominent leaders of the African Methodist Episcopal Church met in Atlanta and after discussing the situation issued a report upon it. The report set up that the colored people "are giving away the earnings of a lifetime; they are ruining our church membership; they are breaking up our churches to the extent that they often take the pastor with them." The report makes a plea for fair treatment. On this point the report as published in *The Atlanta Constitution* says, "The *Constitution* has pleaded for years that, while we are separate here from a social standpoint, our interests are common and that the Negro should be given a fair chance to make the most of himself and family."

We can easily understand how the leaders of the colored churches in the

51

South feel about this movement. It will very seriously affect their organizations. But the churches will not be the only ones to suffer. Colored business and professional men will suffer just the same. What the colored religious, professional and business leaders ought to avoid in this situation is exactly what some of them did when the movement was on several years ago. They should not appeal to the white people to help make it an opportunity to demand the removal as far as possible of the main causes for the exodus. These leaders are in a position where they do not need to make an appeal. They can make a strong, unqualified demand and place the burden of responsibility upon the white people. For example, we have one of these religious leaders commending the following statement which occurred in an editorial of the *Constitution*.

> The Negro belongs in the South. He has shown remarkable physical, mental, moral and material development in the South. He deserves fair treatment.

That sort of statement is too wishy-washy and sentimental. Why does the Negro belong in the South? Any man worth his salt belongs where he can do best. There is nothing sacred about the Negro having been born in the South. History is filled with examples of men who have left the lands in which their forefathers have lived for thousands of years when their conditions became oppressive and they felt that they could better themselves. If the Negro can come North and better his condition economically, educationally and politically, he would be nothing less than a fool to stay in the South simply because he was born there.

We hope that this movement will assume such proportions as will make the white South realize that it can no longer treat the Negro as he has been treated and still keep him in the South. We hope that the colored leaders in the South will take advantage of the opportunity that this movement offers to demand fairer treatment, treatment that will at least include freedom from peonage, a fair share of the educational fund, the right to vote under the same qualifications required of other citizens, common justice in the courts and the abolishment of lynching. However, whether the South concedes fairer treatment to the Negro or not, we hope the movement will keep up. The longer it keeps up, still more will the South be inclined to give fairer and still fairer treatment.

But under all circumstances the Negro will be better off if a million or two of them can come out of the South. As we said before, there are too many of them packed up there. This condition makes Negroes cheap in every respect, not only as labor but as life. It will be far better for them to spread over the country. We only hope that they will not crowd into the cities in large numbers. As many as are able should try and get on the land in the Middle West and in the Northwest.

Let the exodus keep up and let Negroes North and South, leaders and masses, endeavor to take the fullest strategic advantage of the movement.

2 | Lynching and Mob Violence

Undoubtedly, some people will find it difficult to understand why a supremacy of which we have heard so much, a supremacy which claims to be based upon congenital superiority should require such drastic methods of protection.

James Weldon Johnson, "Anglo-Saxon Supremacy
in Mississippi" (December 3, 1914)

James Weldon Johnson cited the "Jim Crow" laws of the South as a means to legalize the wide range of white America's prejudices toward African-Americans. Aspects of these prejudiced attitudes took the form of mob violence and lynchings.

Johnson himself had nearly been a victim of mob violence in his hometown of Jacksonville in 1901. And white America made the issue even more critically important when a series of race riots against black residents occurred in Wilmington, North Carolina (1898), New York City (1900), Atlanta (1906), Springfield, Illinois (1917), and some twenty-five other locations (during the "Red Summer" of 1919, as James Weldon Johnson termed it). In a wave of violence following World War I, seventy-six black people were lynched in 1919, fifty-three in 1920, and fifty-nine in 1921.[1]

Southern political leaders defended mob rule by holding rape out as the main cause of lynching. But Johnson attempted to counter this charge in his editorials when he wrote that of the 3,436 persons lynched in America from 1889 to 1921, only 571 or less than 17 percent was accused of the crime.[2] Consistent in his efforts to attack and expose the irrationality of lynching and its perpetrators, Johnson devoted nearly 50 percent of his editorials in the *Age* to the subject of lynching.[3] Pointing to its stain on American democracy, he believed that change could be brought about through educating all Americans and the world on the horrible details of these savage acts. He committed himself to the widest use of publicity against the crime of lynching during his tenure with the *New York Age*. "I am of the opinion that this can be done only through the fullest publicity," he wrote.[4]

After winning the support of the Harlem NAACP branch, he called for a silent parade to protest the many lynchings that had occurred in July 1917. During this march, he and W. E. B. Du Bois led over 12,000 blacks of all ages down Fifth Avenue to the sound of muffled drums.

Because several states had done little or nothing to eradicate lynching or even to treat it as a crime, Johnson looked to the federal government for protection against this heinous act. There had been several legislative possibilities, and finally in 1921 Congressman L. C. Dyer of St. Louis wrote to Johnson at the NAACP about reintroducing an anti-lynching bill in Congress. Johnson made a series of trips to Washington during the greater part of 1922 to lobby for passage of the Dyer Anti-Lynching Bill. The bill passed in the House but failed in the Senate. Afterward, Johnson reflected, "The Dyer Anti-Lynching Bill did not become a law, but it made the floors of the Congress a forum in which the facts were . . . brought home to the American people as they had never been before."[5]

Although the Dyer bill did not pass in the Senate, Johnson and the NAACP laid up a store of dividends for the black community in the process.[6]

The Frank Case Again

October 29, 1914

Atlanta Georgia, is still being stirred by the Leo M. Frank case. Every effort is being made by the defense to saddle the murder on the colored man, Conley.

Whether Frank murdered Mary Phagan or not we do not know; but the mere fact that Conley did not long ago make his exit from this terrestrial sphere, via a chariot of fire, is convincing proof that he, at least, is not the man who committed the deed.

Politically, the Negro of the Northern, Western and North Western States is the keeper of his brother in other sections of the country. Here, he has a vote, his vote is counted and, what is more important, his vote is a factor, in deciding the results of elections.

This is real political power, and it should not be traded for a mess of pottage. It should not be squandered for just some petty local advantages. It is a power that the nation should be made to feel.

The strongest lever for raising and maintaining the civil and political status of the entire race throughout the country is in the hands of the colored voters in these states; but results will depend upon the wisdom, the unity of purpose and the altruistic spirit with which it is used.

Lawlessness in the United States

November 12, 1914

There is a certain sort of American who never tires of proclaiming, in a loud and cacophonous voice that the United States is the biggest, the richest, the most powerful, the most highly civilized, etc., etc., etc., country in the world; since this sort of American's patriotism is expressed wholly in superlatives he might add that it is the most lawless.

Recent statistics show that the number of murders for each one hundred thousand of population is higher in the United States than in any other country. There is such a wide gap between the figures for the chief of Europe and of the United States that it makes comparison almost ridiculous.

The following tables show the number of murders per 100,000 inhabitants in principal European and American cities:

London	0.9
Berlin	2.0
Paris	3.5

That is, in London there was less than one murder committed for each one hundred thousand inhabitants; in Berlin two, in Paris three and one-half.

Compare the above figures with the following for three principal cities in the United States:

New York   7.1
Chicago   9.0
San Francisco 13.4

But, to be appalled, consider the rates in these less important cities:

New Orleans   24.
San Antonio   28.
Charleston   30.
Atlanta   33.
Savannah   48.
Memphis   68.

In London, less than one murder for each one hundred thousand inhabitants; in Memphis sixty-eight murders for each one hundred thousand inhabitants! On its face that looks like the difference between civilization and barbarism, and it comes very near being what it looks like on its face.

Of course, it will be cited that the greater rate shown by the Southern cities is due to the larger Negro population. Indirectly, the Negro is responsible for this; for if they were fewer in number there would be less of them to be murdered.

The statistics do not state whether the lynchings in this country are included; at any rate, the lynching record of the United States multiplies, instead of adds to, its figures.

It is an unenviable distinction. The United States, the great example of democracy, yet the only civilized states where lynchings are a common practice, and the only spot on the entire globe where would be tolerated the burning alive of human beings.

Anglo-Saxon Supremacy in Mississippi

December 3, 1914

The white chivalry of Byhalia, Miss., got together last week and vindicated Anglo-Saxon supremacy by lynching a Negro and his wife on suspicion of burning a planter's barn; and so the Mississippi brand of supremacy is safe for a while at least. The next time it is in danger it may be found necessary to throw stronger protection around it. This may be done by lynching a Negro and his wife, with the baby thrown in. After the baby stage is reached there will not be much that can be done. Of course, there still remain the unborn babies; they might be lynched together with the others; but after all, a limit must be reached some day, and when that is reached we fail to see what more can be done.

Undoubtedly, some people will find it difficult to understand why a supremacy of which we have heard so much, a supremacy which claims to be based upon congenital superiority should require such drastic methods of protection. They will, perhaps, feel that great superiority would be its own protection. However, these people are mere mollycoddles who do not know "Southern conditions."

The tragedy of this incident is of such proportions as to lead us almost to the verge of laughter—hysterical laughter. Here is what is called a civilized and Christian state of great democracy, a man and his wife, citizens of that state, are lynched on suspicion of burning a barn, and the affair doesn't attract one one-hundredth part of the attention attracted by the announcement of the foot and mouth disease among western cattle. The average man read it in his newspaper as an ordinary news item. A great many readers skipped it as unimportant news.

One of the great New York dailies took it up and treated it editorially. The "New York World" it was that spoke out again in a strong article which we reproduce here in full:

THE USUAL CRIME

The mob that lynched a Negro and his wife near Byhalia, Miss., on suspicion of burning a planter's barn was actuated, we are quite sure, solely by desire to protect the honor of Southern women. Northern people may wonder what barn-burning has to do with criminal assaults, but it is none the less "the usual crime" where a Negro is concerned, just as insulting a white man or striking a policeman or any offense perpetrated by a Negro is "the usual crime" for purposes of immediate and condign punishment at the hands of the mob.

In saying this the "world" is well aware that it will be reminded by forty or more Southern newspapers that it is slandering the South and that it is utterly ignorant of the conditions of racial relationship which necessitate the use of the rope burning at the stake to safeguard womanhood.

There is, of course, ample testimony to the contrary, showing that only a small percentage of Negro lynchings are due to assaults on white women or even to rumors of such assaults. Of thirteen lynchings in the entire country in the first quarter of 1913, not one, Booker T. Washington demonstrated at the time, was caused by "the usual crime." Of forty-five lynchings in ten months of that year, only seven were for assault. But what have figures to do with the case? The one satisfactory thing about them is that the general decrease of lynching the country over necessary effects a diminution of lynchings for "the usual crime."

Reaping the Whirlwind

February 25, 1915

In last week's issue we called attention to despatches relating the lynching of two white men, one in Georgia and another in Kentucky. We also quoted an editorial from the Atlanta "Constitution" which closed with this sentence, "If several Negroes can be lynched for a crime that was not even a capital offense, and the lynchers go unwhipped of justice, what guarantee is there that the lives of white men and women under similar circumstances are safe?"

In these lines the "Constitution" is making an appeal for justice. Of course, as is natural, its ideas of justice and all the other humane virtues are very much twisted. Suppose the lives of white men and women "under similar circumstances" were absolutely safe, would that make the lynching of Negroes any more excusable? If anything, it ought to make the deed less excusable.

However, the communal conscience in places where mob law is allowed to rule is in such a condition that [it] cannot be touched except by some such argument as that put forth by the "Constitution." The people of such a community must be told that if white men are allowed to lynch colored men and women with impunity it will not be long before they will also lynch white men and women. So we must give the great Atlanta daily credit for using the strongest argument (in words) it could lay hands on.

The warning uttered by the "Constitution" is rapidly becoming a fulfilled prophecy; another recent despatch says:

MOB TAKES WHITE MAN FROM JAIL; LYNCHES HIM

Forest Hill, Mo., Feb. 28—A white man believed to be W. F. Williams of Hot Springs, Ark., who took part in a pistol battle in which a policeman and an unidentified man were killed, was taken from the jail here and lynched by a mob.

Early risers discovered the body riddled with bullets hanging from the fire bell tower above the City Hall, where it remained till noon.

But just a word to the Atlanta "Constitution" and to the State of Georgia. Why argue about the matter at all? Or why wait for a number of what might be innocent white men and women to be lynched, in hope that it will result in stopping the lynching of colored men and women? There is a method so simple, so direct, so sure and, withal, so obvious that it could not have been overlooked by the "Constitution" except purposely. It is nothing more than to hang the leaders of each lynching mob.

The leaders of the mob that recently lynched a Negro father, his son and two daughters at Monticello can easily be found out. We have no doubt that their identity is already common knowledge.

If the "Constitution" is in earnest, if Judge Parks and Jasper County are in earnest, if the State of Georgia is in earnest, let the leaders of the Monticello mob be hanged; and lynching, in Georgia, at least, permanently go out of fashion.

A New Crime

April 22, 1915

It has been a good many years since the phrase "For the usual crime" has lost force. As a cause for lynching the "usual crime" has come to be almost negligible. This being the case, the promoters of lynchfests have had to cast about for new crimes. Sometimes they have been hard put to find them. Murder for a while headed the list, but it was found that not sufficient murders were committed to furnish reasons for the desired number of lynchings.

An enumeration of the various deeds that are now regarded as just causes for lynching would require the making of an alphabetically arranged catalog. These "causes" run all the way from heinous offenses down to being impudent to a white man.

One might think that including impudence to a white man among the "causes" for lynching would be as far as inhuman ingenuity could go, but such a one is mistaken; a despatch comes from Valdosta, Georgia, which states that a Negro who had been accused of stealing some meat from the smoke-house of a white preacher was taken from jail and shot to death.

One might also think that we are wrong in classing the stealing of meat from a smoke-house as a more trivial "cause" than being impudent to a white man; we repeat, such a one is mistaken.

According to the ethics of professional Anglo-Saxons, a Negro in being impudent to a white man makes a denial of the white man's infinite superiority; he, in fact, implies Negro equality; and, according to professional Anglo-Saxon ethics, few things deserve to rank higher in the catalog of "causes for lynching." Whereas, to steal a ham from a smoke-house is a clear demonstration and acknowledgement of Negro inferiority. Now, looking at it from the professional Anglo-Saxon point of view, we can see why a Negro might be lynched for asserting equality, but we fail to understand why he should be lynched for demonstrating inferiority.

It is clear that the Georgians who lynched the Negro who was accused of stealing meat from a smoke-house have established a new record. It would be a hopeless guess to venture to say what "cause" will next be added to the catalog of "crimes."

Concerns Not Even the Sheriff

August 5, 1915

Not satisfied with the fact that statistics show an increase in the number of lynchings for the first six months of the present year, some citizens of Texas a few days ago resolved to raise the percentage with respect to cruelty. A Negro who was accused of murder—mind you, not rape, was taken from the court and burned at the stake. If we remember correctly, Texas was the American pioneer in this form of inhuman savagery, but it seems that she wishes not only to be recorded as the pioneer, but hailed as the reviver of a practice that would shame cannibals.

But of graver import than the action of the Texas mob is the apathy of the country; some of the newspapers did not even carry this incident as an item of news, and we have yet to see an editorial protest against it.

It does seem like hollow hypocrisy that this nation is now standing as the protector of human rights before the world, that it is ready to raise armies and navies to uphold the principle of international law which guarantees protection to non-combatants aboard merchant vessels; even when those vessels belong to belligerents; and yet, the fact that within its own borders one of its own citizens is taken from the custody of the lawfully constituted courts and burned at the stake by a mob will not call for the raising of even a sheriff's posse.

Not So in Mississippi

August 12, 1915

Last week, in an article on capital punishment, we expressed the belief that the time must soon arrive when executions for crime will be abolished or when the newspapers will discontinue their present manner of handling notorious criminal cases, because our civilization is growing too high-minded and too tense for such exhibitions. The belief we expressed may apply to New York and some other communities in the effete East, but it applies in no way to the pristine and undergenerate civilization of Mississippi.

Despatches of a few days ago report at Starkville, Miss., the hanging of two Negroes was made the occasion for a general holiday. We learn that the merchants of Starkville advertised the hanging widely, and, as a result 5,000 farmers, white and black, with their wives and children, from adjoining communities attended.

The executions were arranged to take place in a sort of natural amphitheatre where the gallows served as a stage. The festivities began with the free distribution of sandwiches and lemonade; soda fountains and watermelon wagons did a rushing business. Before the main event of the program several candidates for office took the platform, or rather the gallows, and delivered political speeches.

If the despatches are to be believed, the two condemned men were super-humorists; they occupied seats to the rear of the speakers and joined with the audience in appreciation of the oratorical efforts. They are also reported to have eaten several large watermelons with keen relish and with profuse thanks to the donors, and to have joined heartily in the religious exercises which preceded the executions.

So it appears that everybody had a pleasant time, even the condemned men. The women had a chance to wear their best clothes, the children had an outing, the local politicians had a chance to reach their constituency, and merchants of Starkville were, no doubt, repaid for their generous outlay by the resulting increase in trade.

A Sign of Hope

January 20, 1916

No more hopeful sign for us as a race has appeared than that contained in the news columns of last week's "Age," where were recorded the resolutions against lynching adopted by the University Commission on Southern Race Questions which recently held its session at Trinity College and the University of North Carolina.

The Commission is composed of eleven white professors of colleges in as many Southern states. The states represented are Texas, South Carolina, Mississippi, Louisiana, Tennessee, Georgia, Virginia, North Carolina, Florida, Arkansas and Alabama. That about covers all the ground. We say this is a most hopeful sign, because it is not only an evidence of the awakening of conscience on the part of the best white Southern elements, but that these elements have reached the point where they are no longer afraid to speak out against a public opinion which has heretofore compelled and exacted silence.

When a large enough proportion of Southerners have reached this point, then, and not before then will the race question find adjustment; for say or do what we will, no matter how many friends we may have on the outside, the final adjustment of the question lies between the white man and the Negro in the South. It has got to be settled there and by them, but it will be completely and righteously settled only when common Southern sentiment is in line with what the University Commission is striving to do.

Anarchy in Georgia

January 27, 1916

Only a few weeks ago Georgia published a declaration of superiority by lynching seven Negroes and burning down the meeting places of several colored lodges. Now comes the news of a mob in the same state hanging five Negroes who were suspected of implication in the murder of a Sheriff. The mob of forty or fifty men, as in the Frank lynching, did its work with the aid of automobiles. The automobile is finding uses in Georgia which might justify manufacturers in designing and advertising especially for that state a "lynching car." Some of the features of such a car might be a noiseless engine, tires adapted to deep clay or sandy roads, each car fitted with an adjustable, steel limb guaranteed to sustain the weight of from one to six Negroes—this latter feature would save the necessity of hunting up suitable trees. If room for more than six "lynchees" were required, several cars could be used. Of course, any clever inventor could think of a dozen other useful accessories.

When the lynching epidemic broke out in Georgia some months ago, in several articles on the Empire State of the South, we about exhausted our vocabulary of protest; in order to avoid an anticlimax we can now only ask a few questions.

Can the law-abiding element in Georgia continue to look with complacency upon the record which the mob element is making for the state?

If the law-abiding element is not strong enough in numbers to rise up and crush out this sort of lawlessness, is it not strong enough in moral courage to speak out against it?

Is this action of the mob Georgia's answer to the resolution condemning lynching adopted a week ago by the University Commission on Southern Race Questions which met at the University of North Carolina?

Committing and allowing to be committed such lawless deeds as have taken place within the past twelve months, wherein lies the real superiority of Georgia over Mexico.

The only salvation for Georgia, both as to its internal welfare and its outside reputation lies in the hands of the law-abiding and law-loving element of its white citizens. That there is such an element we know, and that its moral courage as well as its conscience is being aroused we are hopeful. But it must act, and it must act quickly and effectively. Even if it does not care to act to save the Negro especially, it must do so to save the state and save itself.

Those Valiant Texans

June 1, 1916

During the past three years which we have been harrassed by Mexico, in which Americans have been murdered and despoiled, both on this and on the other side of the Rio Grande, the nation has been made to look upon the fierce and fearless denizens of Texas as hounds straining at the leash. The growls and barks that came up out of Texas seemed to mean but one thing, "Let us get at the greasers!"

Somehow or other the country was reassured. It was led to feel whatever might be our state of unpreparedness, whatever might be the shortcomings of our regular and our irregular army, whatever might be the daredevilishness of the Mexicans, the American nation was safe so long as there was a Texas full of gallant Texans. Away down in their hearts, the rest of the people in the United States have felt that if worst came to worst, it would be necessary only to give these Texans permission and they would sweep across the border mowing down Mexicans before them like wheat before a modern machine scythe.

It was all a dream. We woke up to find that we have been putting our trust in a broken reed. The hour of need came, Texas itself was invaded. American soldiers and Texas citizens were killed upon Texas soil, our army commanders confessed that they did not have sufficient force, and the President called out the Texas militia.

We feel that neither the President nor the country at large would have been surprised if not only the Texas militia, but every able-bodied citizen in Texas between the ages of sixteen and sixty had sprung to the colors. But not only the able-bodied citizens, but even the militia have failed to do any noticeable amount of springing. Worse still, some of the members of the militia refuse point blank to mow down Mexicans or even to protect

Texans and other Americans in the danger zone; as a result, some one hundred and sixteen officers and men will be courtmartialed.

In the meantime, out on the hot Mexican desert there are thousands of black men who honorably wear the uniform of the United States army, who are fighting to protect the property and homes and lives of the citizens of Texas. What are these Texans who, in violation of their oath, refuse to answer the country's call, who refuse to defend and protect the soil of their own state, what are they doing in return for the loyalty and bravery of those who are fighting? They are burning black men at the stake.

When it comes to tramping across the hot sands of Mexico, and being shot at by bandits, the valor of the precious Texan does not appear to rise to the boiling point; but when it comes to a mob of several thousand seizing a Negro boy, dragging him through the street, chaining him to a stake and burning him alive in the public square of one of their cities, the gallant Texan is Johnny-on-the-spot.

The Silent Parade

July 26, 1917

The colored citizens of New York are arranging to hold on Saturday a silent parade of protest on Fifth avenue. It is proposed to have ten thousand men, women and children march with banners bearing inscriptions that set forth the services of labor and loyalty which the race has given to the country and the wrongs and injustices which it has been made to suffer in return.

If this purpose is successfully carried out, it will be the most effective effort ever made by the American Negro to let the nation know that he resents these wrongs and will be satisfied with nothing less than the treatment which is the rightful due of every American citizen.

It ought to be a great success. Out of the colored population of Greater New York, there should be not ten thousand but twenty thousand marchers. Such a sight as that, twenty thousand colored school children, men and women marching in silent dignity as a protest against the treatment to which the race is submitted in the United States would be so impressive that New York City and the entire country would be compelled to take notice. In fact, the effect would be felt all over the world. No mass meeting, however great, and no speeches, however eloquent, could accomplish as much.

And this is just the time for such demonstration; with Waco and Memphis and East St. Louis still fresh in our memory and, with America waging a war in the name of humanity and democracy. Such a demonstration should be made not only by the Negroes of New York, but by the Negroes in each city in the country where it is possible to do so. These demonstrations should be made now and simultaneously.

An Army with Banners

August 3, 1917

Last Saturday the silent protest parade came off, and it was a greater success than even the committee had dared to hope it would be. Some of the New York papers estimated the number of marchers in line as high as fifteen thousand. It was indeed a mighty host, an army with banners.

No written word can convey to those who did not see it the solemn impressiveness of the whole affair. The effect could be plainly seen on the faces of the thousands of spectators that crowded along the line of the march. There were no jeers, no jests, not even were there indulgent smiles; the faces of the onlookers betrayed emotions from sympathetic interest to absolute pain. Many persons of the opposite race were seen to brush a tear from their eye. It seemed that many of these people were having brought home to them for the first time the terrible truths about race prejudice and oppression.

The power of the parade consisted in its being not a mere argument in words, but a demonstration to the sight. Here were thousands of orderly, well-behaved, clean, sober, earnest people marching in a quiet dignified manner, declaring to New York and to the country that their brothers and sisters, people just like them, had been massacred by scores in East St. Louis for no other offense than seeking to earn an honest living; that their brothers and sisters, people just like them, were "Jim Crowed" and segregated and disfranchised and oppressed and lynched and burned alive in this the greatest republic in the world, the great leader in the fight for democracy and humanity.

The impact of this demonstration upon New York City was tremendous. And it is not strange that it was so. More than twelve thousand of us marching along the greatest street in the world, marching solemnly to no other music than the beat of muffled drums bearing aloft our banners on which were inscribed not only what we have suffered in this country, but what we have accomplished for this country, this was a sight as has never before been seen.

But, after all, the effect on the spectators was not wholly in what they saw, it was largely in the spirit that went out from the marchers and overpowered all who came within its radius. There was no holiday air about this parade. Every man, woman and child that took part seemed to feel what it meant to the race. Even the little six-year-old tots that led the line seemed to realize the full significance of what was being done. And so it was that these thousands and thousands moving quietly and steadily along created a feeling very close to religious awe.

When the head of the procession paused at 30th Street I looked back and saw the long line of women in white still mounting the crest of Murray Hill, the men's column not yet in sight; and a great sob came up in my throat and in my heart a great yearning for all these people, my people, from the helpless little children just at my hand back to the strong men bringing up the rear, whom I could not even see. I turned to Dr. Du Bois at my side and said, "Look!" He looked, and neither of us could tell the other what he felt.

It was a great day. An unforgettable day in the history of the race and in the history of New York City.

More Toll for Houston

February 9, 1918

When the news was suddenly flashed over the country that thirteen soldiers of the Twenty-fourth infantry had been hanged, without any opportunity to appeal their cases, and that several score men of the same regiment had been sentenced to imprisonment for participation in what has been termed "The Houston Riot," colored Americans experienced a feeling that can never be expressed.

In the heart of every Negro man, woman and child in the United States there welled up a feeling of pain, bitterness and anguish, made more acute by a sense of importance. And it was not because they did not realize that these soldiers had been guilty of violating the military law and even more than the military law, but because they knew so well the devilish and fiendish baiting that had goaded the men to do what they did.

A few weeks ago the news was given out that five more men of the Twenty-fourth had been condemned to death as the result of a second court martial but even this does not seem to be the end; as the following recent despatch shows:

> SAN ANTONIO, *Tex., Jan. 30*—Forty Negroes of the 24th Infantry, now at Fort Bliss, El Paso, were ordered brought here today for court martial in connection with the riots at Houston, Tex. The tentative date was fixed as February 12.
>
> Thirteen men were hanged as a result of the first court martial, and five

were given death sentences in the second, but these sentences await Presidential approval.

The record for a half century proves the men of the Twenty-fourth Infantry to be brave, loyal and orderly soldiers at all times and in all places—except Texas. Why they were otherwise in Texas is easily answered. Of course it was a crime for them to go out and kill citizens of Houston, so is it a crime for revolutionists to rise up and chop off the heads of their overlords. But already thirteen of these men have hanged for the lives of the thirteen Houston citizens killed in the riot; and among the thirteen hanged was Blatimore, the colored soldier whose brutal treatment by the bloodthirsty Houston police led to the outbreak.

More than forty men of the regiment were sentenced to life imprisonment on the first trial; since that, five more have been condemned to death, and now forty more are to be tried. No doubt, according to Texas values the execution of an entire Negro regiment would not make up for the life of one white murderer of Negroes on the Houston police force, but this matter is in the hands of the Government and not Texas, and the Government should be made to know that all colored Americans and a great many white Americans feel that a halt should be called until something is done to punish the men who were primarily responsible for what happened at Houston.

The War Department and President Wilson should be flooded with letters and telegrams. The race should let the Administration and the country understand that we are concerned about the fate of these men, and that we are not satisfied with the sort of justice which extorts such an overwhelming toll, without even inquiring into the guilt and responsibility of the other side.

My reader, whoever you are, sit down and write such a letter or telegram to-day. Couch your communication in restrained and respectful language, but let it plainly express the deep feelings of the American Negro on this matter.

Methods to Abolish Lynching

August 24, 1918

The extraordinary announcement of the San Antonio (Texas) Express that it had set aside a fund of $100,000 to be used in combating the crime of lynching in this country has attracted a great deal of attention.

At a meeting of the stockholders of the Express Publishing Company

67

on the first of this month, it was determined to devote this sum of money to the purpose of rewarding persons who shall be directly responsible for the arrest and conviction of those who incite riots and mob outbreaks that result in lynchings, and of those who perpetrate the lynching crime itself. The terms of the fund provide that a reward of $500 will be paid to each person who shall be directly responsible for the arrest, with subsequent conviction and punishment, of any person or persons who were instrumental in arousing a mob to commit a lynching or in putting through the lynching itself, when the individual lynched was a Negro.

The newspapers of the country, and especially the colored newspapers, have commented upon and commended this sincere effort on the part of this great Southern daily to do something practical to remove the stain of lynching from the South and the country; and the effort deserves all the commendation that may be given it. However, it is our opinion that the most promising thing about the anti-lynching fund of the Express is that it is a sign of the awakening of a public sentiment against lynching; if that sentiment becomes general and dominant the days of lynching will be numbered; but as to the effect the fund itself will have, we do not entertain any very great hopes.

The unsurmountable difficulty which the providers of this fund are going to find is this in a community where there is a sentiment and public opinion which permit and uphold lynchings there will also be a sentiment and opinion which will make it next to impossible for any person to gain a reward by giving information and testimony against those guilty of lynching. In such a community, any colored person who gave the necessary information and testimony would do so at the risk of his life; any white person who gave this information and testimony would do so at the risk of his economic, business or social position; both of these considerations would make a reward of $500 or even $1,000 seem too small for risks involved.

Just consider what it would mean for any reputable white person in or around Valdosta, Ga., to go before the authorities and for a reward of $1,000 give testimony that would lead to the arrest, conviction and punishment of the men who took part in the recent lynching of a half-dozen or more Negroes in that vicinity. If he had a job he would lose it, and nobody would dare give him another. If he had a business it would be ruined. If he had social position he would become an outcast. We need not consider what it would mean for a Negro to be the informer.

Moreover, the terms of the fund contain a provision that is necessary but which will act as a drawback; it is that no reward will be paid except in cases where arrest is followed by conviction, and conviction by punishment. This provision is necessary, because without it there would be a temptation for giving information against innocent persons; but it also entails the ordeal of testifying in the court and following the case through to end an ordeal which most people shrink from even in ordinary cases. It is our opinion that when a community has a public sentiment that will permit persons living in it to gain a reward by informing against lynchers, it has at the same time a public sentiment that will not permit lynching.

There is still another consideration which makes us less hopeful about the results that will be accomplished by the Express antilynching fund. Information as to the persons who perpetrate lynchings is not the thing most lacking. The thing most lacking is the courage of the authorities and the community to arrest, try and convict those who are guilty of the crime. It may be said that in ninety per cent of lynching cases it is generally known who the leaders of the mob were; at any rate, it would require only very little effort for the authorities to find out, and this could be done without offering a reward. The great difficulty is to find officers of the law with the courage to arrest and try, and juries with the courage to convict those who are guilty. Perhaps it would be more effective to offer rewards for officers who arrest lynchers, and even for juries who convict them.

The fact that it is almost impossible to convict persons who are guilty of lynching is deplorable, but it is not so much to be wondered at when we consider how often it is difficult in law abiding communities to convict persons who are guilty of common murder. We can reason that it is much harder to get a jury to pass the death sentence upon a crowd of fellow citizens who are murderers than upon a solitary murderer; yet it is often impossible to get them to do the latter. So the question naturally arises, even if persons are found who will come forward and earn the rewards offered by the Express how much nearer will it bring us to the conviction and punishment of lynchers?

Since it is so difficult to secure the conviction and punishment of lynchers, it seems that the best way to fight lynching is to adopt means for preventing the crime. And so we are inclined to place more hope in a bill that is being considered by the Georgia Legislature than in the Express fund. This bill provides for the removal from office of any sheriff who permits a prisoner to be taken from his custody or the custody of the deputies and lynched.

It would be a better law if it provided for the removal from office of any sheriff who permitted a lynching in his county. Such a law would not be unfair to sheriffs. If the captain of a ship allows his vessel to run on the rocks or ashore or to suffer any other accident which is in any degree due to his negligence or incapacity, he is dismissed, and his career as a sea captain is over. Now whenever a lynching occurs, it is due to the incapacity, cowardice or inaction of the sheriff of the county in which it happens. This is for the simple reason that no one man nor two men nor three men ever commit a lynching. Lynching is a cowardly crime, and it always takes a crowd to commit it. To raise a crowd and work up the mob spirit takes time and is something that cannot be done in secrecy. Therefore, if a sheriff has a sufficient number of capable deputies stationed throughout the county, no lynching could occur without his knowledge of what was likely to happen. If he knows what is likely to happen and does not take steps to prevent it, he ought to be removed from office.

It has been repeatedly proved that as few as three brave men with loaded guns in their hands and backed by the law and determined to carry it out can stop any lynching mob that was ever formed. One man can do it if he is brave enough to shoot. We believe that even sheriffs in Georgia, if confronted by the alternative of losing their jobs or shooting to uphold the law and protect their prisoners, will shoot, and shoot to kill. And every sheriff who shows a determination to shoot to kill, will find mobs melting away like mist before the rising sun.

We think plans to prevent lynching will be more productive results than plans to punish those who have committed lynchings; yet we are glad of this effort on the part of the San Antonio Express. For even if it leads to no convictions and punishments of lynchers, it will serve to waken and strengthen public sentiment against the crime; and that, after all, is what the country must have before lynching can be entirely abolished.

Teaching Negroes "a Lesson"

September 13, 1919

Many of the lynchings and other outbreaks which are now taking place are for the sole purpose of "teaching the 'niggers' a lesson." All over the South and in some other sections of the country there is the opinion that the colored soldiers got some "bad ideas" in ther heads over in France, and they need to be taken out. This opinion grew out of letters written by white soldiers on the other side, and has been greatly spread since their return.

So, those whites who are the upholders of a special brand of "Anglo-Saxon superiority" feel that the most drastic steps must be taken at once to let the Negro know what his place is, now and for all time. They think that by lynching and mobbing they can force the Negro to cease aspiring for the things which the nation so recently called on him to fight for.

The poor fools! Can't they understand that the more Negroes they outrage, the more determined the whole race becomes to secure the full rights and privileges of freemen? And this determination cannot be destroyed by lynching a dozen Negroes a day.

Thousands of colored men died in France fighting for liberty; so the race is not panic stricken by the mere thought of death.

Dealing with Mobs

October 11, 1919

It would be a hard matter to put more blame than belongs on the unconscious or premeditated assininity of police authorities for the results which have attended recent outbreaks of mob violence.

This is especially true of Omaha, where a costly public building was almost destroyed, the life of the sheriff threatened and the mayor all but lynched.

Naturally a great deal of admiration and sympathy has gone out to the mayor of Omaha for the heroic stand which he took and for the grave consequences which he suffered; but, after all, his stand and the consequences should and could have been made absolutely unnecessary.

What would anyone think of the chief of a fire department who, on seeing a fire starting, keep his men squirting water on it through atomizers until the whole building was ablaze; and then, at risk of his life, plunge into the burning structure to put out the flames? His act of plunging into the burning building might be a proof of bravery and heroism, but the fact that such a chance on the building and such a risk to the lives of himself and his men were avoidable would make the whole course of his action assinine.

This is just the sort of thing which was allowed to happen in Omaha. The fire of the mob spirit began to kindle and blaze and spread for several days before it became a great conflagration; and all the while the police were busy squirting on it through atomizers.

A mob is never the result of the spontaneous and simultaneous uprising of ten thousand or one thousand or even one hundred people. A mob is always the result of the activities of one person or of a very few persons. Around this small nucleus the mob begins to gather and grow until it becomes a raging, surging mass of humans turned, for the time, into beasts and fiends. When the mob reaches this stage it is beyond control.

The plain duty then before police authorities when the mob spirit is sensed—and it is easy to sense—is not to allow any nucleus to be formed. In the two or three days before the mob reached the uncontrollable stage the Omaha police should not have allowed any gathering on the streets whatever. Whenever small knots of people came together they should have been promptly dispersed. This should have been done, even if it took guns to do it. If such a policy had been carried out no mob would have been formed.

The Omaha authorities are now seeking a man named William Francis. This man is said to have ridden a horse at the head of the mob on the afternoon of the outbreak. The newspapers report that Francis carried a rope on his saddle, with which he said he would "string him up": and that he threw the rope out into the crowd several times and lectured to the mob when it seemed to weaken. It is all very well to arrest Francis now and punish him for his part in stirring up the mob, but the proper thing to have done was to arrest Francis while he was stirring up the mob. This should have been done by taking Francis alive, if possible; but dead, if necessary.

When General Wood took charge in Omaha he gave a lesson to the police departments of every city in the country. The prime lesson which He gave was contained in the order which he issued to his men. He said to them:

> When you go to make an arrest use no more force than is necessary and use all the force that is necessary. Remember you are sent for a certain man. Come back with him. Bring him in alive, if possible. But bring him in.

The chief weakness of police authorities all over the country is that they temporize with mobs whenever the intended victim of the mob is a Negro. And they do this because ninety-nine out of every hundred white men whose sworn duty it is to uphold the law cannot bring themselves to the point of enforcing the law TO THE UTMOST against white men for the protection of a Negro.

Away down in their hearts they do not believe that white mobbists should be killed in order to give a Negro a fair trial before the law. Until officers of the law are men of sufficient courage to believe and act otherwise they will always be at the mercy of mobs.

3 Women

There is a class of men and women that can stand on their own initiative, their own courage, and their own power, asking for equal opportunity and a fair chance. Also there is a class of women and likewise of men who cannot do this but require to be sheltered or provided for in one way or another.

James Weldon Johnson, "Equality of Privileges for Women"
(September 2, 1922)

In his column, James Weldon Johnson aggressively supported the Woman Suffrage Movement. He stated that every argument against woman suffrage is based on ignorance. His interest in the women's movement centered mainly on the issue of voting rights. He laid before his readers both sides of the argument. The right to vote should not depend on qualifications such as education, wealth, color, or sex; these restrictions are wrong in principle, he wrote.[1] Johnson believed that if women were given the right to vote, the political effectiveness of the African-American vote would become doubled, and the "colored" vote would become an instrument of power.[2]

Johnson's respect and admiration for all women in general is apparent, but he expressed a particularly special sentiment for black women. He was especially sensitive to the black woman's double burden of race and gender. "She is confronted by both a woman question and a race problem, and is as yet an unknown or an unacknowledged factor in both."[3] Johnson praised black women to his readers for their strong and active participation in the women's movement. Citing their courage, he noted that Southern white men concluded that black women were less intimidated than black men in their attempt to vote.

Johnson underscored the similarities between the race problem and the question of prejudice against women. He acknowledged, however, that the women's movement had learned and was following the practice that money was needed to place their cause before the public. He challenged his readers to donate more money to counter the prevailing public opinion about African-Americans. If black publications like the *Age* received more financial support from the black community, they could become better and larger instruments for shaping public opinion on African-Americans, he noted.

The Letter from a Colored Wife and Mother

April 20, 1915

Elsewhere we publish a letter from "a colored wife and mother" which is more than interesting, it is disquieting. It is more than a heart cry against war from a mere woman, it is a heart cry from a colored woman and those who read the letter will understand how much more that means.

Our correspondent makes no pretense of setting up a logical argument why colored men should not enlist to fight; she is speaking not for her head, but from her heart; and, possibly, she is speaking for the hearts of thousands of other colored wives and mothers. The letter is disquieting because it makes us pause and consider what the result would be if the women of the race lost heart. It also makes us realize how bravely they have struggled, in spite of the double burden which they bear. Further, we are led to speculate upon how much the American Negro could bear before he would take his fixed gaze off the beckoning star, and turn with empty eyes back upon black despair.

Woman Suffrage

October 21, 1915

On the 2d of November the voters of New York are to decide whether or not the women of this State shall have the right to the ballot.

Some weeks ago we discussed this question in its general aspects, and tried to meet the stock arguments that are advanced against woman suffrage.

We tried to show that every argument against woman suffrage is founded in prejudice or ignorance or in some sort of sentimental hallucination about "the ballot dragging woman down from her lofty throne and tearing the sacred halo from her brow." No doubt, there are men who will indulge in this rot whose wives help to support the family.

If working for a living does not "drag woman down from her lofty throne," etc., we should like to know how taking an interest in good government and casting a vote once or twice a year is going to do it.

So much for the general objections to woman suffrage; as we covered them in a former article at considerable length. Let us now see if there are not special reasons why the right of women to the ballot should be supported by all colored voters in New York. And not only in New York, but in all the Northern and Western States where the question is submitted to the electorate.

Woman suffrage should be supported by all colored voters because the gaining of the ballot by the women will be a blow against all arbitrary limitations of the right to vote in this country.

The right to vote should not depend upon such qualifications as education, wealth, color or sex. Every honest, law-abiding citizen of sound mind and legal age should have the right to say how and by whom he is to be governed. One may be a perfectly good citizen and yet never have the opportunity to reach a certain standard of education or wealth; and it is certain that no one can change his or her color or sex. All such restrictions are wrong in principle. They were devised by those who wish to perpetuate themselves in political power, by those who believe that the few have some sort of divine right to govern the many.

Abraham Lincoln said that no man was good enough to govern another man without that man's consent. Truer words were never spoken.

Colored voters, in casting their ballots for woman suffrage, will strike a blow against these oligarchic principles, which have so often been invoked to rob the Negro of his political rights.

There is another good reason why we as a race should support the cause of "votes for women." If women are given the ballot the political effectiveness of the colored vote will be doubled. This will not be the case with other classes of people; for, whereas, our vote is almost a unit, theirs is divided amongst various parties and factions. In Harlem, for example, our voting strength will be practically twice as great while other classes of voters will each gain only a fifth or a sixth more strength than they now possess.

This doubling of our political power would be especially effective in those states where we already hold the balance of power when elections are close. If a woman suffrage is adopted throughout all the Northern and Western states, the colored vote will become an instrument of power not only for our betterment in the North and West, but also for the protection and defense of our brethren in the South.

Let every colored voter in New York, and in all other states where the question is submitted, cast their ballots for Woman Suffrage.

The Suffrage Parade

October 28, 1915

It was impossible not to be impressed with the Woman Suffrage Parade which took place in this city last Saturday. It is estimated that more than 25,000 women marched, and that the procession was viewed by more than a quarter of a million spectators.

There were no attempts at making the affair a pageant. Symbolic floats and costumes were conspicuous by their absence. The one, impressive thing was the sight of column after column of earnest women steadily marching on. There was a dignity and majestic beauty about it that made a deep and, at times, solemn impression.

In the line were old women, bent under their three score and ten years, but marching along bravely; there were thousands of women in the prime of life; and there were thousands of girls just reaching womanhood. There was no talking, no laughing, no glancing around, no mincing gait; column after column swung along with free stride in time to the martial music of the bands; all eyes fixed forward; the faces of the older women tense with earnestness and those of the younger ones alight with enthusiasm.

The colored women in the parade showed up splendidly. They were scattered promiscuously in many of the companies. One body of colored women that marched together made a fine impression. Several companies were under the command of colored captains.

In fact, the women cannot be too highly complimented upon the success they made of such a large undertaking. There is no doubt that the parade made many friends for the cause of Suffrage, and that it will have an effect upon the coming election.

While on the subject of Woman Suffrage we wish to supplement our article of last week by meeting another argument which is being advanced against the right of women to vote. It is held that the ballot in the hands of women will by no means solve our political and social problems and bring about the millennium. Well, suppose it doesn't and nobody with practical, common sense claims that it will—what has that to do with the justice of the case? Why should it be demanded of women to accomplish something with the ballot that men have never yet been able to accomplish? Thousands of young men each year as they become of age are given the ballot, but no such demand is made of them.

Of course, the granting of the suffrage to women will not bring about the millennium, and it is unfair and unreasonable to demand that it should; however, it is certain that it will bring higher and better influence into politics.

A Comparison

November 11, 1915

Woman Suffrage was defeated in the recent elections in four great states, New Jersey, New York, Pennsylvania and Massachusetts; however, the women do not feel themselves beaten, they are organizing for a wider and more aggressive campaign than they have yet made. They have announced the plan of taking their case to Congress in order to secure an amendment to the Constitution.

This action will have the effect of still farther removing the question of woman suffrage from the category of "crank" issues, and will add to its weight and importance as a national issue. Whether it will be easier to force an amendment to the Constitution and have that amendment ratified than it would be to win finally in each of the states, we are not prepared to say. At any rate, this much is certain; by carrying out the plan which they have now decided upon, the women will keep their cause prominently before the public during the coming year, and also give the dominant party in Congress considerable additional worry.

That the women, at least those of New York, mean business, is shown by the fact that at a recent suffrage meeting in this city the sum of $100,000 was raised for campaign purposes. This demonstrates that the politicians of the gentler sex are learning the hard, practical rules of the game. In politics, a cause does not win merely because it is a just cause; its justice must be made known, it must be placed before the people and made clear to them; and that is something which requires money for its accomplishment.

To digress for a moment; it is just upon this point that we, as a race, fall short. We have a just cause, but we do not put up the money which is necessary to place that cause before the great American public in the proper manner. There are a great many things about us which, if they were generally known, would gradually win public opinion over to our side. As it is, most of the publicity which we obtain is of the kind that turns public opinion against us.

Of course, our present financial weight is not sufficient to control the instruments of publicity in this country which are opposed to us or not in sympathy with us; but we do not even properly support those that are fighting for our cause. Whatever just criticism that may be brought against Negro newspapers and magazines is outweighed by the fact that the race does not give the support which would enable these publications to become better and greater and able to wield a wider and stronger influence. As a race, we do not assist the propaganda in our behalf even by buying the books written by white or black men to set our case in the right light before the people of this country.

The women know that their cause is just, but they have learned that it will take money to place their cause before the public so that the people at large will have the opportunity of forming the same opinion.

But we started this article with the intention of drawing a comparison; let us get down to that.

No one who has studied the woman suffrage movement can fail to be impressed with the fact that in spite of the numbers, intelligence, wealth and influence from within and without which the women have been able to bring to bear they are up against obstacles in the East and the South which may yet require years to entirely overcome. Seeing this, the writer has been led to speculate upon what chances would the Negro now have to gain the right to vote if the Fourteenth and Fifteenth Amendments had not been adopted when they were.

There are those who declare that the adoption of the Fourteenth and Fifteenth Amendments was a blunder; some go so far as to call it a crime. There are those who say that the nation should have waited until the Negro was prepared for the ballot; we have heard colored men who were asinine enough to say the same thing. Witnessing the difficulty which white women are having, we ask, "When would it have been possible for the Negro to convince the country that he was 'prepared' for the ballot?" Not in five hundred years.

Of course, in certain states, the Negro has been denied his right to vote; but he has the right. Being denied the exercise of a right is an entirely different thing from not having the right at all. And even the most unprincipled Negro-hating politician knows that that right cannot forever be denied, for it stands written in the basic law of the land.

If the Fourteenth and Fifteenth Amendments were not already a part of the fundamental law of the nation, we venture to say that the great-grandchild of no Negro now alive would live long enough to see them made so.

The Colored Nurses

July 20, 1918

The Red Cross rally at the Palace Casino in Harlem last week was one of the best attended meetings ever held in that large auditorium; and the audience was one of the best that ever gathered there, made up as it was of thoughtful and intelligent people. The striking feature of the audience was, of course, the colored nurses. There were perhaps a hundred of them in uniform, and they occupied the front seats. They are a fine body of young women and attracted a great deal of attention. They were undoubtedly a surprise to many colored people who did not know there were that many trained nurses of the race in the city.

The program was a splendid one and was well carried out. Colonel Anderson presided suavely and displayed a good deal of his well known ability for eloquence in his introductory remarks and in presenting Mrs. August Belmont, the speaker of the evening. Mrs. Belmont gave an interesting and graphic account of her experiences in Red Cross work over there. Several musical numbers were also rendered.

It was mentioned that this [was] no time for complaint; that all must put their shoulder to the wheel. So far as we are able to understand, the only complaint the colored nurses have is that up to this time they have not been allowed to put their shoulder to the wheel.

Protesting Women and the War

September 21, 1918

Miss Alice Paul has issued to the members of the National Woman's party an appeal to protest with all the strength and vigor they have in order to get the Suffrage Amendment through the Senate. She declared, "If enough women protest, and protest with sufficient vigor, the Federal Suffrage Amendment will be passed." She urged all who would not be able to take part in the protest demonstration in front of the White House on September 16, to contribute financially to the fall election campaign in the West, when voting women will be called upon to protest through their votes against the Democratic party's continued blocking of the amendment enfranchising women.

Miss Paul said further: "the Suffrage Amendment is still blocked in the Senate. The Administration and the Senate show no signs of acting on it."

Of course, Miss Paul must know the reason why the Suffrage Amendment is being blocked in the Senate. It is being blocked because the Southern senators, and they control the Senate, are opposed to it. And the Southern senators are opposed to it because they are opposed to the enfranchisement of colored women in the South.

This is the irony of the whole Negro problem; the white people of the South have to deny themselves many of the good things that they need and want because they are not willing for the Negro to have them. They deny themselves compulsory education laws because these laws would also compel the colored child to go to school. The white women of the South evidently would like to have the vote, but their Senators must fight against the national enfranchisement of women because they do not want colored women in the South to be enfranchised.

The question might arise in the minds of some, why are these politicians so afraid of giving the vote to the colored women of the South, could they not disfranchise them as easily as they have disfranchised the men? There comes the rub; we believe the Southern politicians know just what we know, and that is that the colored women, if given the vote, could not be kept out of their rights so easily as the colored men have been kept out. Often as a matter of compliment men say that the women are the most worthy sex. That is no compliment when applied to colored women, it is simply a statement of fact.

Three-fourths of what the Negro has amounted to in America is due to the colored women. For the past fifty years they have struggled on patiently and bravely, never shirking. Negro fathers who are lazy, trifling and no good, who have deserted wife and children when the load grew a little heavy, can be counted by the thousands; but Negro mothers have stuck, they have slaved and sacrificed to keep these same children fed and clothed and in school. The colored mother who deserts her post is such a rara avis that she may be said not to exist.

If these women who have struggled so heroically for fifty years and held the race together are given the vote, it may be depended upon that they will put up a better fight to hold it and exercise it than the men have put up. Perhaps the Southern politicians know this.

But this is the thought that struck us when we read Miss Paul's call upon the women of the country to protest; the white women of the United States have more privileges and power than any women in the world; it seems that they have about everything that the feminine heart could desire; the only thing they appear to lack is the symbol of political power, the ballot, and for this they are protesting. They are not only demanding it in spoken and written language and by all the pressure they are able to bring upon the national law making body, they are protesting by demonstrations in front of the President's house.

Now, if it is right for these women who have so much to go to such lengths while the country is at war because they have not yet been given the ballot, why is it wrong for the Negro to protest during the war because members of the race are burned alive at the stake?

This war is going to bring many changes; but it is not going to work any miracles fo the Negroes. It is simply giving him the chance to work out his own salvation, and if he doesn't start to working out that salvation now, he had just as well leave the job alone. If he thinks that by merely going along and doing his duty humbly and faithfully, somebody is coming along after the war and say, "Well done, thou good and faithful servant, come up higher," he is in for the biggest disappointment in his history. The Negro just as the women of America and the laboring classes of England have got to take intelligent thought and action now to insure the future benefits which they hope to gain.

Smoking Women

February 20, 1920

One of the Boards of the Methodist Church is very much alarmed over the increase in the use of tobacco among women, and appeals to them to refrain from it in the name of the country's welfare. The Board utters the warning that unborn children are drugged by tobacco in the blood in the smoking mother.

The opinion seems to be general that smoking is a vice or a habit of the "new woman"; but is that really the fact? It is not. Any one who is familiar with the rural sections at least of the South, knows that the older women have smoked for generations. It is a common sight there to see an old woman comfortably seated enjoying her smoke. The difference is that the new woman sits in a cafe or in her boudoir and smokes scented cigarettes, while the old woman sits on the front porch or by the fireplace and smokes a clay pipe.

The women of South America, probably, have always smoked. The women of the classes smoke cigarettes in their homes, and the women of the masses smoke everywhere—at work, at play, in their homes and on the streets. They do not smoke cigarettes; they smoke little, black cigars; and they smoke one after another, all day long.

In the matter of smoking, the new woman cannot be blamed with introducing a new vice; the worse that can be said of her is that she is introducing an old habit and making it fashionable.

There is no question of morals involved. If it is morally wrong for a woman to smoke, it is morally wrong for a man to smoke. Of course, there is a question of health, still it is just as foolish for a man to smoke when he knows it is injurious to his health as it is for a woman.

The whole matter is one of good form, of good taste. A man objects to his women folks smoking because he feels it is not good taste, that it is vulgar. Some women object to smoking by women because they themselves would not dare. It remains to be seen whether smoking by women can ever become good form in the United States.

The Colored Woman Voter

September 18, 1920

We have more than once stated in these columns our belief that the colored women will be less easily intimidated and kept out of voting than the colored men have been. This has been realized all along by the opponents of Suffrage especially those in the South. Senator John Sharp Williams said on the floor of the Senate, "Negro women will not be as easily handled as Negro men have been."

But as courageous and determined as the colored women may be, they cannot succeed even as voters unless they have the necessary information and knowledge. They should begin everywhere at once to learn all the preliminary steps to voting and to get the actual practice of marking a ballot. To this end study classes ought to be formed in every community. The groups that make up these classes ought not to be too large. The persons in each community who already have a knowledge of the machinery of government and politics should get together and begin to organize these groups.

Careful attention should be given to each section of the city or the county. The study classes should rotate from church to church, from hall to hall and from home to home. Every colored woman who can possibly be reached should be brought into these classes. The work can be made quite interesting if the leaders will thoroughly prepare themselves. The classes might open with twenty to thirty-minute talks on the structure of our government, from the town on up through county and state to the national. There should also be talks on the machinery of politics from that of the precinct up to that of the national convention. However, the leaders of the classes ought to avoid any temptation to display how much they know about these subjects; rather they should strive to make everything they say as simple and understanding as possible. They should get down to the A.B.C. of it.

Then there should come painstaking instruction in the requirements and qualifications for voting in the community and the state. Information regarding registration and the places for registration, about marking a ballot and the proper polling place at which to vote should be given.

It may be that those who would like to begin and carry out the work outlined above do not feel that they possess the requisite knowledge and information to do it as well as it should be done. Any such lack may be easily supplied. The National American Woman's Suffrage Association began the publication of a comprehensive course in "The Woman Citizen" in the issue of April 3, 1920. Each lesson is followed by an amplification of the subject from the program of lectures delivered before the School for Political Education, conducted under the direction of Mrs. Carrie Chapman Catt. State laws vary; party customs and usage vary in the different states. In these lessons will be found the laws and political usages for each state. "The Woman Citizen" is published monthly in New York City.

The New York League for Women Voters has also issued a splendid course of study for groups, each lesson being prepared by an authority on the subject treated. These lessons are made very simple, but are none the less extremely interesting. The course embraces the following topics:

Politics and Woman's Interest,

Town and County Government,

State Government,

National Government,

Political Parties,

How Candidates are Nominated,

Elections,

Direct Primary or Convention: Which?

These lessons are issued in pamphlets which are sold at ten cents a copy or fifty for three dollars; they are, therefore, within the reach of all.

This matter of forming groups for civic and political education offers just now the most useful and interesting service that well informed colored women can undertake. Of course, there is no reason why they should not permit the men to assist them in it.

Beautiful Women

November 26, 1921

Professor Frederick Starr, a noted anthropologist, lecturing at the Chicago University to the "co-eds" made a statement which startled his class and caused a great deal of comment throughout the country. He said: "There are no beautiful women in the United States. It is only our American good nature that makes us call a girl that is not phenomenally ugly a pretty girl." The professor then went on to state that the most beautiful women he had seen in all his travels were among the Africans. This latter statement was so astounding that most of the newspaper paragraphers seemed to think that the professor was merely joking.

I made a similar statement in these very columns about three years ago. A statement which a good many of my own readers found very hard to swallow. I said that colored women in the rural districts of the South were more beautiful than the white women and that the only reason that we did not realize it was due to the fact that our education had made us almost incapable of seeing human beauty in darker colors.

Some of the papers in New York, however, took Prof. Starr seriously and they invited him to come to New York and take a glance at the parade of feminine beauty that could be seen any day on Fifth Avenue. They assured Prof. Starr that he could see the most beautiful women in America and in the world on Fifth Avenue.

I agree with the New York papers as far as they go, but they should not stop on Fifth Avenue. If they wish to see a more fascinating phase of beauty they should see upper Seventh Avenue. Undoubtedly the prettiest women in America can be found in New York City and New York City contains no prettier women than can be found in colored Harlem. Anyone who has attended a large social affair among the colored people in Harlem cannot but agree with the above statement. The color and warmth of beauty at such an affair is something that cannot be approached in any "dead white" gathering.

Equality of Privileges for Women

September 2, 1922

Mrs. Anna Garlin Spencer in a recent lecture at Teachers College, Columbia University, said "Women cannot have freedom, equality of rights, economic independence and equal opportunity of self-development with men and at the same time claim from men, as many women are, I am sorry to say, trying to do today, the same kind of privileges that chivalrous and good-hearted men use to give to their mothers, sisters and friends when those mothers, sisters and friends were absolutely dependent upon them."

Mrs. Spencer is an advanced woman, is a Unitarian minister, an educator, a peace advocate and a prominent suffragist; and so, naturally, she takes the position that women should be willing to forego the privileges and indulgencies which spring from so-called chivalry and should take her chances in the open field of equal opportunity. She cited a number of advantages to be gained by following such a course. She pointed out that women have only recently had any real freedom of choice in marriage and that the economic independence of a woman now gives her the opportunity, when a man asks her to marry him, to take into consideration the question whether she likes the man well enough to give up her economic independence for the sake of living with him.

She admitted that the new freedom has increased divorce because women now can no longer be held to intolerable conditions in marriage any more so than can men. Following up the theme of marriage, she expressed the opinion that women being now economically almost free are again to a large extent the selective agents and that they will choose and thereby create the type of men they desire. Formerly the type of man most desired, she said, was a good provider: [but] that "now character and self-control have become part of our masculine ideal and women, if they are wise, will use their new power to help make a race of men as good as they are strong, as far removed from the barbaric heroes of former days as one can imagine."

All that Mrs. Spencer says is true as far as it goes, but it does not go so far as she proposes. Her generalities are too broad. When she speaks of women she has in mind women who are actually or potentially the kind of woman she is. But it is easy to see that this supposition leads to error. All women are not alike, either actually or potentially. There is a class of women more or less like Mrs. Spencer who not only in these modern times but through all ages have chafed under and protested against conditions which gave them privileges and indulgencies but the class of women that has incessantly struggled for a wider field and for independence and which has today emerged as the new woman, the woman who has achieved her economic independence and who is ready to compete with men in constructive and creative work.

But there is another class of women and it is the larger class that has neither the desire nor the power to achieve such independence. The women of this class make up what might be called the "sheltered type" of women. The very thought of struggle and competition for the necessities of life and for position would be not only distasteful to them but overwhelming. Such women shudder and shrink from the very thought.

And so Mrs. Spencer's appeal to women to seize the new freedom is an appeal, after all, to only one class of women, the women who are fitted mentally and physically to answer the call. It is an error to think that all women will ever answer such a call, because all women are not and never will be alike.

But in this respect women do not differ from men. It is an error to think that all men are fitted for competition and struggle and combat in an open and equal field. Most men are workers, it is true, and earn a livelihood; but for that matter, so are most women, even of the sheltered class. The average housewife works about as hard as the average man and earns every nickel that her husband may give her; and the average man is dependent upon his employer for his livelihood as the average housewife is upon her husband for her food, clothes and lodging. The men who are able in the face of struggle and competition to make a place of relatively economic independence make up a class of men that do not constitute a majority. There is a class of men and women that can stand on their own initiative, their own courage and their own power, asking only for equal opportunity and a fair chance. Also there is a class of women and likewise of men who cannot do this but require to be sheltered or provided for in one way or another.

4 Economics and Employment

Where is the Negro who can rise to the opportunity of becoming a real labor leader for his people?
James Weldon Johnson, "More About Employment"
(September 30, 1915)

There is a distinction between being without money and being without economic opportunity, Johnson wrote. The issue of economic parity is one of the most perplexing that black Americans have had to endure. Johnson saw the economic question as one that black leaders, in general, had given very little attention. Education and politics had been considered the conduits to solving the race problem. Because black leadership had virtually ignored the economic factor, many within the race lacked the necessary comprehension of its fundamental importance. Johnson explained to his readers in the following editorials how much the status of black Americans was tied to this nation's existing economic order.

Johnson emphasized the need for organization and strong leadership to address the economic and employment issues. He pointed out that African-Americans should educate themselves in labor and business philosophies just as they had educated themselves to obtain their rights as American citizens. This self-education, he believed, would enable them to better understand business practices that might lead to providing jobs for members of their own race. He cited the objective of economic education by the Business League to underscore his point.

Dr. Washington's Practical Suggestion

November 19, 1914

The open letter which Dr. Booker T. Washington sent out a short time ago to the farmers of the South, urging them not to confine themselves to cotton, but to raise an extra pig, or pigs, and other products of an immediate cash value, is stirring up a great deal of favorable comment in the white as well as the Negro press of that section. The suggestion is an extremely practical one, and applies to the white farmer of the South, perhaps, as fully as to the black. If acted upon and carried out it would mean a tremendous increase in wealth.

As it is now, the farmer plants his cotton in the spring, tends it during the summer, picks and markets it in the fall, and loafs all winter. There is no other serious work in the world where so much valuable time is left unutilized as in ordinary, unintelligent farming.

The small Negro farmer who relies solely upon cotton is absolutely powerless. He is a nonentity when it comes to the price and the marketing of his crop. Many of these farmers eat all winter on the cotton they expect to sell the next summer. They do not trade; they do not buy and sell; they do not handle cash money; they simply live eternal debt to cotton.

The danger and stupidity of depending upon a single crop is illustrated in the present condition of cotton. Some twenty years ago it was illustrated in Florida. At that time, the only crop given any attention was oranges, and it constituted almost the sole wealth of the state. The Florida farmer would fish all summer, and pick and market his oranges in the fall and winter. Then came the great freeze of 1905, and the growers who had gone to bed the night before worth hundreds of thousands of dollars woke up the next morning bankrupt.

It was a disaster, but proved to be the best thing that ever happened for the state. The growers replanted their groves, but while waiting for the trees to mature they devoted themselves to raising celery, lettuce, tomatoes, Irish potatoes, pineapples, grapefruit, poultry and eggs. These are to-day the principal products of Florida, and they are products with a ready cash value. As a result, Florida is feeling the present stringency less, perhaps, than any other Southern state.

If Dr. Washington can awaken the Negro farmers and induce them to diversify intelligently the products of their land; to raise, in addition to cotton, those things for which they can find a daily or weekly cash sale or, in lieu of that, with which they can feed themselves and their families, he will, as the magic, add greatly to the wealth and prosperity of the entire race.

The Negro press can do a great good by giving this suggestion the widest possible circulation.

The Harlem Gold Mine

December 24, 1914

For centuries the natives in South Africa literally slept over a gold mine. Around the Kimberly region it is likely that many a native stubbed his toe against a diamond and kicked it out of the way.

The gold and diamonds were useless to them not only because they, probably, did not know that these precious stones were right under their feet, but because they did not know how to make use of their value.

Now, it might sound startling to say that there are colored men and women sleeping over a gold mine in Harlem, stubbing their toes against diamonds and kicking them out of the way; nevertheless it is true.

There live in Harlem within a radius of a mile more than 50,000 colored people; this makes that section of the city the most unique Negro settlement in the country. It is, in fact, a city in itself. There are cities in the South with a total population of less than 50,000 where Negroes have built up successful establishments and do a business of thousands of dollars. If this can be done among a colored population scattered around the fringe of a Southern city, what are the limits to the possibilities in Harlem?

Every nationality is making money out of Negroes in Harlem—except Negroes. The few Negroes who are doing business only emphasize the statement. Is there any good reason, is there any good excuse for this?

Of course, the first excuse to be offered will be that the race will not patronize Negro business enterprises. There may be a slight disinclination among some classes and in some localities which, however, can be overcome; but, generally speaking, this charge is not true. The race will and does patronize Negro business enterprises conducted on a business basis.

Nine out of every ten colored men that fail in business blame their failure on the race. That is not fair. If the race was loyal to the last penny some of these men would be bound to fail anyhow. A certain percentage of white merchants fail every year. But the truth is, most of those who fail do so because they do not conduct business on a business basis.

When a colored man goes into business the principal thing he should remember is that a Negro is a human being first and a Negro afterwards; that is, his human nature lies deeper than his color. So a Negro, no more than anybody else, is going to buy from a man unless that man's stock is as good, his prices as cheap and service as attentive as are those of his competitors; and it is foolish to expect him to do it, because it is contrary to human nature. Through race pride and enthusiasm he may do it once or twice or three times, but he won't keep it up. Mere race pride is no sound basis on which to do business.

Colored men who go into business must study it not only from the race's point of view, but from the business man's point of view. They must study the science of business management—and it is now a science, with books and magazines devoted to its study. They must learn the difference between profit and loss. They must learn how to figure on 1/8 of a cent. They must learn the advantages of advertising. These are the only methods by which they can compete in the modern business world, and the only solid foundation on which to build a business.

One of the common causes for business failure among colored men is overshooting the mark; that is, trying to create a demand rather than trying to supply one. Creating a demand generally requires unlimited capital.

Take for example the average Southern city. Some colored man will conceive the laudable ambition of opening an up-to-date restaurant where respectable people of his race can get a first class meal. He invests his capital and, generally, he fails, Why? Because in the average Southern city the people who would eat that sort of a meal eat at home.

If the same man will open a lunch-room and furnish fried fish and bread, coffee and other ready cooked dishes at prices ranging from 5 to 15 cents, the large laboring and floating colored population of the average Southern city will make him rich.

Another cause of failure is, bleeding the business. Take again for example the average Southern city. A colored man opens a family grocery on one corner and a Syrian opens the same sort of a store on the opposite corner.

Now in the first place, the colored man has no time to loaf, his competitor is a merchant by heredity; the Syrian's ancestors were trading on the Mediterranean before the Pyramids were built.

Suppose they are both successful and reach a business of $45,000 a year. How does the Syrian manage? Why just the same as he did when his profits were only $500 a year. He and his family still live in the back of the store; they keep the place open all day and half the night; his wife stands watch for him while he sleeps; next to nothing spent for food or clothes; at the end of ten years he is rich.

Do we need to draw the other picture? Hardly. A fine house, horse and buggy—no, an automobile, good clothes, social entertaining and an occasional trip North—ending, most likely in failure.

We do not write this to blame the colored man who has thus failed. He made the money and he wanted a good time in preference to a good business, and he got it. But we do object to the blame being saddled on the race.

But let us get back to the gold mine in Harlem. There are great opportunities in that section for colored men with some capital and intelligence. There are opportunities for combinations of colored men of small capital, if they also have intelligence.

But we have already pointed out, these opportunities will not yield if they are gone after in a haphazard way.

The field should be carefully studied. A business should be decided upon that one already knows or feels that he or she may become adapted to. You cannot carry on any business unless you yourself know the business or can easily and quickly learn it. To pay somebody else for knowing how to run your business is always disastrous.

Observe the lines of business that are already successful in Harlem. Observe the grades of goods that are carried. This is important. For instance, it would be a waste of capital to try to sell goods in Harlem that are usually bought on Fifth Avenue. The secret is to learn to cater to the trade as well, if not better than your competitors.

But catering to the existing trade of a locality does not mean that one should not use his best judgment and the judgment of experienced friends in deciding upon some new line of business that might prove successful.

The main point is, business to-day is a science which must be studied. Studied form every angle. From the angle of the person in business, from the angle of the people to be served, from the angle of the locality, the market, the times, etc.

Harlem offers the opportunities. One hundred colored men and women can establish successful business enterprises there if they will only go at it in a whole-hearted and intelligent way.

Don't sleep over a gold mine! Don't stub your toe against a diamond and kick it out of the way!

Girl Waiters on Dining Cars

January 14, 1915

Out of Detroit came the following dispatch:

> BUSINESS INCREASED IN MICHIGAN SINCE NEGROES WERE REPLACED
>
> *Detroit, January 2*—Detroit executives of the Michigan Central Railway are having tested a plan whereby Negro waiters in dining cars will be replaced by white women. Employees say the business has greatly increased since the young women, dressed in plain black dresses and white caps, were put on duty.

The test is hardly a fair one for the men. White girls, colored girls, Indian girls, Japanese girls, or any other pretty girls neatly dressed, would increase business. If, however, the white girls prove to be more efficient waiters than the colored men, then the matter is serious.

It is bad enough for Negroes to be forced out of work, but when, through their own lack of efficiency, they lose certain lines of employment, it is criminal on their part.

This has often been the case, especially with waiters. Negro waiters once controlled the hotels of New York, the white waiters displaced them through sheer superiority of efficiency.

There are gray-haired waiters in the Waldorf-Astoria and other such hotels who can buy and sell many of the people they wait on. These men make a study, no, more than that, they make an art of their business. They stick to their work as steadily as a bank clerk sticks to his.

Colored men lost their grip on the New York hotels for several reasons: one was, they did not care to work in town the entire year; when the weather got warm they preferred to work at some seaside resort. It is sad to see all this lucrative work taken absolutely away from them.

If success in life can be summed up in any few words they would be "whatever you are engaged in doing, do it to the best of your ability." If a man is a waiter he should make himself the very best waiter possible. This does not preclude him from aspiring to be something else, a lawyer, for example; it simply means that while he is a waiter he should be the best possible, it is then quite likely that he will make a decent lawyer.

The Business League

August 26, 1915

Perhaps, the things most worth while that we can say about the recent meeting of the National Negro Business League at Boston can be set forth in a few paragraphs giving the most striking impressions we received while attending the sessions. These impressions may be of some value to the reader, for the reason that the writer had not before had the privilege of attending a Business League convention, so his mind was open to receive fresh impressions.

We were first impressed by the sight of colored speakers addressing an audience from a public platform, and making use of figures of arithmetic in preference to figures of speech. Usually at large conventions among our people there is an unstinted use of oratory but here there was an entire absence of it.

More strongly still were we impressed by the sight of a large colored audience listening to a long program of addresses, which consisted almost wholly of unadorned recitals of facts or strings of figures. It was almost curious to see them bending forward to catch the words as they fell from the speakers' lips.

We also received the impression that the colored women seem to be distancing the men in business enterprise and activity. The women who made addresses were particularly interesting. They handled their subjects in a logical and forcible manner, using direct and well chosen English. All told, they succeeded in arousing more enthusiasm than did the men speakers.

Our composite impression of the whole convention was that the race is fast seizing the idea of the present age; that is, the idea of efficiency. That we are learning that business does not mean merely the opening of a little shop, but keeping it open and making it a bigger shop. That we are coming to understand that our economic progress does not depend merely upon individuals of the race saving a thousand dollars each, but upon ten, twenty, fifty such individuals putting their savings together to establish business enterprises on a big scale; business enterprises that will make money earn money, that will give our young people employment and demand for the whole race consideration in the financial world. That we are realizing that we cannot do business merely as colored business men and women; that we cannot appeal to members of the race for patronage solely upon the ground that we are all colored; that the Negro is a human being before he is a Negro, and we cannot expect him to give up his money unless he gets value; that if we want the patronage of our race or of anybody else, we must compete for it and deserve it; in a word that we must study and practice efficiency.

More about Employment

September 30, 1915

Last week we had something to say about the practice among wealthy people of this city and other large northern cities of employing in their homes anarchists and nihilists from every far corner of the earth, in preference to colored people who are Americans by birth, by customs and by mode of thought. We made the plea that the largest part of this employment should go to colored men and women. It is likely that the murder of Mrs. Nichols through the connivance of her Russian butler will awaken such people to the fact that here at home they can find capable domestic employees to whom even lesser crimes would be unthinkable.

There is now another interesting phase of the employment question. Italy has gone to war, and Bulgaria and Greece have mobilized; it seems to be only a question of time when the other Balkan states will follow suit. These countries have called and will continue to call their reserve forces to the colors; thereby taking out of this country a large body of men usually employed as laborers on the railroads and public works throughout the North and East. Why should not their places be filled by colored laborers?

It has been said, that a Negro can get anything in the North except the opportunity to earn a living. This statement, like all epigrams, cannot be taken too literally. In New York a colored man may be a bank clerk, a private secretary or the manager of some mercantile concern—there are a number of colored men holding such positions—while in this same city it is almost impossible for one to get steady work as a carpenter or a brick mason.

This, however, is true; the race in this section cannot reach a solid economic plane solely because it is possible for a few of its members to hold higher positions. What is absolutely necessary is that the great mass of the race be able to obtain honest employment and steady wages through as many channels as possible. Steady employment in varied occupations and at good wages for the mass of the race would quickly lead to the solution of most of our problems in this section.

So we repeat the question, "Why should not the work which has usually been done by Italians, Greeks and other foreigners be now seized by colored men?"

One man's ill is another's good. The war is devastating Europe but it is bringing golden opportunities to the big business men of the United States. We, as a race, can benefit only in an indirect way from the opportunities that are coming to the American captains of industry and finance, but we can gain direct and lasting benefit if we seize the chance to broaden our economic foundation, to secure and hold these wider fields of employment.

There is no question that this can be done. The Negro is better fitted in every way to take and hold this work than are the foreigners. His greatest advantage is that he speaks the English language. To this great advantage he would only need to add numbers and steadiness.

Prejudice would not be an obstacle. If anyone has taken the time to watch the work on the subway, the aqueduct of the deep foundations in this city, he could not have failed to notice that the Negro workmen generally ranked above the green foreigners. He must have observed that the majority of the men handling shovels were foreigners while the majority of the steam-drill operators were colored men. Perhaps one of the reasons why the skilled labor of operating the drills is given to colored men is that they speak English.

If Negroes can crowd the green foreigners out of the more skilled jobs on our public works, why can they not also crowd them out of the common labor?

For many years certain political exigencies made it difficult for colored men to secure employment on the public works of this city. It was more convenient to the powers who had the allotment of the work that it be given to foreigners who would vote in large numbers as one man, rather than to native American citizens; but that political day is fast fading. It can be noticed that each year colored men are being employed in large numbers upon the great works being carried on by the city.

We should have more of this work; and we should have more of all other kinds of work in this city and throughout the whole North and East.

Where is the Negro who can rise to the opportunity of becoming a real labor leader for his people?

Where Is The Man?

June 7, 1917

Recently we had an article on the present need for a Negro labor leader of national influence and power. This article brought from W. A. Armwood of Tampa, Fla., an interesting letter, full of information on labor conditions as they affect the race, which we publish elsewhere. Mr. Armwood's letter prompts us to say more on the subject.

For more than a year we have been pointing out in these columns the vital effects that the exodus from the South may have on the race. Effects that it certainly will have, if the race exercises foresight and wisdom enough to take full advantage of conditions. We have said that this exodus is the most important thing that has happened in the history of the race since the adoption of the Fourteenth and Fifteenth Amendments to the Constitution. We have shown that the direct results will be the securing of better treatment in the South and the gaining of larger economic independence and political power in the North.

Of course, the blind forces that are at work will bring about these results in some degree, whether the Negro takes intelligent thought of them or not, but the best results cannot be secured unless the Negro himself takes a hand in intelligently directing these forces.

All of the benefits to be gained from the exodus depend in degree upon the number of colored people who are able to come North and stay; the larger the number, the greater the benefits. The mere fact of their coming North will produce no permanently good results, unless they are able to stay. In fact, a tidal movement back and forth of large numbers of colored people might have very bad results. Now, it needs no argument to prove that large numbers of colored people can come North and stay only if they can get jobs and hold them. So the whole situation hangs upon the ability of these people to adjust themselves industrially and economically. Reduced to the simplest terms, the whole situation hangs upon jobs.

The demand for laborers and workmen is so great that up to the present colored men have found very little difficulty in getting employment; but there are two dangers that must be guarded against. Some steps should be taken to prevent the irresponsible, shiftless class from making a bad name for Negro labor, and something should be done to prevent any serious clash between colored workmen and the great labor union organizations. Already there have been too many complaints about the shiftlessness of Negro labor. A number of northern employers who are accustomed to steady workmen have had good reason for complaint. They threw their doors open to colored men and found that after pay day the men would not show up for work at all. The Pennsylvania Railroad which was the first of the great northern concerns to seek colored labor in the South is loudest in these complaints. There is reason. As our correspondent says concerning the Pennsylvania Railroad, that company sent agents South and had them spread the news that they had free transportation for as many men as wanted to go North to work; these notices gave only a day or two to those who wished to take advantage of the offer. As a result, many of the most shiftless and unreliable of the race, attracted by the prospect of a trip North, were gathered in. The steady, reliable class would demand more time and more information before they would be willing to pull up and leave.

But notwithstanding the fact that there is a reasonable explanation of the disappointment which some northern employers have experienced with the shiftless, unreliable class that came up in the first great rush, it is also a fact that the explanation will not entirely remedy the damage that has already been done. Some of the employers who have been disappointed will always declare and believe that Negro labor is no good.

However, by natural process, this condition is being rectified. Since the first great rush, the people coming North are more and more largely of the steady, reliable class. This is due to the fact that agents are no longer recruiting wholesale in the South. The people who have come North and secured jobs are writing back to their relatives and friends to come on. This is by far the better method, for in most cases, those who write have their eyes on a job for those who come. This process is selective, and in time will produce a steady flow northward of the best element of colored working people who will become adjusted economically and socially as soon as they arrive. The wholesale and indiscriminate method of the recruiting agents would have led eventually to chaos.

Nevertheless, the reputation that is to be made by Negro labor in the North should not be left wholly to chance and natural tendencies; there should be some sort of intelligent, organized effort to supply the right employer with the right kind of men.

As to the second danger, clashes between colored workmen and the great union organizations, there are already some signs. The East St. Louis riot is a symptom. Up to now there has not been much trouble in this direction because the great mass of Negroes brought North has been employed in only the roughest grades of labor. But when the employment of colored skilled laborers and artisans reaches a certain mark, there is sure to be opposition on the part of the white labor unions. This opposition will probably take on the form of race riots and will be so heralded to the world by the newspapers; but the fundamental reason for these outbreaks will not be racial, it will be economic. As to whether or not the Negro should seek to become an integral part of the white labor unions, there is much to be said on both sides. It is a question that we shall discuss at a future time.

All the thoughtful colored men must at least realize this truth: the issues at stake in this movement of our people from the South to the North are too great to be left to chance or to adjust themselves through a series of costly errors. The great need of the hour is for intelligent organization. There must be organization that can direct the economic and industrial forces involved. To accomplish this, there must arise a single man, a man of vision and power. Such a man must be wise, he must be brave, and above all, he must be honest.

We say that such a man can send his name down in race history alongside the names of Frederick Douglass and Booker T. Washington, but we ask, "Where is the Man?"

Cotton Is King

September 21, 1918

For a while cotton was dethroned monarch, but he has again come into his kingdom. And this time it is no constitutional monarchy; it is no triumvirate, shared with corn and wheat; it is an absolute autocracy, and no one dares to dispute his rule.

Before the war cotton was selling at from eight to ten cents a pound and growers were glad to get that. Cotton was a beggar in the marts of the world. We all remember the buy-a-bale movement, the time when cotton was dependent on charity, on fairs where bales were raffled off, and on the hasty pledges of some ladies to deny themselves all the pretty, flimsy things that women love so much and to wear garments throughout made of cotton.

But there has come a great change. Cotton is selling today at 35, 36 and 37 cents a pound, and may go still higher. We say it may go higher because nobody dares to say that it shall go no higher. The prices have been fixed for wheat and corn and coal and other necessities of life, but cotton has the sky for its limit.

A few days ago it was intimated that Mr. Baruch of the War Industries Board, in view of the fact that the board is at present without authority to fix a maximum price on raw cotton, would ask for a report and a recommendation from an investigating committee on the cotton situation. It seems that legislation must be passed by Congress before the board can move or hold the growers to a low price. This news of an investigation caused something of a panic among the Southern senators. They immediately came together and held a conference in the office of Senator Simmons of North Carolina. At this meeting it was resolved "to see President Wilson if any attempt was made to fix the price of cotton."

Recently a correspondent writing to the New York Tribune on the question, "Why should not a tax be put on cotton," quoted Congressman Kitchin as saying in a speech in Boston that this is the North's war and the North should pay for it. Mr. Kitchin denied ever having made any statement and said that he never expressed or entertained such a sentiment.

It is easy to believe that Congressman Kitchin never made the remark charged to him, for even if he thought it, he would have been a fool to say it, and Mr. Kitchin is no fool. Nevertheless, the fact remains that cotton is the only great staple commodity that has not been regulated in price. Why there is a maximum price on wheat and none on cotton can be explained only on the theory that Southern members of Congress are in better position to look out for the interests of their constituents than are the members of Congress from the West.

A New Wrinkle in
Civil Service Discrimination

May 10, 1919

Our attention has been called to a new method of appointment of civil service employees in Hampton, Va., that warrants the attention of the heads of that branch of government and definite action. The clipping referred to reads:

> WANTED—TWO WHITE MAIL CLERKS in Hampton Post Office. Send in written application.
> F. W. Shield, Postmaster

Strange and devious are the ways in which new symptoms of prejudice and un-democracy are cropping out in this land of the free. According to the Civil Service regulations and laws, whenever vacancies occur in the higher branches of the service, those in lower positions who have given efficient and faithful service are promoted and their places are filled by others who are able to pass examinations and qualify otherwise for the vacancies. These examinations are open to all persons and appointments are supposed to be made from the list of the successful ones in the order which they rank in competitive tests. Yet here is an example of a postmaster deliberately advertising for white mail clerks and doing so with impunity and in open violation of the civil service law.

The deliberate discrimination of officials of the Civil Service Commission shown towards colored applicants has long been known, but this is the first time to our knowledge that one has dared to come out openly in the manner of the postmaster at Hampton. Hitherto it has been done in a sub rosa fashion. One case in point which comes to mind is that of a young woman living in a western city who successfully passed an examination and was ordered to report on a certain day in Washington to begin work. This young woman was the sole support of a widowed mother. They sold their home and all of their possessions at a great sacrifice, went to Washington, and on reporting for duty, the young woman was told that there had been a mistake, and that the position had already been filled. The case of this young woman is not an isolated one, but many more can be cited. Following a number of such cases, some genius in the department thought of a shrewd plan of having all applicants send photographs of themselves with their applications. Even this plan, however, was not entirely successful because, due to certain obvious reasons, the colored race in America has so many shades and complexions that it is frequently difficult to differentiate between the two races.

If the United States government, through the Civil Service Commission is thus going to practice or at least assent to such intentional violation of civil service laws then colored and white people alike will have another reason to wonder if Fiume and Czecho-Slavakia are to be the only recipients of that illusive quantity known as democracy.

The Future Harlem

January 10, 1920

Have you ever stopped to think what the future Harlem will be? It will be a city within a city. It will be the greatest Negro city in the world within the greatest city in the world.

In the next thirty years the Negro city of Harlem, roughly speaking, will embrace the territory from 110th street to the Harlem River and from Fifth and Madison avenues above 110th street to Morningside Park. This territory will contain a colored population in the neighborhood of a half million.

In that time 135th street will have become a great business street, and 145th street will be following fast behind it. More than that 125th street will have passed under the control principally of colored business men. The great stores and shops and the theatres and hotels and office buildings of that thoroughfare will be controlled and patronized chiefly by colored people.

Some may fear that the Negro will be driven out of Harlem as he was in years gone by driven out of the Thompson and Bleeker street neighborhood into the Thirties; and out of the Thirties into the Fifties and upon San Juan Hill; and from there into the Nineties and into Harlem.

In my opinion he is in Harlem to stay, because his condition in this section is entirely unlike it ever was in any of the other sections. In the first place, there are perhaps 125,000 colored people in Harlem now, and there is no place for them to go unless they leave the city. In the former moves, there were only a few people to move, five, ten or twenty-thousand; it is almost inconceivable to think of moving these 125,000 colored people anywhere at all.

In the second place, Harlem is a sort of natural pocket bounded almost on two sides by the river. To move again these colored people would have to cross the Harlem River into the already thickly populated Bronx.

But a stronger reason still is the fact that the Negroes are beginning to own Harlem. In the older sections they owned only their churches. In Harlem they own not only their churches, but are fast buying homes; and not only homes, but large apartment houses. I am informed that in the past twelve months colored people in Harlem have taken over more than five million dollars worth of property. Among the great colored property holders St. Philip's Church heads the list with more than a million dollars worth.

And so I feel confident that the Negro is in Harlem to stay. And what a fine part of New York City he has come into possession of! High and dry, wide and beautiful streets, no alleys, no dilapidated buildings, a section of handsome pivate houses and of modern apartment and flat houses, a section right in the heart of the empire city of the world.

We take just this first glimpse of the Harlem of the future; at another time we shall consider some of the possibilities for the race which it will offer.

A New Danger To Be Met

January 1, 1921

There is a new danger facing colored people in Northern cities, especially the large industrial centers. Business depression has brought about curtailment in employment, and colored laborers and workmen are the first to be made victims of this curtailment. But there are some other forces besides the natural curtailment that has followed the artificial expansion of war times. News from Buffalo, Cleveland and Detroit shows that a definite effort is being made to get rid of the colored worker in many lines. Just what these forces are and where they originate is yet to be found out. It is not improbable that they are behind a plan to compel the majority of colored men and women who migrated North during the war to return South.

Whatever the causes may be the condition is one which must be met with intelligence and energy by colored people in all northern cities. This can be done only through organized effort. In all northern cities where these conditions prevail or are likely to prevail colored organizations should at once get in touch with the proper authorities and keep their fingers on the situation. And above all, the action of such organizations should be united.

A precaution of this kind will be found especially useful in the question of crime, which is sure to arise in most of these communities. When men are suddenly thrown out of employment there naturally follows a "crime wave." Now, all the great cities of the North are suffering from "crime waves," and the criminals are white men. The police are struggling as best they can to preserve safety and order; nevertheless, they are dealing with the situation by methods wholly within the established police powers. But let two or three of these crimes be committed by colored men, and you will hear cries of "Run the Negroes out of town!" and even cries of "Lynch 'em! Lynch 'em!" With such cries as these ringing in the people's ears, not even the most honest and respectable colored people will be safe. This latter is a danger we should prepare at once to meet.

Southern Political Economy Exploded

July 7, 1922

The exodus of colored people from the South has exploded a good many Southern theories. One of the most tenaciously held theories in the South is that theory of political economy which holds that those persons whose names are on the tax rolls pay all public schools and public improvements. Southern cities and counties and states have long proclaimed that the white people of the South were taxing themselves to educate colored children. This statement was made to justify the inequitable apportionment of public school funds. They have held that since all the money, or the overwhelming part of it, for public schools came out of the pockets of white taxpayers, the colored people might be thankful for whatever part of it might be doled out to them.

Of course, no such theory is sound. Every person in any community who rents a house or a hut or a shop, or who works, or who buys goods from the merchants of the community, pays taxes.

Suppose such a theory as is advanced in the South should be held to in a city like New York where, relatively, only a very few people own real estate and pay taxes on it. What would become of the right to public school education or the thousands and thousands of children whose parents rent houses and apartments?

We have often said that if the Negro were suddenly taken out of the South the white people would very soon realize how much less money there would be left in the public funds for public schools or any other purposes. The exodus from the South is in a large measure demonstrating the truth of that statement. It is a demonstration which proves that every child in the community is entitled to equal participation in the public school's funds. When states like South Carolina expend $10.70 per year for the education of each white child and only $1.09 a year for the education of each colored child, it is nothing less than highway robbery. Each colored child is actually being cheated out of $4.30 each year.

Landowners in New York City would not for a moment think of saying after they had collected rent from their tenants, paid their taxes and other fixed charges on the property, and put the rest of the income in their banks, that the children of their tenants were not entitled to equal participation in that part of the taxes devoted to public schools. Every Negro in the South must live somewhere and therefore he must own the property where he lives and his children are entitled to the same rights as the children of tenants in New York City.

The exodus, as we said, is exploding a great many false theories that hold good in the South. We hope it will be kept up long enough to explode the one about the apportionment of public school funds.

5 Education

Accomplishment in life depends upon brain-power, and the magic of securing increased brain-power consists in thinking. Not in memorizing, but in thinking.
James Weldon Johnson, "What Is Your Brain Power?"
(November 26, 1914)

"Nothing has been more persistent in the twentieth century than the tendency to constitute the disparity between money spent for education of white children and that spent for the education of Negro children," wrote historian John Hope Franklin.[1] In the following editorials, James Weldon Johnson addressed some of the challenging issues that confronted his people regarding education, including: (1) the inequities of the apportionment of public school funding across the South; (2) race discrimination in higher education; and (3) the need for blacks to take advantage of the limited educational resources available to them.

Since emancipation, education had been regarded as a main gateway to freedom by African-Americans. Johnson believed that this original faith in education was almost childlike. There was a general belief that an education could almost eradicate the race problem.[2] Because of this belief, blacks attacked education with a fervor. Notwithstanding, Johnson believed that this desire to acquire knowledge and assimilate it constituted the cornerstone of all that African-Americans have reared since slavery ended. Nevertheless, by

1900 every southern state had laws on the books that provided for separate schools.[3] By focusing its resources on a superior education for whites rather than for blacks, the South's concept of white supremacy was aggrandized significantly.

Even out of this irrational educational paradigm, African-Americans reared a group of highly trained men and women who were regarded as scholars by any criterion, including W. E. B. Du Bois (1868–1963); Benjamin Brawley (1883–1939), Carter G. Woodson (1875–1950); Charles S. Johnson (1893–1956); George Washington Carver (1864–1943); Ida B. Wells Barnett (1862–1931); and others.[4]

The Harlem Public Library

November 5, 1914

The public library on West 135th Street is located in the center of the densest Negro population in the Borough of Manhattan, and it should be more generally used by the colored people of that section of the city.

I suppose if we were denied admission to this institution we would be hammering for entrance—as it is, we are admitted on the same terms as all other persons and we fail to take full advantage of our opportunity.

Listen my readers, there is not a young man or woman who is able to read who could not, by devoting a certain number of hours each week to the proper sort of reading, obtain for himself or herself a liberal education.

You say you haven't the time. That means you haven't the inclination or the will. As Arnold Bennett says in his book "How to live on 24 Hours a Day"—

> We never shall have any more time. We have, and we have always had, all the time there is.

In another place he says:

> The chief beauty about the constant supply of time is that you cannot waste it in advance. The next year, the next day, the next hour are lying ready for you, as perfect, as unspoilt, as if you had never wasted or misapplied a single moment in all your career.

Ponder the following magical words by the same author and see if you do not derive new inspiration from them:

> In the realm of time there is no aristocracy of intellect. Genius is never rewarded by even an extra hour a day. And there is no punishment. Waste your infinitely precious commodity as much as you will, and the supply will never be withheld from you. No mysterious power will say: "This man is a fool, if not a knave. He does not deserve time; he shall be cut off at the meter." It is not affected by Sundays. Moreover, you cannot draw on the future. Impossible to get into debt! You can only waste the passing moment. You cannot waste tomorrow; it is kept for you. You cannot waste the next hour, it is kept for you.

Doesn't that paragraph give you a greater feeling of responsibility regarding the waste of time, the very stuff that life and all of its opportunities depend on?

What Is Your Brain-Power?

November 26, 1914

The essential differences among engines are differences of horse-power. The essential differences among men are differences of brain-power.

A 10 horse-power engine cannot accomplish the work of a 60 horse-power engine; nor can a 10 brain-power man accomplish the work of a 60 brain-power man.

Then why are you content to run around as a 10 brain-power man when it is possible for you to be a man of 20, of 30, of 40, of 50, of 60 brain-power?

There is no mystery about developing and increasing brain-power; it is as simple as developing and increasing muscular strength. We develop muscular strength by physical exercise. We develop brain-power by mental exercise [which] consists in thinking.

Do not confuse the development of brain-power with the securing of an education. Securing an education may result in increased brain-power, and it may not. There is many an educated fool, and there are not a few unlettered wise men. A man with an education is one who has learned something. A man with developed brain-power is one who has thought out something.

In the vaudeville theatres there are often given exhibitions of educated horses and dogs and monkeys, etc., but these are in no degree exhibitions of brain-power.

Reading does not necessarily produce increased brain-power. A man may read one thousand books and never have an original thought about what he reads, such a man is not developing brain-power, he is merely educating himself, storing his mind with information, useful or otherwise. On the other hand, to read one great thought and then to think it through, to unravel it, to get at the inside of its meaning, to chew, swallow and digest it mentally, will produce increased brain-power. Thinking the thought through gives the brain the proper exercise; making the thought your own gives the brain the proper food, and it gains strength and power.

In truth, without reading any book at all, a man may observe life about him, and, by thinking over his observations, increase his brain-power. Indeed, this has been the method followed by those men who are the world's mental giants.

Do you wish to make a simple experiment in measuring brain-power? Well, you can do it at any place where you catch people at leisure, with nothing to do; just watch and see how they do it. The best place, perhaps, is in a subway or elevated train or in any street car. You get into the car and

108

you have a twenty minute ride before you; use your eyes on the people around.

Notice that fellow doubled up in the corner seat and fast asleep with his mouth open; you will be liberal if you give him credit for more than 10 brain power. See that young girl gazing vainly around or listlessly out of the window; do not give her more than 20 brain-power. There are some people who are reading; according to what and how they are reading, you may mark them 30 or 40 or 50 brain-power. There is a man sitting there, oblivious to everything around him; you can see by the expression of his eyes and his face that he is thinking, thinking out some important question, weighing it up and down and deciding how he shall act; promptly mark him down 60 brain-power.

Accomplishment in life depends upon brain-power, and the magic of securing increased brain-power consists in thinking. Not in memorizing, but in thinking.

Brain-power is the power to take hold of the problems of life and reduce them to the best solutions possible. It is, in a word, the power to decide. It is the power to decide questions ranging all the way from the small affairs of everyday life to the problems of metaphysical philosophy.

Brain-power is employed not alone in building a great bridge or in arguing a great law case or in writing a great book; it may be employed in running a farm or in digging post-holes.

Men who possess developed brain-power become the directors of men who are lacking in it, and thereby their superiors. If it is necessary for one man to decide for another where and how the post-holes should be dug he becomes that man's superior.

As it is with individuals so it is with races. Those races which are to-day the backward races are those running on a low mental speed. They are those races that are not thinking and, so, are not developing increased brain-power. Perhaps at one time they were running at higher speed, but they have allowed their mental engines to slow down, and, as a result, they have fallen behind.

How shall we increase our brain-power? By thinking. And how shall we do that? Why, simply by doing it. In most people the mind is lazier than the muscles. It is difficult to keep it on the job. It likes to loaf. It shirks and runs away. When you begin to think you will probably find that after a few moments concentration the mind is wandering far off in other fields. You must take hold of it bodily and put it back to work. The oftener you do this the less you will find that you need to do it; the mind will begin to stick to its work and to enjoy it. The time will come when you will find yourself able to tackle a thought, to think it through logically and clearly to the end, and to decide what action to take.

Don't be a 10 or 20 brain-power man. Make yourself a man of 30, 40, 50 or 60 brain-power.

Howard University Attacked

February 18, 1915

The Southern Democrats in Congress are determined not to lose any chance to boost their record of anti-Negro legislation. The latest addition to the already high record comes from Representative Sisson of Mississippi. The gentleman from Mississippi, on a point of order, had the Howard University appropriation totaling $101,000 dropped from the sundry civil bill, and the measure passed the House without this item.

The point of order raised and sustained was that Howard University is not a Government institution and that appropriations for it have no authorization by statute.

The unanimous consent request to have the Howard items returned to the bill, made by Representative Parker, was not granted because of the refusal of Representative Sisson to concur. The latter maintained that with him it was simply a question of the illegality of appropriating the money without original authorization by statute. The fact that Congress has regularly made this appropriation for the past thirty years had no weight with him.

It is a refreshing sight to see Mr. Sisson so concerned about the strict observance of the law, inasmuch as he comes from a state in which love and reverence for law is about on a par with the observance of the Ten Commandments in Hades. We sincerely hope that he will not expend all of his righteous enthusiasm on the Howard appropriation, but that he will reserve some of it for much needed work when he gets back home. Some of it, for example, could be very properly used in the community which recently lynched a Negro and his wife on suspicion of burning a barn.

What do these .22 calibre statesmen think will be the result of this Negro baiting which they are so tirelessly carrying on in Congress? Of course, they know that they are injuring the race, but do they also know that they are hastening their own political doom and that of their party? The fair-minded people of the United States will not tolerate the injustice and inhumanity which these Negrophobists are too plainly displaying.

Perhaps, following a strictly technical construction of law, Howard might be deprived of its appropriation, but the long established precedent of Congress and the merits of the case outweigh any slight technicality.

We believe the items will be returned to the bill and that Howard will receive its appropriation. We are glad to note the work being done toward this end by Representative Fitzgerald of New York, Parker of New Jersey and Mondell of Wyoming. It is also gratifying to see that, at least, one Southern Congressman, Sherley of Kentucky, is working in behalf of the University.

The Apportionment of Public School Funds in the South

March 11, 1915

The city of Jacksonville, Fla., recently voted a million-dollar bond issue for the erection of new school buildings. The school board has completed its program and has decided to expend for white schools the sum of $800,000, and for colored schools the sum of $115,000. These figures are not secret, but have been published in the Jacksonville daily papers; which fact goes to prove either that the school board is not conscious of any unfairness in such a division or that it is not ashamed to be unfair.

According to the census of 1910, the colored population of Jacksonville amounted to 50.8 per cent of the total population; that is, a little more than half. There are now, perhaps, 35,000 colored people living in that city; and it is safe to say that there is not a community in the South that has a more industrious, enterprising, progressive and law abiding Negro element than Jacksonville. That this is not a mere assertion is proved by the fact that the Florida metropolis is one of the fastest growing and most prosperous cities, not only of the South, but of the whole country; and if more than one-half of its population was backward and shiftless and lawless it could not make such progress. No matter how energetic the white people might be, they could not carry that amount of dead weight.

The colored people of Jacksonville are engaged in every kind of business, from peanut vending to banking. (It is needless to mention how much support they give to white business enterprises.) They work at all the mechanical trades, from mending shoes to building skyscrapers and steamships. They do all of the hard labor. Many of them are homeowners, and pay a fair share of taxes. In fact, they are essential contributors to the wealth and prosperity of their city.

On the other hand, what do they get? They get no such returns as come from holding office and municipal jobs. They benefit only to a small degree from the funds appropriated from public improvements. They have no share in the money spent for public recreation. The only direct return they get is the pittance spent upon the education of their children.

This being the fact, is it not just and right and righteous that they should receive a fairer share of the public school fund than is now contemplated by the board of education?

We cite this case because it applies in a general way to nearly every city in the South.

Look at the figures given below. They are from the Negro Year-Book for 1914–1915, and show the amount expended per child of school age in the following eight Southern States:

Virginia	for whites $10.92	for colored $3.43
Florida	for whites 4.75	for colored 3.10
North Carolina	for whites 6.69	for colored 2.50
Louisiana	for whites 16.60	for colored 1.59
Mississippi	for whites 8.20	for colored 1.53
Alabama	for whites 8.50	for colored 1.49
Georgia	for whites 9.18	for colored 1.42
South Carolina	for whites 9.65	for colored 1.09

By way of comparison, look at the following figures prepared for the World Almanac of 1915, showing the amount expended per child of school age in eight Northern States:

New Jersey	$58.51
New York	49.73
Massachusetts	49.13
Pennsylvania	40.09
Connecticut	39.92
Rhode Island	37.06
New Hampshire	36.88
Vermont	34.80

A glance at these two tables brings up the problem in higher arithmetic often propounded by Dr. Booker T. Washington. "If it costs $49.13 a year to educate a white child in Massachusetts, how much education can a black child in South Carolina get for $1.00?"

We cannot complain because South Carolina does not spend as much as Massachusetts for education, for the simple reason that she hasn't got it to spend; but we are justified in complaining of the fact that South Carolina pays out $9.65 a year on the education of each white child, and only $1.00 on each colored child.

Going back to the case of Jacksonville, the statement made above that the colored people of that city pay their fair share of the taxes has nothing to do with the merits of the question. The theory of political economy which recognizes the landowner as the one who really pays the taxes is not tenable. It is obsolete, and the school boards of Jacksonville and every other Southern city know it.

The 35,000 colored people in Jacksonville live in houses either their own or belonging to somebody else; and they pay either taxes or rent; in either case, they pay taxes. Besides, they contribute their pro rata of all indirect taxes, and no reduction is made for them in fines and licenses. So, for the white citizens, because their names are in the majority on the tax books, to claim that they have to stand the cost of educating the Negro children of the community is as absurd as it would be for the relatively few landowners of New York City to complain that they have to stand the financial burden of educating the thousands and thousands of children whose parents pay rent for tenements and flats.

The South often makes the boasts that it has spent hundreds of millions for Negro education, and that it has of its own free will shouldered this awful burden. It seems forgetful of the fact that all of this money has been taken from the public tax funds for education. Let the millions of producing and consuming Negroes be taken out of the South, and it would very quickly be seen how much less of public funds there would be to appropriate for education or any other purpose.

As the conditions set forth above are general and concern the whole race, let us consider what we are going to do about the matter. To narrow it down to the case before us, what are the colored people of Jacksonville going to do about it? I can almost hear some reader answer, "Nothing."

But something should be done. The matter should at first be laid before the school board in a comprehensive, direct and intelligent manner. If this step should fail, the question should be appealed to the white citizens at large. It is difficult to believe that there are not enough fair minded white people in Jacksonville to influence such a case as this.

If there are not enough so fair minded as to be able to see the justice of a more equable, if not equal, division, there ought, at least, be enough who from an economic point of view could see the advantages of it. They evidently want their city to continue to develop and prosper; well, it can't if more than half the population is kept back and down. It can't if eight times as much is spent upon a white child in order to give him a chance to become a good citizen as is spent upon a colored child. It would be common sense and good business to reverse the figures.

If neither of these steps succeed there is only one left, and that is for the colored citizens to raise sufficient money to legally oppose the spending of the proceeds of the bonds in the manner designated by the school board. Let them raise a sufficient amount to take the case, if necessary, to the Supreme Court of the United States.

"Let Down Your Buckets"

April 29, 1915

A meeting of the Public Education Association will be held this week, at which the question of helping colored children in the public schools toward a more helpful future will be discussed. The Association has just issued a report on "Colored School Children in New York." Miss Eleanor Hope

Johnson, chairman of the committee on hygiene of school children, says in the introduction of the report:

> We are constantly learning, through interpretation of sympathetic students of various races of immigrants, the several ways in which these aliens may contribute to our national life; and each discovery, especially in the different Negro to be considered in the light of a national asset, and his loyalty, patience, of art, is hailed with joy by constructive patriots. Surely it is time for the sympathetic kindliness, and artistic instinct be counted on as real contributions to our national welfare.

Here is an effort that shows real intelligence and humanitarianism. The only sort of effort that can possibly bring about stable racial adjustment. And, sooner or later, our white fellow citizens all over the country must and will come to this method of dealing with the problem: the method of sympathetic co-operation. The consideration of their own best interests, if not ours, will demand a change.

It is interesting, in reading Miss Johnson's introduction to note her catalog of our virtues. It is not a complete catalog, and it is not likely that she meant it as such, but see what an array there is! "Loyalty, patience, sympathetic kindliness, and artistic instinct." Has any of the races coming to these shores to help make up the American nation of the future brought a finer contribution than that? The thought brings back to mind the famous admonition to our white fellow countrymen given years ago by Dr. Washington at Atlanta, "Let down your buckets!"

An Open Air Lecture Course

May 6, 1915

As the pleasant weather comes on the lecturers who speak in the open air upon subjects of varied and vital interests [they] will begin to gather their audiences around them. Colored people are, in a general way, interested in what these lecturers talk about, but only in a general way. It is regrettable that we are not more deeply interested.

But since for various reasons—some good and most of them bad—we, as race, are not interested in sociology or economics or eugenics or even woman suffrage, would it not be a good idea to establish in Harlem an open air lecture course upon subjects in which we are vitally interested.

The open air lecture course has grown to be a great institution. It is university extension carried to the farthest point. On a hot day men will gather around an open air speaker and listen for an hour or more to an informative talk on some topic of the day. The majority of these men would never think of going to a lecture, but they will listen when the lecture is brought to them.

There are a great many things that the colored people of New York should be taught and told, things they do not hear either at school or in church. If the proper sort of open air lecture course could be established in Harlem these things could be brought to their attention and they would listen to them.

There is one colored speaker who, if he could be secured, would give series of lectures that would be more than equivalent to a year at college, and of incalculable benefit to the community.

If the public spirited colored men of Manhattan wish to do something of great practical value at a relatively small cost, let them take steps to establish in Harlem an open air lecture course for the summer upon subjects of importance and interest to colored people as a race.

We should be glad to receive suggestions from our readers.

The Importance of the Negro to the South

August 16, 1916

There is no great question more paradoxical than the one which embraces the relations of white and black people living together in the South. This is forcibly brought out by the furor about the migration of colored laborers to the North, which is stirring so many Southern communists.

From most that has been said and done by Southerners for the past fifty years, one would conclude that the Negro was a terrible burden on the South, a burden that it would be only too glad to get rid of at the first opportunity. He, the Negro, has been declared a general nuisance, a handicap, a blot, a curse, and as many other things of that kind as can be thought of. Southern leaders have, even in Congress, advocated his deportation. Others have gone so far as to advocate his annihilation. It has time and again been proved that the Negro was the one thing that stood between the South and all the blessings of peace, prosperity and perfect happiness.

Now comes a time when large numbers of colored people propose voluntarily and without expense to their white neighbors to leave, and what is the result? Why, the powers of city, county and state are invoked to prevent them from doing so.

Instead of being a burden to the South, the Negro is an element of great strength. He is both a producer and consumer, and so he is doubly a tremen-

115

dous asset. It is often charged that he is especially a heavy economic burden. This charge is based on the old and worn out theory of political economy which recognized the land owner as the one who really pays the taxes. The unequal distribution of the public school funds between whites and blacks is defended upon this theory. It is often stated that the South has spent millions for the education of colored children; and the statement is made as though the spending of this money were an act of philanthropy or charity. The fact that these millions have been taken from the public tax funds for education is entirely disregarded. Each child in the South, white, or black, is justly entitled to an equal share in the public school fund. And when white Southern land owners claim that they stand the financial burden of educating colored they are wrong. It would be just as reasonable for the relatively few land owners of New York to claim that they stand the financial burden of educating the thousands and thousands of children whose parents pay rent for tenements and flats. Let millions of producing and consuming Negroes be taken out of the South, and it would quickly be seen how much less of public funds there would be to appropriate for education or any other purpose.

The New President of Howard University

November 22, 1919

Howard University last week installed its new president, Stanley Durkee. The ceremony in every way befitted the importance of the occasion. In addition to the inaugural exercises there was a conference on readjustment and reconstruction which was attended by educators, social workers and leaders of thought from many parts of the country.

Dr. Durkee in his address outlined the new program for the University and stated clearly his views on education. From his views it can be seen that no mistake has been made in the choice of him as the head of the foremost university for colored youth. We feel confident that Howard will see great growth and development under his administration.

The Proposed Department of Education

January 28, 1922

There is now before Congress a bill which proposes to create a Department of Education, this department to be one of the executive departments of Government and to be headed by a Secretary of Education who shall be a member of the President's cabinet. The proposing of the new department, as stated in the bill, is to assist the states by Federal aid and, in the removal of illiteracy and the equalizing of educational opportunities. For this purpose the bill appropriates $7,500,000 for the removal of illiteracy, to be divided among the states according to the number of native-born illiterates. It also appropriates $7,500,000 to be divided among the states according to the number of foreign-born illiterates. It also appropriates $50,000,000 to be divided among the states, to be used in public, elementary and secondary schools for the partial payment of teachers' salaries and providing better instruction and extended school terms, especially in the rural districts.

The purposes set forth in the bill are in accord with what thinking colored people have been demanding for a long time, that is, Federal aid to public school education. It is easy to demonstrate mathematically that at the rate at which most of the Southern states are spending money on education in colored schools, the removal of illiterate young colored people is nowhere in sight. An approximate average of the money being spent for the education of white children and colored children in the states where a dual school system exists, shows that throughout the South about $10.32 is being spent on the education of each white child and about $2.89 for each colored child.

Of course, as long as there are separate schools this average will be very little altered and the situation will be very little changed. It appears that the only remedy lies in Federal aid given under strong guarantees against discrimination in the administration of the funds.

But it is upon this very point that the Sterling-Towner Bill falls down, for in the latter we find the following provision:

> All funds apportioned to a State to equalize educational opportunities shall be distributed and administered in accordance with the laws of said State in like manner as the funds provided by State and local authorities for the same purpose, and the State and local educational authorities of said State shall determine the courses of study, plans and methods of carrying out the purpose of this section within said State in accordance with the laws thereof.

The bill needs to be amended, for as much as colored people desire to see Federal aid given to public education, especially throughout the South, they would prefer not to have it than to have it under conditions which would allow the Southern states to use these Federal funds as they now use the public school funds of the states.

Democracy at Harvard

June 24, 1922

The universities of the world have always been considered the well-spring and the refuge of liberalism. This has been so regarded in all countries and in all times from the middle ages down. Among the great universities in the United States none has held a higher place in this respect than Harvard. Harvard University has always been looked upon as the strong-hold of liberalism. This is especially true as it touches the Negro. Not only were a great many men who championed the Negro's cause cradled at Harvard but in turn became the cradle of numbers of aspiring youth.

Today the question of color and race is raised as a bar to the enjoyment of what Harvard has to offer. A few weeks ago the question of Jews, and reducing their number at the university, became a public one. A few days ago the same question as applied to colored students became public. This question as to colored students has been simmering for some time at Harvard. A number of strong influences have been at work in an attempt to do away with the practice of discrimination against colored students which was fast becoming a fixed policy. An effort is now being made by certain members of the Alumni headed by Mr. Moorfield Storey of Boston [who drafted] a petition presented to the governing body of the university asking that Harvard return to its old tradition as regards the Negro and that the exclusion of colored men from the Freshman dormitories be discontinued.

The most disheartening aspect of this whole situation is the attitude of President Lowell. President Lowell is reported as stating quite frankly that Harvard is catering to students from the South and that he is not going to let a little matter of democratic principle stand between Harvard University and white students of the South. Dr. Lowell is quoted as having written a letter containing the following statements:

> No agitation will force us from doing our duty toward the rest of our students. If it is better for them, as we believe it is to have compulsory residence in freshman halls, we shall not be deterred from doing what is best for this overwhelming majority of our students because there are perhaps one percent of colored men to whom the policy be applied.
>
> In fact, their inclusion would make it impossible to carry out the compulsion for the rest. Men from the South and Southwest come to us in con-

siderable numbers, and cannot be compelled to room or eat with colored people. We owe to the colored man the best possible opportunities for education but we do not owe him inclusion in a compulsory social system with other people when it is not mutually agreeable.

If President Lowell had been reared in Mississippi instead of Massachusetts he could hardly have put up a stronger defense for discrimination. Evidently Southern students at Harvard have been working up this situation for a great many years but now that they have President Lowell's official endorsement of their attitude and their reasons, it is likely that they will stop at no ends in their efforts to keep colored men out of Harvard University entirely.

If this matter had transpired at Yale University where there has always been some degree of prejudice against the Negro or at any other large university in the country it would have been bad enough; but for it to have transpired at Harvard is discouraging beyond expression.

Exclusion in Our Universities

October 14, 1922

What is coming over the universities of this great democracy, this land in which a popular education is supposed to be one of the foundation stones of its security and greatness? Harvard University has deemed it necessary to place arbitrary restrictions upon the privilege of entering her portals; that is, she has placed exclusive bars up against men on account of race.

And now comes along President Hopkins of old Dartmouth with a still more exclusive policy. His statement is that entirely too many men go to college anyhow. The Harvard policy seeks to reduce the number of Jewish and colored students, but President Hopkins is in favor of the policy of excluding a large part of the regular white variety of American students.

Dr. Hopkins says that if democracy is to be preserved it must be a "quality product rather than simply a quantity one." He feels, therefore, that men who are "incapable of profiting by the advantages which the college offers, or indisposed to do so, shall not be withdrawn from useful work to spend their time profitlessly, in idleness acquiring false standards of living." He feels, too, that on the other hand, "the contribution which the college is capable of making to the lives of competent men through them to society shall not be lessened by the slackening of peace due to the presence of men indifferent and wanting in capacity."

This is dangerous ground on which to build democratic ideals. Who is able to judge which students are capable and worthy of taking a university education? Who can tell before he gets it what this or that man will do with a college education? We have it of record that some of the most useless students have become most useful men. Undoubtedly many of our colleges are being taxed beyond their capacities and there must be a selection of the fittest for the advantages which they have to offer, but this selection should not be based on any grounds of race or color or upon the fallible judgments of any Board or Committee as to which students are worthy of these advantages. The only wise method will be to raise the qualifications, raise them as high as necessary, but let them apply equally and impartially to all men, white or black, Gentile or Jew, classes or masses, rich or poor.

6 Black Leadership

In a word, we can do the Africans more good and give them greater help by achieving our full American citizenship rights than we can by colonization schemes. Mr. Garvey and those with him are either deceiving themselves or deceiving others.

James Weldon Johnson, "African Colonization Schemes"
(August 12, 1922)

Real leadership is not a distinction to be assumed; it is an office to be achieved, wrote James Weldon Johnson. Moreover, "Of the real leader the people some day become aware, and say: This man serves well, let us follow him." he added.[1] He acknowledged two necessary elements of leadership: radicalism and conservatism. Radicalism was needed, he wrote, to keep the race from becoming too complacent; conservatism was needed to give balance to radicalism. When both elements are present, the leader is not fearful to act radically when necessary and not afraid to act conservatively when it is necessary to stand still.[2] Believing that the race should guard against being stagnant on the one hand or wild eyed on the other, as a race leader, Johnson generally was guided by his own principle.

The other prominent black leaders during his tenure with the *New York Age* were Booker T. Washington (1856–1915); Marcus Garvey (1888–1940); and W. E. B. Du Bois (1868–1963). Alienating neither the conservative Washington nor the so-called radical Du Bois, Johnson centered his political position between their two philosophies.

He wrote more vitriolic about Garvey's leadership and race philosophy than he did about any other black leader. He acknowledged, however, that Garvey stirred the imagination of the masses as no African-American ever had. Johnson's strong disagreement with Garvey is evident in the following editorials. According to Johnson, Garvey fought practically every "Negro" organization in the country, especially the NAACP, mainly focusing his attacks on W. E. B. Du Bois.

Johnson joined the staff of the NAACP in 1916 and became its executive secretary from 1920 to 1930. In the dual role of editor and NAACP official, he used his *Age* column to explain the NAACP's goals and its apparatus for attacking the race problem. Johnson wrote that the NAACP should be the nucleus, the synthesis, the clearinghouse for all black forces.

The Norfolk "Get Together" Conference

December 10, 1914

Recently a conference was held at the Hampton Institute between representative colored and white men of the city of Norfolk. The object of the conference was to effect co-operation between the two races for the betterment of both. This is a very significant sign of a better understanding and better conditions in the city.

Major R. R. Moton of Hampton Institute spoke frankly and directly to the white men present. Among other good and sensible things, he urged upon them to acquaint themselves with what the Negroes of their city were doing and trying to do with the manner in which they live and with what the best ones want.

Here Major Moton touched what we believe to be the key to this whole vexing problem. Intelligent colored men feel that if they could get Southern white people to listen to them patiently and become interested in them sympathetically the whole Negro question would at once be more than half solved. They feel that if they could get their white neighbors to know the better elements in the race, to know how they live, what their aspirations are and how great is their desire to co-operate with the white race for the mutual benefit of all, they feel if this could be done the present misunderstanding and bitterness would soon be overcome.

As the situation now is, the Southern whites know us only through their contact with the less intelligent and less progressive class of the race, and they continue to look with contempt and disdain upon the intelligent and progressive class with which they have almost no contact. A glance into the homes of some of the colored people in their very midst would be a revelation. But it is next to impossible to get them to take that glance.

The most pathetic phase of the whole Southern situation is that as the progressive colored people advance they constantly widen the gulf between themselves and their white neighbors, that the very colored people who most need and who could best appreciate sympathetic co-operation are forced into an isolated position.

But the Norfolk "get together" movement is a bright sign; and, if the committees continue to confer in the proper spirit the results for good will be far-reaching. If such conferences could be carried on in all the principal Southern cities the present condition would be changed for the better within an astonishingly short time.

Honorable Charles W. Anderson's Record

December 10, 1914

In his handling of the intricate income tax and of the more recent war tax, Mr. Charles W. Anderson, Collector of Internal Revenue, has made a remarkable record. Not merely a record of which he may personally be proud and of which we, as a race, should be proud, but a record which goes to the high water mark in the whole Revenue Service of the United States.

It is not based upon the fact that Mr. Anderson has collected hundreds of thousands of dollars each year without any discrepancies in his accounts that his high record is based—the average functionary with the normal amount of honesty and intelligence could do that—but it is principally based upon the way in which he measured up to the demand for initiative and for quick and sound judgment in the interpretation and application of an untried law.

When a law is placed upon the statutes it is merely fundamental. Its entire effect and effectiveness will depend upon the decisions made in its interpretation and application. These decisions grow to be the commentary on that particular law and always exceed it in bulk. Often the law itself is complicated or vague, and the makers themselves are not absolutely sure as to what it means. These various decisions which are reached in putting the law into execution serve to give it clarity and point.

This was true in a larger degree of the Income Tax law than of, perhaps, any other law passed in the United States. Here was a law without precedent in this country, and every day there arose questions of detail which could not have been foreseen by the makers, nor which, had they been foreseen could have been included in the original law.

The majority of these questions came up first to Mr. Anderson, for it is in his district that the great bulk of the income tax is collected.

How well he acquitted himself is a matter of record. It is safe to say that no man connected with the Revenue Service has had more to do with forming the mass of decisions through and by which the Income Tax law is interpreted and executed than Mr. Anderson.

No tax is popular; and, of all tax laws, an income tax law is the least popular. The fact that although Mr. Anderson's district contains the people who were the hardest hit there was little or no complaint speaks in the highest terms not only for his intelligence but for his skill, his diplomacy and his great common sense.

The Passing of Jack Johnson

April 8, 1915

It is the old, old story of one fight too many. It is a demonstration of the old truth that in a contest of age with skill and experience against youth, strength and endurance, youth, in the end, will always triumph.

From a pugilistic point of view, it was a great fight. And, however much we may cultivate the finer sensibilities, however much we may decry the exercise of brute force, still there is something in a great fight and a clean and fearless fighter that stirs every man with red blood in his veins. Johnson fought a great fight. He showed no sign of the yellow streak, and it must be remembered, too, that it was the fight of one lone black man against the world. And he proved that he has not only been a great winner, but that he could also be a good loser. After the battle was over he was manly and sportsmanlike enough to say:

> It was a clean knockout and the best man won. It was not a matter of luck . . . I have no kick coming.

Johnson was the perfect athlete, the master boxer and always the square sportsman. Even those who hate him concede that no greater fighter ever put on a glove. Had it not been for certain bad personal breaks, he would have been the most popular idol pugilism ever had; for he possesses all the elements that make for popularity. Even so, it is hardly probable that Willard will ever become the world known figure that Johnson is. There is not, perhaps, a spot on the globe where Jack Johnson's name is not familiar; while it is doubtful that Willard's name will ever go beyond English speaking countries.

Johnson's bad personal breaks deprived him of the sympathy and approval of most of his own race; yet it must be admitted that with these breaks left out of the question, his record as a pugilist has been something of a racial asset. The white race, in spite of its vaunted civilization, pays more respect to the argument of force than any other race in the world. As soon as Japan showed that it could fight, it immediately gained the respect and admiration of the white race. Jack Johnson compelled some of this same sort of respect and admiration in an individual way.

One of the delusions fostered by the Anglo-Saxon is that white men are superior to those of "lesser breed" not only intellectually, but also in physical strength and stamina; that physical stamina is a matter of mind, and the white man's mind being superior he can stand the gruelling grind that takes the heart out of other men. Before the Johnson-Jeffries fight, the papers were full of statements to the effect that the white man had the history of Hastings and Agincourt behind him, while the black man had nothing but the history of the jungle; that when the white man looked the black man in the eye, the black man would wilt. But the black man did not wilt. He not only looked the white man in the eye, but hit him in the eye. Johnson effectually punctured this old and pet delusion; and so we say his pugilistic record is something of a racial asset.

Frederick Douglass had a portrait of Peter Jackson hung on the wall of his library, and he use to say that Peter was doing his part to solve the race question. Were it not for the unfortunate "breaks" referred to, Jack's niche would be greater than Peter's.

When Johnson licked Jeffries, most of the states passed laws prohibiting the exhibition of moving pictures of prize fights. Of course it would be degrading to the morals of the people to see a black man conquering a white one. (Some of this moral fervor expended against the "Birth of a Nation" would be very creditable.) Now that a white man has licked Johnson, the law looks funny, doesn't it?

We notice that Willard will draw the color line. He labels himself, by this, not as the greatest fighter in the world, but merely as the greatest white fighter. So, after all, Jack Johnson goes down as the last real champion, a fighter who was ready to match his strength and skill against all comers.

Sam Lucas

January 20, 1916

The death of Sam Lucas removes from the theatrical profession the man with the longest and, perhaps, most varied career of all colored performers who have made their reputations in this country.

In his long career, Lucas represented on the stage roles ranging all the way from a knock about "Darkey character" to a fine and sympathetic portrayal of the gentle "Uncle Tom." To properly estimate his ability in legitimate characterization, it is well to remember that his "Uncle Tom" was played in a white company under the direction of no less a person than Charles Frohman. Only a few months ago, Daniel Frohman, in his biography of his brother, which is running in the "Cosmopolitan" magazine, paid a tribute to Lucas, both as an actor and a man.

Sam Lucas was one of the few colored men in the profession to whom the term actor might be properly applied. he was not a performer by main strength; he had brain, and he always put his brain into whatever he did, no matter how small or insignificant the part might be. Anyone who saw his performance of the minor part of Chairman of the Board of Education in "The Red Moon" must have been impressed with this fact.

To those who knew Sam Lucas, the most remarkable thing about him, more remarkable than his long career or his ability as a performer, was his eternal youth. He never grew old. Up to the last, his optimistic outlook on life was an example and an inspiration to younger men. There was always the cheerful greeting and a story at parting. How he could relate so many stories without monotonously repeating himself will always remain a mystery.

A couple of years ago he was engaged to play the part of "Uncle Tom" for the great moving picture production which was made of the play; and so he had the satisfaction of seeing what was his greatest pride, his portrayal of Harriet Beecher Stowe's hero, preserved on the screen.

Sam Lucas leaves an honorable record behind him. He enjoyed the respect of both white and colored members of the profession and the special love and esteem of those of his own race.

Dean Pickens

May 17, 1919

William Pickens, Dean of Morgan College, made a remarkable speech at the session of the National Conference on Lynching that was held at the Ethical Culture Hall. Dean Pickens has long enjoyed a great reputation as an orator, but perhaps not every one who has heard him realizes what his most unique quality is. Mr. Pickens is eloquent; but many other colored speakers have the gift of eloquence. What Mr. Pickens has which no other colored speaker we know anything about has, or, at least, in such a high degree, is the power to satirize race prejudice. He has the power to make race prejudice such a fool and absurd thing that even those who practice it are compelled to see that it is something ridiculous. This is a wonderful power.

Then when Mr. Pickens has them laughing at their own folly, he jabs them with a bitter truth. At the Ethical Culture Hall he said:

> The primary right of self-defense is denied the Negro. No mob will allow a man universally judged to be by his own inherent nature unfit to vote, to defend his life against a man who is supposed to be of superior nature and fit to vote. Juries will not put dogs and men on terms of equality in court. That man is a dreamer who hopes to degrade the Negro politically, economically and socially, and yet defend him from the mob.

This expresses the absurdity of expecting that a judge who is merely an ordinary human being—and most judges are—or any other officer of the law is going to have any special regards about the rights of a Negro, when that Negro has not the right to vote him in or out of office.

Rabbit-Hearted Leaders

October 11, 1919

Every week sees a declaration in the newspapers issued by some rabbit-hearted "leader" or group of "leaders" condemning the men and women of the race who are to-day making a determined fight for equal justice and equal opportunity, and asserting that all that is now needed to settle the problem is to leave it in the hands of "our best friends," the Southern white people.

Any man or woman who has watched the development of events and forces during the past two or three years must realize that if the American Negro fails at this particular moment, he has failed for the next fifty years. If the American Negro fails to hold the front line trench in which he is now fighting, he is in for a long and disastrous retreat. The forces against us in this country are to-day making a gigantic effort to stamp out once and for all every hope of equal rights and equal opportunity that the race has. To destroy our progressive organizations, and to destroy our progressive press. In a word, to compel the Negro to accept and be contented with a permanently inferior position from which he will never dare to aspire.

If the American Negro cannot to-day, when the masses of the entire world are stirred to ideals of common democracy, stand firm for those ideals and die for them, if necessary, he will not get another chance to share in them, perhaps, for another century.

Now, if there is any Negro in the United States who hasn't sense enough to see and understand that this is true, he has a brain so small that if he tried to get a hat to fit it he would find that a thimble would come down over his ears.

But most of these rabbit "leaders" take their position not because they lack brain; they take it because they lack courage, either physical or moral.

Of course, if a man is born with a heart of a rabbit, there is some excuse for him. It is unreasonable to expect courage from such a man. So for colored men who are sincerely frightened at the critical state of affairs and are counselling peace, peace at any and every price, submission, if necessary, in order to obtain peace, for those men we have sympathy, if not pity.

But for the other fellow we have no respect. For the fellow who is using this crisis to batten off his craven utterances; to hold on to his job; or to get a fatter job; for that fellow we have nothing but contempt.

I understand and realize that a job means bread; and that bread is a vital thing. I know that men who have been willing to sacrifice bread for the sake of principle have been few in the history of the race. Those men are of the stuff that heroes are made of; and [are not] made every day or every year, or every century.

So I know that there are colored men in many places who are not in positions to speak out frankly and fearlessly for the things which they know to be true and right. But if such men cannot carry out the obligation to speak out for what is true and right, they should at least carry out the obligation to keep their mouths shut.

For myself I will say that if I were dependent on the good-will of the reactionary white South for bread for myself and for those who looked to me for bread I might be forced to realize that I could not speak out as loudly and boldly as I wished for the rights of manhood and citizenship for myself and my people, but by any god that lives I swear that I would cut out my tongue before I would be forced to repudiate those rights.

These are trying times, but let us stand firm; firm for what is true and what is right. We are right and truth is on our side. There is nothing that we should fear.

"A Crime Against Nature"

September 24, 1921

Recently Mr. Marcus Garvey, President-General of the Universal Negro Improvement Association, was quoted in one of the daily papers as making the following statement:

> The Universal Negro Improvement Association stands in opposition to the Pan-African Congress and to the leadership of Dr. Du Bois because they seek to bring about a destruction of black and white races by the social amalgamation of both. The Dr. Du Bois group believes that Negroes should settle down in communities of whites and by social contact and miscegenation bring about a new type. The Universal Negro Improvement Association believes that both races have separate and distinct social destinies, that each and every race should develop on its own social lines, and that any attempt to bring about the amalgamation of any two opposite races is a crime against nature.

This is a statement in which Mr. Garvey consciously or unconsciously, plays to the most deep-seated prejudices of the white man in America. It is the very sort of thing that Vardaman, Cole Blease and the rest of that ilk sayand wish to have accepted. Does Mr. Garvey realize the full implication of his statement when he says that any attempt to bring about the amalgamation of any two opposites substitute black domination for white domination? By what feasible plan then does Mr. Garvey propose to secure it?

The only possible end of the race problem in the United States to which we can now look without despair is one which embraces the fullest cooperation between white and black in all the phases of national activity. If that end can be reached save through the recognition of all kinds of equalities, we should be glad to have Mr. Garvey tell us.

Of course, there may some day arise one or two or three great empires in Africa that will compel the recognition of the full rights of men of African blood everywhere. Or there may come sooner than expected the ultimate downfall of the white race. But as Kipling would say, that is another story— in fact a couple.

African Colonization Schemes

August 12, 1922

The question of the colonization of the Negro in Africa is again in the public mind, more or less. The idea has been given some publicity through the utterances of Marcus Garvey.

We say the question is again more or less in the public mind because it is an error to suppose that this idea is a new one. It has been coming up periodically for more than a hundred years. It has been tried out on various scales ranging all the way from steps taken by individual pioneers to movements of colonies of considerable size. Some of these movements have been backed by large amounts of money.

But taking the whole history of African colonization schemes for American Negroes, we must say that the idea has been a colossal failure; nor do we see any greater chance of success for the present movements, either the one sponsored by Mr. Garvey or that of Dr. Thorne. Indeed, the political conditions in Africa for the founding of independent Negro colonies are less favorable now than they were one hundred years ago.

To anyone who considers this matter practical, the first question to be decided is: Where will the Negro go in Africa? Mr. Garvey talks about a great Negro state, or republic, or empire which he hopes to found. Can Mr. Garvey put his finger on any spot on the map of Africa and say, "Here we will found our state," and say so with any regard to the possibility of carrying out his plan?

There is only one spot in Africa where American Negroes might go in any numbers at all, and that is Liberia, and we doubt very much if they would be welcomed even there if the numbers were too large. We have not the slightest doubt that the Liberian government would object to the immigration of a hundred thousand or even fifty thousand American Negroes, and what effect would even that number have on the twelve million in America?

American Negroes may, after securing proper passports, visit the countries on the northern coast of Africa which are under the suzerainty of England, France, Italy and Spain, but they are not allowed even as tourists to visit the great states to the south in which the majority of the Negroes in Africa live. Mr. Garvey talks about carrying millions of Negroes to Africa. We doubt very much whether Mr. Garvey himself as an individual could possibly get into Africa.

Mr. Garvey, from his utterances, appears to include conquest in his plan. He speaks of conquering. We suppose he means by this, conquering some of the overlording European nations in Africa and seizing the territory. It is quite possible that Africa will some day be redeemed for Africans by conquest, but if that is to be the method of redemption the initiative will have to be taken by Africans in Africa instead of by any society or organization in the United States. Such societies and organizations could do little more than support an African movement.

Mr. Garvey's last step is the action taken by the the UNIA now in convention, appointing a Delegation to confer with the British Government and ask for one of the former German African colonies. On the face of it this step looks practical, but is it? England has never been known to give away anything and if she gives the Garveyites one of the German colonies which she now holds possession, it will be nothing short of a miracle.

But there is a still greater obstacle. The former German African colonies do not consist of large tracts of vacant land. All of these colonies, with the exception of one, are already filled with people. German East Africa, with an area of 384,180 square miles, has a population of nearly eight million Negroes according to the latest figures; Kamerun, with an area of 191,130 square miles, contains more than two and a half million Negroes; and Togo, with an area of 33,700 square miles contains more than a million Negroes. The only one of the four which is not already well populated is German West Africa, with an area of 322,450 square miles and a population of eighty thousand Negroes.

The reason why the population of German West Africa is so sparse is because most of the tribes inhabiting it have been decimated by the Germans or they have been killed off, because they are nomadic and fighting tribes, they would give American Negro colonists almost as much trouble, perhaps, as they have given the Germans.

It is needless to say that the Negro natives of the three thickly populated colonies would not tolerate any overlording or governing on the part of the Negroes from the United States or the West Indies.

Dr. Thorne's plan is not so big as Mr. Garvey's neither is it so impractical. His idea, as reported in the New York "World," is to obtain a concession to ten thousand or more acres of land in Nyassaland on the Zambesi River. This territory lies in southcentral and southeastern Africa and the concession would need to be granted by the British Government.

Now comes up the practical objection to Dr. Thorne's plan. What would American Negroes gain by swapping not only their residence in the United States by their American citizenship for the status of colonists under British rule in South Africa? They would gain nothing. In fact, they would lose a great deal. Negroes under British rule in South Africa, as we know have neither the rights nor the opportunities of Negroes even in the Southern States.

But to all of these African schemes there is a psychological difficulty which one of the promoters of these schemes appears to take under consideration, and that is that the Negro is a human being before he is a Negro. In spite of the fact that the American Negroes and the African Negroes are blood brothers. American Negroes will never migrate in any numbers to Africa until Africa can offer them better and greater advantages than they have in the United States. Men have often left their homelands and gone to new lands but always the new lands offered at least the prospect of more than the old lands gave.

Furthermore, these promotors of African colonization schemes fail to realize that a common origin and even color do not make American Negroes Africans. Peoples are not related and united by physical aspects or even by blood. They are united by common cultures, common ideas, common ideals, common languages, common educations. The fact that the Chinese and Japanese are half brothers does not unite them. The average American Negro thrown into the midst of primitive African conditions would feel just about as much out of place as the average white American.

All of these facts must be taken together in any scheme for the redemption of Africa so far as the American Negro is involved. No mere sentimental or emotional appeal about our kinship with the Africans and Africa being our ancestral home is going to take the American Negro back there. In this the American Negro is not an exception to the common laws of human nature. It can be said with equal truth that, even with more favorable guarantees and conditions, the Jews in the United States, in spite of the sentimental appeals of Zionism, are not going to leave America and settle in Palestine.

In a word, we can do the Africans more good and give them greater help by achieving our full American citizenship rights than we can by colonization schemes. Mr. Garvey and those with him are either deceiving themselves or deceiving others.

The Apotheosis of the Ridiculous

August 19, 1922

One can discuss calmly the African colonization scheme of Mr. Garvey and his followers, impracticable as that scheme might be because it is related to a great question of world politics, the question of the saving of Africa for native Africans. But no such state of equanimity can be maintained in discussing the "court ceremonies" held at Liberty Hall last week at which time a large number of titles were conferred and debutantes were presented to "His Supreme Highness." We read that "dukedoms" and "knighthoods" and other orders were conferred upon a number of men. There were created "His Grace, of the Niger," "Commanders of the Order of the Nile," and "Commander of the Order of Ethiopia." We also read that deputies and delegates in evening dress were presented to "His Supreme Highness, the President," Mr. Garvey, and each was required to kneel.

If some satirical humorist were to write a burlesque depicting life in some actual or mythical Negro country and showing what is commonly spoken of as the Negro's childish vanity, love of show and "high-sounding emptiness," he could hardly produce anything more absurd than what is reported to have actually taken place at this Garvey court ceremony; and if such a writer did produce such a story, it is likely that all of the thoughtful colored people in the country who read it would become indignant. But here is the thing actually happening.

If the Garveyites were actually in possession of a country and had established a government and were handing out dukedoms and knighthoods, it would be bad enough, but there would be some substance behind the title. The dukes and knights would probably constitute a parliament of congress that legislated for the nation. But to be creating dukes and duchesses and lords and ladies in Harlem, N.Y., USA, is the apotheosis of the ridiculous.

And it brings up the question, what sort of a government does Mr. Garvey propose to establish in Africa? Seemingly there is no intention of establishing a democracy or a republican form of government. It looks as though his aim is to establish a government based upon hereditary class distinctions, the very thing that most of the enlightened peoples have abolished or are seeking to discard.

The report of this ceremony in *The New York World* stated that this court reception is held each year at the annual convention of the UNIA, to remind the Negro race of what are considered the past glories of Ethiopia and the future possibilities of Africa. As regrettable as it might be, we are nevertheless faced with the fact that past glories of Ethiopia, however great they may have been, will not fit into the future possibilities of Africa.

133

Marcus Garvey's Inferior Complex

September 2, 1922

In reply to certain statements made by William Pickens regarding the Universal Negro Improvement Association, Marcus Garvey is quoted in the "Negro World" of August 19 as delivering himself as follows:

> You know some of us lose knowledge of ourselves sometimes. In the tropics where I come from, you will find every well-to-do Negro losing knowledge of himself. That is, the moment a white man smiles with him, pats him on the shoulder and invites him to dinner for once, he loses knowledge of himself, and starts to believe that he is a white man. I wonder if anybody has patted Pickens on the shoulder; I wonder if anybody has taken Pickens by the hand; I wonder if anybody has invited Pickens to dinner and I would not doubt that he has been invited to dinner, because I have seen him recently very much in the company of white folks, and any time a Negro gets into the company of white folks he becomes a dangerous Negro.

Has Mr. Garvey any realization of the revelation he is making of himself when he expresses such a sentiment as the above? Evidently, Mr. Garvey does not see that he is placing himself in a position far more contemptible and ignominious than the one in which he seeks to place Mr. Pickens. When Mr. Garvey expresses the belief that at any time a Negro associates with white people he feels so flattered that he becomes a boot-licking syncophant and a parasite, he is revealing what the Freudian psychologists would call an inferiority complex.

What becomes of Mr. Garvey's boasts about the equality and even the superiority of the Negro if within himself he feels that a Negro cannot sit down with a white man, look him in the face and talk with him, or eat with him—in a word, that a Negro and a white man cannot extend to each other the simple courtesies of life—without the Negro feeling himself greatly flattered and having his head turned? If this is true, any boasts about the Negro's equality is sheer humbug. If this is true, the future of the UNIA under Mr. Garvey's leadership hangs on a very slender thread.

Suppose some day a white man should invite Mr. Garvey to dinner and he did summon enough courage to go. According to his beliefs, the Negroes of the UNIA would from that hour henceforth be minus a Moses. It appears that Mr. Garvey's only security in maintaining his sense of equality and superiority is to steer clear of white folks.

Mr. Garvey pretends to speak for the colored people in the tropics where he came form. We feel more inclined to believe that he is speaking for his subconscious self and that he is expressing the way he would feel if "patted on the shoulder" by a white man. However, Mr. Garvey knows more about

134

the people of his home than we do. But we can give him the information that in the United States, at least, there are hundreds and thousands of colored people who can and do associate with white people and without feeling themselves in any way flattered by the association. They take it simply as matter of common human relations, as a matter of course. We can also inform Mr. Garvey that there are masses of white people with whom these same hundreds and thousands of colored people in the United States would refuse to associate.

We can also inform Mr. Garvey that there are a great many white people in the United States who can and do associate with colored people without being in any degree condescending or patronizing; they, too, take such association simply as a matter of common human relations, as a matter of course.

Any colored man who feels, like Mr. Garvey, that no Negro can associate with white people without feeling flattered and becoming a bootlicker may well question whether or not he actually does believe in his own equality.

If Mr. Garvey cannot understand the implications of his attack on Mr. Pickens he ought to go and have himself psychoanalyzed, and he will find that he has an inferiority complex. His over loud boastings about his own equality are obvious indications of that complex.

A Negro Benefactor

September 2, 1922

We are no longer surprised when a Negro wins a prize as an orator at Harvard or Yale or develops into an athletic star, or writes a remarkable book, or accomplishes any other feat that depends upon his own powers. But when a Negro leaves $100,000 to a worthy cause, we must confess that it does attract unusual attention because it is so rarely that such a thing is done. Not that many Negroes have not died and left $100,000 and even more, but the cases in which they have left $100,000, $50,000, or even $10,000 to any worthy cause or institution are so few and wide apart that most persons would be compelled to say that they had never heard of a single one.

A dispatch in the Cleveland "Plaindealer" states that James M. French, a business man of Sandusky, left practically all of his $100,000 estate for the benefit of Oberlin College; the income on the principal for fifty years to be given to the trustees for the benefit of "deserving Afro-American students," and at the end of fifty years the principal to be used for same purpose. The will specifies that the bequest is to go to Wilberforce University if Oberlin does not accept it.

135

Just why Mr. French did not leave his money to Wilberforce in the first place we do not know. He may have felt that his gift would be instrumental in turning Oberlin's attitude toward colored students, which in recent years has changed so much, back to what it was years ago.

Mr. French accomplished a remarkable achievement by gathering a fortune of $100,000. In bequeathing his fortune to a great institution for the benefit of the youth of his race he has achieved something more vital, far-reaching and noble.

Garvey

June 30, 1923

Mr. Garvey has been convicted and given a full sentence. Regardless of what this means to Mr. Garvey personally, the bursting of the bubble of the Black Star Line is somewhat in the nature of a disaster to the Negro.

It appears that during his trial Mr. Garvey had the opportunity to make an exhibition of what has been his greatest strength and what ultimately proved to be his greatest weakness. It was undoubtedly the vain glorious posturing which he indulged in before the court in which he was tried that had much to do with attracting and holding together the large number of people who followed him; but it was this same trait which largely contributed to his final undoing.

Religion

Here is a great work which must begin with the intelligent and progressive ministers. The work of making this powerful organization not only the instrument for promoting our spiritual welfare, but our welfare as men and citizens.

James Weldon Johnson, "Responsibilities and Opportunities of the Colored Ministry" (February 8, 1917)

"The most complete and powerful organization in the race is the Negro church. No other medium that we have can compare with the church in strength of appeal, breadth of influence and finality of authority," Johnson wrote.[1] In this power rests upon African-American ministers greater responsibilities and opportunities than upon any other single group, he added.[2]

Johnson told his readers with deep disillusionment that the problem within the black church was due mainly to its leadership—a leadership that inhibited the church from meeting the exigency of the African-American plight in this nation as it confronted it during slavery days and in the post–Civil War period. He complimented the progressive preachers of the day, but his lamentations were founded in his thinking that too many preachers had gone after social position and wealth. He believed that these preachers had lost their spiritual influence over the hearts of their members. Admonishing many preachers as bootleggers of religion who peddled a spurious brand of religion at a relatively exorbitant price, Johnson noted that they were letting a critically important opportunity slip through their fingers. In his column, he wrote that the ministers should not only make this powerful organization an instrument to promote spiritual needs, but an instrument to educate its members on the issues of the day—issues that affect their daily lives.

Challenging African-American youth in colleges and universities to consider the ministry as a career, Johnson wrote that the ministry as a college-based career could make the role of preacher as desirable for well-educated and progressive youth as the fields of medicine, law, and denistry have become in recent years.

Because of the unique problems that African-Americans faced in this nation, Johnson believed that the race was being ill-served by its most powerful institution.

Florida's New Christian Colony

November 5, 1914

According to a full page advertisement in "The Philistine," Dr. Geo. F. Hall of Chicago, is the "Founder, Owner and General Manager of Christian Colony." The "Colony" is being settled at Hall City, De Soto County, Florida. The advertisement, among other inducements, sets forth the following: "1,200 farms already sold and 2,000 lots in Hall City, the booming temperance capital of the Colony. Perpetual prohibition clause in every deed. No Negroes. No dagoes."

These two last sentences seem not to ring with a very true Christian spirit, and we venture to suggest that the colony is starting out under a misnomer. Furthermore, and we know whereof we speak. Dr. Hall is as wrong on another important matter as he is on his principles of Christianity. If he thinks he can build up a successful town in Florida without Negroes, he is doomed to everlasting disappointment. It might be done around the suburbs of Chicago, but in Florida—impossible.

Catholic Gains

March 25, 1915

The Official Catholic Directory shows that the Roman Catholic church has increased in numbers a quarter of a million in the last year. It also shows a gain of nearly four million in the past ten years and more than seven million in the past twenty years.

These figures will alarm a great many good people, who will see in them the ultimate downfall of the Republic and a lot of other dire disasters.

For our part, we should like to see more of the Catholic spirit instilled into our great Protestant and other denominations. The Catholic church in this country is that religious body in which wealth, social distinction, class and race count for the least. The humblest, poorest and most ignorant immigrant entering New York can go up into the great Cathedral on Fifth Avenue, and feel that he is welcome, and the truth is, he is welcome. Anyone in such circumstances would hesitate for some time before entering a rich Protestant church.

It is almost impossible to think of a Catholic priest preaching race discrimination or urging his congregation to go out and lynch somebody.

If all the great Christian organizations in this country had the religious and moral courage to openly disapprove the injustice, lawlessness and cruelty which the Negro has to suffer, those sins and crimes would soon be stopped.

But they haven't got it.

Pagan Temples

April 13, 1915

Some months ago we said in one of our articles that if Christ came to New York, we doubted whether he would make his home in one of the pagan temples erected in his name. No doubt, some of our readers considered the statement irreverent. We had no intention of being flippant or irreverent; we meant exactly what we said.

A short while ago one of the congregations of this city decided to erect a new church building at a cost of three million dollars. Later, it was decided to increase the cost to four million, two hundred thousand dollars. It is easy to understand why four million or more dollars might be put into an art museum or a public library or any other building built for show as much as for use, but what reason or excuse can be given for putting that amount of money into a church building? A church building should be comfortable and commodious; its beauty should be the beauty of simplicity and dignity.

Four million dollars to build a church where a strong man, standing on one of its towers, could hurl a baseball into the midst of poverty and human suffering. Four million dollars to build a church in the name of Him who founded the Christian religion as He trod his way from town to town. Four million dollars to rear a glittering temple in the name of Him who was the humblest among men; in the name of Him who had no where to lay His head; in the name of Him who chose to live and labor among the lowly. It is mockery!

What will such a building stand for? It will stand for pride. Pride of the congregation, pride of the city. Pride, that is it! Worldly pride, the thing most directly opposed to the very essence of all Christ's teachings.

Look into such a church. A high-salaried, well groomed, soft-voiced, perhaps, over-fed minister addressing from week to week an audience of those who are, supposedly, already saved; an audience with which straggling, sinful, needy humanity would not dare to mingle, even to hear the words of Jesus. Contrast this scene with the Christ, sublime in His simplicity, standing in a fisherman's boat preaching to the throngs along the shores of the Sea of Galilee.

There you have an answer to the question, "What is the matter with the Church?" There you have a reason for the fact that the church is again losing its power over men's souls. Its strength is being spent in producing gorgeous flowers and delicate perfumes.

Billy Sunday Cleans Up Paterson

May 27, 1915

Paterson, N.J., is not a very large city; so when we read that Billy Sunday for his seven weeks' campaign in that city received as his own individual share $25,000 in cash besides other valuable gifts, we can only exclaim in Billy's own vernacular, "He certainly did clean up Paterson!"

We do not mean to say that Billy did not earn the money. His drawing power would net him just about that much in vaudeville, and he wouldn't have to work near so hard. However, we cannot believe that saving souls and making money out of it as a business is looked upon with favor by God, or will be very much longer by decent men.

Billy Sunday's methods, especially that of getting the money, are far from the direct example set by Jesus Christ that no allowances for 20th century civilization can excuse them. The early apostles trudged about with scarcely clothes for their backs, and laid the foundation that made Christianity the religion of the Roman world. Billy Sunday has gained for himself more than $25,000 for seven weeks' work, and it is probable that within three months there will not remain in Paterson one single beneficial effect of his efforts.

Billy has a right to make all the money he can, but he ought to do it where he seems to belong rightly—in vaudeville.

What's the Matter with Church?

October 14, 1915

A prominent New York minister discussed at considerable length in one of the daily papers a few days ago the following question. "Why is the house of God forsaken?" He went on to say a great many things in his discussion, but when he had finished he had failed to answer the question.

The question as stated goes too far; the house of God is not forsaken; nevertheless, the church has lost and appears to be still losing influence and power. This is evidenced by lack of interest and falling off in attendance on the part of the people. Why this is true, is a serious question for the church, a question to which it should bestir itself to find an answer.

Why is it that people show a growing tendency to stay at home or go elsewhere than to church? There may be someone who thinks he is smart enough to point his finger at the single cause; we make no pretensions to such smartness. We believe there are numerous causes, some of them the direct fault of the church, and others entirely beyond its control.

One cause which may be cited is the fact that the church has stronger competition than it ever had before. There was once a time when, on Sundays, people who were socially inclined had no where to go but to church. In those days the church was the social center of the community; and there is no doubt in our mind that the majority of people attended, on Sundays in particular, because it gave them the great, and sometimes only opportunity of the week to put on their best clothes and to see and meet people similarly arrayed.

In those days most of the sweethearting was done through the church. The decent young fellow would escort the young lady he was courting to church; now he takes her to the "movies" or to the "sacred" Sunday concert or out automobiling.

The old condition may still prevail in small communities, but in the cities it is past. And it is a state of affairs beyond the control of the church. As a social attraction, the church is up against competition which it is powerless to overcome.

Another cause which may be cited is the extreme ultilitarianism of the age. The spirit of the times is to throw aside everything which has no practical bearing upon every day life. Even the oldest universities have had to bend to this spirit. Young men no longer spend four years at college to broaden and elevate their minds; they spend four years preparing themselves to be able to make a living.

The same demand is being made on the church. A sermon explaining the mysteries which John saw on the Isle of Patmos sounds idle to people who want light on the realities they are facing. Directions for securing a starry crown and golden slippers are mockery to those who are worried about how to get a hat and a pair of shoes.

But is not this also a condition beyond the control of the church? We agree that the majority of sermons could well be made more practical; but is it within the power of the church to compete in utilitarianism with the schools and colleges, with the lecture platform and the press? We think not.

There are, however, causes of decrease in the power and influence of the church, for which the church is directly responsible and which it could remedy.

There has developed in the church a gross mercenary spirit which does not harmonize with what Christ taught nor with what most people feel to be proper.

The church is supposed to deal in spiritual things, but it charges hard cash. It is money, money, always money. There is no longer such a thing as free gospel, unless it is picked up on the street corners. And for what purpose is this money gathered? Does it go to feed the hungry? To clothe the naked? to care for the widow and the orphan? To some extent, yes; but the great bulk of it goes to maintain costly temples.

Does this bear any resemblance to what Jesus taught by word and example? Not the least. He founded the Christian religion as He walked along the shores of the Sea of Galilee, preaching to the crowds that gathered to hear Him. If Christ came to New York today, He could hardly be conceived as making His headquarters in one of the glittering, pagan temples erected to His name.

One of the most pronounced attributes of Christ was His sublime simplicity, his disdain of pomp and glory; the church today needs a new baptism of Christ-like simplicity.

This admonition applies not only to the church as a body, but to the ministry as individuals. Too many preachers have gone after the flesh pots of Egypts, too many have hungered after wealth, preferment and social position; and, thereby, lost their spiritual influence over the hearts of men. Only a few days ago the whole country was listening to the humiliating confession made to his congregation by one of the most distinguished clergymen of this city. With tearful eyes and choking voice he told how the desire for wealth had entangled him in a mesh of evil and brought ruin down upon his head. Most likely that man's greatest usefulness as a minister of the gospel is forever ended.

It is a psychic truth that the only kind of a man who can give out spiritual inspiration is a man of sincere simplicity; whether he does his preaching on a street corner or from gilded pulpit. And so the ministry also, in order to regain its spiritual influence over the hearts of men, needs a new baptism of Christ-like simplicity.

The realm of the church is neither in the social or the utilitarian world, it is in the spiritual world; so there is no use for the house of God to attempt to compete with places of amusement or utilitarian institutions. The purpose of the church is to lift man, if only for a moment, out of the everyday world of work and pleasure up into the higher world where he may renew his spiritual inspiration and strength, and so be able to do better work and enjoy purer pleasures. When the church truly fulfills this purpose, it need never fear that it is dead or dying; it will know that it is still a living and vital force, and that the House of God is not forsaken.

Sin and Pleasure

June 1, 1916

The old amusement clause in the Book of Discipline of the Methodist Episcopal Church has been again under discussion. A subcommittee of the General Conference recommended the elimination of the clause which prohibits dancing, attending the theater and card playing, and the substitution of a clause warning members against these diversions. But the Conference rejected the proposal.

Those in favor of the change maintained that the penalty provided for violation of the clause is not now enforced in any church, and that the effect upon young people will be better if this provision, which cannot be enforced, is withdrawn and a general warning issued that the church does not sanction such amusements. Those opposed to the change say that such an action would mean that the church is letting down the bars.

We agree with those who think that the old clause should be eliminated, yet we cannot see what good it will do to substitute a warning, except as a sort of concession to those who are opposed to the change. If an absolute prohibition did not stop members from indulging in these diversions, a warning will have no effect. The most probable effect of entirely abolishing the clause will be to bring many people into the church, who, otherwise, might not join.

There are a great many good and intelligent people who believe that dancing, going to the theater and playing cards are acts which are in themselves wrong. This notion comes down from the time when sin and pleasure were considered to be one and the same thing; from the time when people who got any fun at all out of life were looked upon as lost; from the time when, in certain religious bodies, it was considered almost sinful to laugh heartily. It is not so long ago that the singing of a song which has anything about love in it was a sufficient cause in some denominations to bring a church member to trial.

What is sin? That is a question which has puzzled theologians in all ages. In an attempt to give a definition in a few words, and entirely apart from theology, we should say that sin is that which is harmful. An act by which one advertently harms another or himself is sinful; and the harm may be physical or spiritual; also the act may be one of commission or omission. Under this definition, murder and theft and excess eating and excess drinking naturally fall into the category of sins; but there are many acts, especially those involving spiritual harm, which are not so easily classified.

It is true that many sinful acts furnish pleasure. There is no doubt that the murderer in his frenzy derives a flash of primitive pleasure in killing his enemy or adversary. The same may be said of him who takes another's goods or of him who eats or drinks to excess. Perhaps it is true that most sins furnish a temporary pleasure of one sort or another. But it cannot be argued from this that every act that furnishes pleasure is a sin. That, however, has been the position taken by a great many religious sects. For example, see the "Blue Laws" of Connecticut. These laws, although they may never have been statutory, nevertheless, were the standard of conduct in the colony. Read the following:

> No one shall run on the Sabbath day, or walk in in his garden, or elsewhere,
> except reverently to and from meeting. . . . No woman shall kiss her child on
> the Sabbath or fasting days. . . . No one shall make mince pies, dance, play
> cards, or play on any instrument of music except the drum, trumpet and
> jews-harp.

Dancing may be as innocent and beneficial as jumping rope. Going to the theatre may be as edifying as listening to a sermon. Playing cards may be as harmless as playing authors. Of course, if one cannot dance in a wholesome fashion, or if his taste for the cards without gambling or losing his temper, he ought to refrain from doing these things, because for him they are sinful. But that does not make it necessary to prohibit them to the great majority of people, for whom they are harmless diversions; two of them, dancing and theatre going, may be made very beneficial.

There are many plays which are harmful; likewise, there are a great many books which no one could read without sinning, because they contain that which works spiritual harm, but nobody, on that account, thinks of advocating illiteracy.

It will be a step forward when the progressive element in the great Methodist Episcopal Church succeeds in having the old amusement clause eliminated from the Book of Discipline.

Responsibilities and Opportunities
of the Colored Ministry

February 8, 1917

No one who travels over the country especially through the South, can fail to be impressed with this fact. The most complete and powerful organization in the race is the Negro church. No other medium that we have can compare with the church in strength of appeal, breadth of influence and finality of authority.

In this respect the colored churches relatively constitute a more powerful organization than do the white churches. For while white people are influenced religiously by their churches, they are influenced in matters social, industrial, financial and political through other well established mediums. On the other hand, the only medium through which many millions of colored people can be reached and influenced is the church. There it goes without saying there rests upon colored ministers greater race responsibilities and opportunities than upon any other single set of men.

The writer has several times said in this column that if the white churches of this country should unite in taking a real Christian stand on the race question, a miraculous change would be brought about; a similar statement may be made about the colored churches. If the colored churches of this country would unite in taking an intelligent and unselfish stand on all questions of vital interest to the race, there would also be brought about a miraculous change. The taking of such a stand depends entirely upon the colored ministers. It is first necessary that they come to realize the responsibilities and opportunities that their position gives them.

Of course, there are many of our ministers who do realize these responsibilities and opportunities, but the great majority, those that reach the mass of millions, have not progressed beyond the standard ante-bellum days. They are still consuming all of their time in the pulpit, and using up some mental and a great deal of muscular energy in efforts to expound what Paul said. The things that Paul said are, of course, important and it is the duty of a minister to preach and teach them, but there are things being said by men living to-day and in this very country important enough to the race to be worthy of some of the time usually devoted to Paul.

Here is a great work which must begin with the intelligent and progressive ministers. The work of making this powerful organization not only the instrument for promoting our spiritual welfare, but our welfare as men and citizens.

The Power of the Negro Church

July 9, 1917

We have said before that the Negro church is, beyond all question, the one powerful organization in the race. We have pointed out that it is relatively far more powerful than the white church. The white people of the country may be reached and influenced through many mediums, but the great mass of our race can be reached and influenced through only one, the church. There is then a correspondingly greater obligation resting upon colored ministers than upon white ministers, and that obligation was never more serious than it is today.

The pressing duty before the Negro ministry is to take the power of the Negro church and make it an instrument for bettering the conditions of the race. It is a time when that power should be used to secure for the race a larger fore-taste of better things right here and now. It is a time when less attention should be paid to larger collections for handsomer churches and some effort be made to raise a great general fund to be used in fighting for our rights. In such an undertaking we would be following the example of the Jews, who are now raising one hundred million dollars to be used in fighting for greater rights for themselves when the war ends. It is a time to put the Negro church into close touch with the practical questions that affect the welfare of the Negro people as citizens. It is a time when less attention may be paid to what Saint Paul said and did and more attention to what is being said and done by the makers of current history. It is a time to put away petty rivalries and to unite with one purpose in view.

Union, that is what we need. Union of the great mass of the race. It does not make much difference what we attempt to do, if we would all do it at one time and together. If one million of the twelve millions could be so organized in taking any step for the advancement of the race as to take that step together and with the same purpose, no power in the country could withstand them.

Such race-wide power could be realized if the Negro ministry would come together and solidify the Negro church. Such a church, working in cooperation with existing protection, and civic organizations would constitute a force within the race that could not be defeated.

The Interchurch World Movement

July 3, 1920

The withdrawal of the General Assembly of the Presbyterian Church and the Northern Baptist Convention from the Interchurch World Movement seems to threaten the very existence of the undertaking. If such should be the result it is to be regretted for two reasons: first, the movement promised to bring about a closer cooperation among the churches, at least the Protestant and Evangelical churches; second, the program as laid down by the movement promised a great many practical benefits in which the colored people were to be included.

The exact reason for the withdrawal of these two strong denominations, without which it does not seem possible that the movement can succeed, are not yet made entirely clear to the public. That they must have been serious and weighty no one will deny.

The published reports of what happened at the Baptist Convention give accusations chiefly of extravagance. Outside there come rumors that the whole movement was designed as a means whereby religious thought and activity could be more completely under the control of the capitalistic powers of the country. The truth will undoubtedly soon come out.

8

The Black and White Press

Negro weeklies make no pretense at being newspapers in the strict sense of the term. They have a more important mission than the dissemination of mere news. . . . They are race papers. They are organs of propaganda. Their chief business is to stimulate thought among Negroes about the things that vitally concern them.

James Weldon Johnson, "Do You Read Negro Papers?"
(October 22, 1914)

Black papers should not be imitations of white papers. African-American editors have a relatively deeper responsibility to their readers than white editors have to theirs, Johnson wrote. The service possible for the black press to render to black America is more vital than what the white press has given to white America, he added.[1] Johnson, as cogent as anyone, used this medium to expose, interpret, and attack the issues that were so vital to African-Americans in their quest for full equality as American citizens.

One of Johnson's principal concerns as editor included the habitual untruths written in the white press about black life to divert attention from the ignominious wrongs inflicted upon his people. In the face of this skewed picture of black life, Johnson exhibited sagacity and skill by systematically exposing these calculated misstatements and by giving the public the facts. In general, the white press repudiated the legitimacy of African-Americans in their struggle for equality.

149

"One can only conjecture as to the influence on the American mind of this . . . evidence of the violations of the basic principles of American democracy."[2]

Johnson believed it important for white people to read black newspapers because the white press manifested scant interest in black achievement. Johnson devoted considerable space in his column to highlight black progress.

It is also important to note that Johnson's primary concern was the eradication of lynching. Probably fifty percent of his *Age* editorials was devoted to educating the public on the subject and keeping them stirred up for political action.

Do You Read Negro Papers?

October 22, 1914

In the last issue of The Age there was an interesting communication from Mr. T. L. McCoy, of Raleigh, North Carolina, regarding Negro newspapers and their readers. Mr. McCoy has been working the journalistic field, and he states that the work is hard and the harvest far from bountiful.

In his effort to secure colored subscribers and readers he had met with a great deal of discouragement. We can well believe that he is not exaggerating the gloomy side of his experiences.

It appears that the chief objection to Negro papers which he encounters from some of the people he approaches is summed up in these words, "I cannot find any news in the Negro newspapers."

The Negro paper is not primarily a newspaper, any more than a religious weekly is a newspaper.

If a man wants news he should buy one of the great dailies with resources for gathering almost instantaneously the reports of happenings from every point on the globe. All the news that a sensible man would expect to find in a colored paper is that growing out of our church, fraternal and other organizations and out of our social life or the record of an event that in some way touches the race.

Negro weeklies make no pretense at being newspapers in the strict sense of the term. They have a more important mission than the dissemination of mere news. It is not their work to herald that there has been a wreck off the Fiji Islands or that the Russians have captured Przemyls.

They are race papers. They are organs of propaganda. Their chief business is to stimulate thought among Negroes about the things that vitally concern them.

Some colored people make an open boast that they never read Negro papers. It is safe to bet that these same people never do anything toward the development and upbuilding of the race.

It is also safe to bet that they wouldn't buy groceries from a Negro even if his stock was as good, his prices as cheap, and his store as convenient as any other man's.

One more safe wager is that they are people who are getting along pretty well, and are not much bothered about how anybody else gets along; especially those of their race.

In effect, they paraphrase the famous retort of old Commodore Vanderbilt, and say. "Damn the race!"

The *New York Times* Solves a Puzzle

November 5, 1914

Every once in a while the New York "Times," contrary to its general policy, strikes an editorial blow in behalf of the colored peoples of the world. Only last week we quoted the rather scathing remarks it made on the insincere and cowardly action of the American Bar Association in repealing the resolution of debarring Negroes from becoming members.

In an issue this week the "Times" seeks and finds a reason for the "widespread, probably general feeling of mingled apprehension and repugnance" excited by the use of colored soldiers in settling the quarrels of white nations. It advances a reason which, it says, may be of the sort called subconscious; and adds that, at any rate, it has not often been mentioned.

The reason given is that even the peoples calling themselves most highly civilized give to physical courage and fighting ability sincere admiration; and though they are supposed to condition this admiration by the merits of the cause for which bravery and prowess are displayed, it is impossible to withhold it from those who show these qualities—especially in a fight against odds. So, white men subconsciously resent seeing men of color given the opportunity to display those qualities which they wish to believe to be possessed exclusively by the white race.

The latter half of this article is so much to the point that it will be well to quote it directly. It reads as follows:

> And since our appreciation for efficient pugnacity is so great, may it not be that we object to the utilization of more or less "savage" troops as auxiliaries in a white man's war simply because, when this is done, the "savages" show themselves practically equal to us in the very things for which we admire ourselves most?
>
> At any rate, the comparison is not so much to our advantage as we would like to have it. As the present war has repeatedly illustrated, the men of color—the Senegalese and the East Indians—are not at all afraid to attack white troops, sometimes do it effectively, and manifest no incapacity for using our weapons or in executing the military operations worked out after profound study by our best experts. We can still believe that the dark folk need white instruction and leadership to make them "good" soldiers, but the great majority of white troops are also more or less nearly helpless when left to their own devices.
>
> The often demonstrated superiority of white armies to those black, red, or yellow seems to be more largely a matter of weapons than of courage or of natural military ability. As far as "atrocities" go there is not so much to choose, if all stories are to be believed, and they all rest on about the same basis of unproven accusations.

Strong Words from the *Globe*

December 17, 1914

On the speech made by John Skelton Williams before the Southern Society of New York and the reply made to him by Ex-Attorney General Wickersham, the "Globe" published the following strong editorial. In these days when the tide of public opinion seems set against us in so many quarters it is gratifying to see such sentiments expressed by a great metropolitan daily. On several recent occasions the "Globe" has taken high ground on the Negro question. The good effect of such utterances cannot be estimated:

THE FEAR OF INFERIORS

John Skelton Williams of Virginia, controller, was moved in his remarks before the Southern Society last night to trot around again the decrepit political back on which so many inferior men have ridden into office to the injury, intellectual, moral, and material, of one of the fairest sections of the Union. "Long ago we determined," said Mr. Williams, in the familiar stump speech manner, "that the Negro should never be our masters." As if there is or ever was danger of 30,000,000 proud and intelligent whites of the south, with a great tradition behind them, falling under the mastery of 10,000,000 members of a race but a few years out of slavery! Mr. Williams insults his neighbors by mentioning such a thing as possible. The world's familiar with the domination of the inferior many by the superior few; and sometimes the superior few have been dominated by the inferior many, but history records no instance of the domination of the superior many by the inferior few.

It is agreeable to note that Mr. Wickersham, who followed Mr. Williams on the speaking list, was moved to reply and did so suavely and effectively. It is even more agreeable to note that the members of the Southern Society, silent during the speech of Mr. Williams, applauded Mr. Wickersham. It is a wholesome and encouraging thing when a gathering of representative southerners, bored by childish appeals to race prejudice, is pleased by declarations that "no people can thrive and advance if side by side and working with them, are 10,000,000 who are disfranchised and denied all voice in government."

Mr. Williams has Skelton as his middle name, and this name is a proud one because among other reasons, it was borne by the wife of Thomas Jefferson. Let this latest Skelton remember that Jefferson, although the owner of slaves and brought up in contact with the institution, declared with respect to Negroes: "Whatever be their degree of talent it is no measure of their rights. Because Sir Isaac Newton was superior to others in understanding he was not lord of the person or the property of others." Jefferson was animated with the true spirit of Virginia, that big and generous Virginia that was the political leader of America, and, more than any other colony, was instrumen-

153

tal in establishing independence and in creating the Union and the nation. The calm and beautiful voice of the Old Dominion, defending the rights of man and the great principles of democracy, will yet make itself heard above all the shrill shouting of race prejudice.

Comment Here and There

January 7, 1915

"Life" is a weekly which is supposed by most people to be a humorous publication, but is more witty than funny. For an example of keen wit, with an added sting of satire, we offer the following:

THE INFERIORITY OF THE NEGRO

Our friends down South, being sure that the Negroes are inferior, deny them advantages and provide inferior schools for Negro children in order that they will continue to be inferior and thus prove the correctness of the contention of the scientists and sentimentalists that the Negro is inferior. After all, there is nothing quite so satisfying as the feeling that you have got things fixed so that you will always have an inferior race in your midst.—Life

There will be some people who, on finding such a sentiment in "Life," will evidently think it is intended as a joke, yet, even they should remember that "many a truth is spoken in jest."

The "Saturday Evening Post" is a serious publication, yet, like "Life," it is not particularly concerned about the Negro. It is, therefore, interesting to note it pointing out seriously what "Life" lays bare with a slash of wit and satire:

A LESSON TO THE COTTON BELT

In big cotton states that single crop comes to considerably more than half the value of all other agricultural products. The disadvantages of so great dependence on a single product are illustrated with the sharpest emphasis this year; but they have been illustrated before, when cotton has been too cheap to yield any profit to the grower, or when the boll weevil has ravaged the plant over large districts. Well-informed Southerners have even said that this cotton crisis would prove a blessing in disguise if it brought greater diversity of crops in the big cotton states. However, ignorant Negro labor, on which agriculture largely depends in some parts of the South, is an obstacle to diversifying the crops. That labor has been taught to raise cotton. To teach it diversified farming would be no light task. There are other factors undoubtedly, but this factor of ignorant, unresponsive Negro labor is one of the anchors that hold the South to cotton. Of course any community anywhere is tied hand and foot to its labor. In agriculture or manufacturing it can go no farther than its labor goes. A Southern community that denies education to Negroes, while depending on Negro labor, fastens a ball and chain to its own foot.—The Saturday Evening Post.

The writer has been much concerned about the fate of Mrs. Boone Little of Detroit whose heartless husband is suing her for a divorce on the ground of a recent discovery that she has Negro blood in her veins. We know Mr. Little must be a heartless man, because otherwise he would not be so cruel to such a charming little lady as Mrs. Little is—judging by her pictures in the papers.

We have been much concerned, because if Mrs. Little has Negro blood in her veins her case is decidedly embarrassing, and if she has not, her case is truly tragic.

Scientists have been baffled; and it is just on this point that we can't understand why, if Mrs. Little is so white as to baffle the scientists, Mr. Little should be so upset over the matter.

However, a Dr. Windsor, who has had long practice in the South, tested Mrs. Little by a method which is said to be considered infallible by Southern planters, and declared her to be white. The following is an extract from a despatch from Detroit to the "New York Sun":

PASSES TEST

Mrs. Little, according to Dr. Arthur Windsor, a prominent Ontario physician, to-day passed a test which he claims beyond a doubt proves the woman has no Negro blood in her veins. It is a test which Dr. Windsor on many occasions in his thirteen years practice in Southern States made to determine racial ancestors of persons brought to him. It is obtained by a pressure of a finger on the tip of the subject's nose where there is what is known as the alar cartilage. In the colored race this cartilage is blunt and solid, while in whites it is separated so that two distinct formations can be felt. Mrs. Little's nose, according to this test, is of Caucasian formation.

Although the racial identity of the writer has never been questioned, we, nevertheless, on reading these words involuntarily pressed a finger on the tip of our nose, and lo and behold! the two distinct formations of cartilage were plainly felt. Poor Mrs. Little!

Of course by now you have pressed the tip of your own nose.

155

Perverted History

April 22, 1915

Several of the great dailies of this city, either on account of their interest in the welfare of the colored people, or from a sense of common justice and fairness, have spoken out against the vicious picture play known as "The Birth of a Nation." Other New York papers for reasons best known to themselves, have remained silent. It remained for "The Press" to come out and editorially commend the picture:

In a recent editorial "The Press" said in part:

> "[The] Birth of a Nation"
>
> We are at loss to understand the persistent attacks upon the motion picture play, "The Birth of a Nation," which is an historic portrayal of that dark time in the late sixties when the Republic was in the terrible agony of a new birth.
>
> It tells in pictures the story of a vital period of our history. It illustrates scenes that were common in one of the greatest cities of the Nation. It is not a cheerful tale. The Reconstruction is not a theme which any American, North or South, can dwell on with pleasure. But that is no reason why our children and children's children should be ignorant of the events of that fateful time. There is little instruction in the bright pages of history. It is only by studying the plague spots of the past brought on by the mistakes of our own forefathers that we can hope to arm ourselves with wisdom against the great problems of the future.

When "The Press" declares that it is at a loss to understand the persistent attacks upon "The Birth of a Nation," it convicts itself of utter stupidity. If the writer of the article has seen the production he ought have no difficulty in understanding why the picture arouses resentment among colored people and fair-minded white people. And we say that we do not believe that any man could rise to be editorial writer on "The Press" and be so dull of understanding as not to be able to see the cause of the attacks upon Dixon's photoplay.

The writer makes himself equally as ridiculous when he says that "The Birth of a Nation" is "an historic portrayal of the dark times in the late sixties." In the first place, the majority of the incidents portrayed in Dixon's play that relate to colored people never happened. For example, when did any Negro lieutenant-governor of a Southern state ever try by force to make a white woman marry him? When did Negro troops, led by Northern officers, ever loot and pillage the homes of the Southern whites and maltreat and murder the occupants of those homes?

But even if every incident in this picture play could be verified as a fact, still "The Birth of a Nation" could not pass as history. History is not a record of isolated facts set down to the exclusion of other counterbalancing facts of equal importance. By such a method as that anything could be proved by history. A happening or two could be taken from the life of King David, which standing alone, would make him one of the grandest scoundrels that ever lived; yet, David's life taken as a whole won the tribute that he was "a man after God's own heart?"

Suppose a Southern white man, or a Northern white man, for that matter, should walk into a London theatre and see a picture flashed on the screen entitled "Life in the South" or "Southern Life in the United States" or something of that kind. And suppose this picture consisted of a series of incidents portraying the wrongs committed by whites against blacks. Now it would be a very easy matter to verify such incidents, all the way from defrauding Negroes out of a few acres of land to burning them alive at the stake; but, does the editor of "The Press" think that any white American spectator, be he Southerner or Northerner, could sit still and accept such a picture as history. And yet, such a picture would be more veracious than are those parts of "The Birth of a Nation" relating to the colored people.

Now why would the American spectator be justified in resenting this supposed picture? For the reason that such a representation would be out of proportion to the history, civilization and development of the South considered as a whole; and therefore, not history.

And so with "The Birth of a Nation"; many hundreds of colored people are used in this production for the purpose of representing Negroes as a race, and they are pictured as the perpetrators of every kind of indignity, crime and barbarity, from shoving white folks off the sidewalk, to committing robbery, murder and rape. The only thing to offset this is the portrayal of a couple of genuflecting old darkey servants known as "the faithful ones." This picture pretends to be a history of the nation in general and of the Negro in particular, yet there is not one single decent, self-respecting, industrious and intelligent Negro represented in the whole production; it fails to give the Negro any credit for the phenomenal restraint and control which he showed both during the war and Reconstruction, and absolutely ignores all progress he has made since that time; there is not in it one creditable thing attributed to the Negro as a race, still, the editor of "The Press" is at a loss to understand why we do not enjoy "The Birth of a Nation," why it arouses our resentment, why we will not accept it as history.

The greatest and truest history is less concerned with incidents than it is with tendencies, with movements, with results. So far as the Negro is concerned, whatever happened during slavery or during the war or during Reconstruction is insignificant compared with the great result into which these happenings have shaped themselves. The great result is that out from slavery, out from a bloody war, out from the red passions of Reconstruction, set free naked and penniless, the dupe of knaves and the victim of oppressors, out from all this the Negro has come, rising as he came.

"The Birth of a Nation" is morally wrong when it ignores this great result, and, while it does, it has no right to be regarded as history.

Why White People Should Read Negro Papers

December 2, 1915

A correspondent writes to us from Tonopah, Nevada, saying that he is making an effort to get as many white subscribers as possible for The Age. At the same time he asks us to state some reasons why white people should read Negro newspapers.

In the first place, we wish to say that our correspondent shows himself to be a wideawake man. How many agents of colored newspapers are there who realize that it is possible to interest white readers? That it is possible, even easy, is proved by the fact that The Age has among its subscribers a large number of white people. The names of some of the white people who read The Age regularly would make an astonishing list.

There are several good reasons why white people should read Negro newspapers; one of them is that the white people of this country ought to know what the ten million colored people who live amongst them think of them. Sometimes our opinion of our white fellow citizens is very high; they would find that gratifying. Sometimes our opinion is just the opposite; they would find that instructive.

However, the principal reason why white people should read Negro newspapers is that it would make them better acquainted with colored people; and, with better acquaintance would come better understanding. The main cause of prejudice is ignorance. People of one race or nation dislike people of another race or nation because they do not know the best things about them. In every people there are more good qualities than bad qualities; and when those good qualities are known and appreciated, blind prejudice is bound to vanish.

Anyone who knows Chinese only by the few Celestial laundrymen in his town is more than apt to have a contemptuous opinion of the whole race and to speak of them as "chinks." But when he learns that many of the inventions which have made human progress possible (notably the mariner's compass and printing from movable type), were originated by the Chinese;

that the Chinese have produced great philosophers and sages; that in spite of all the modern advancement of Japan, the literature of China still constitutes the classics of the Mikado's kingdom, just as Greek and Latin literature constitute the classics of the western world; when he learns that most Japanese banks have Chinese cashiers, because honesty is considered a traditional virtue of all Chinese business men; when he learns as a race the Chinese are exceptionally industrious, frugal and temperate; and that their civilization, on the whole, is the most remarkable that any branch of the human family has yet evolved, having endured for five thousand years or more, and been adequate for the general peace and happiness of the people, while scores of other civilizations have blossomed and perished; when anyone has learned these and other similar facts about the Chinese, how will it be possible for him to think of them only with contempt and speak of the race as "chinks?" To do so would merely be a proof of his own inferiority.

The Chinese are on the other side of the world; but, in many respects, they are no farther distant from the white people of the United States than are the Negroes who live in this country.

Much of the prejudice against us arises from ignorance of our better qualities. Through a hostile or indifferent press the deeds of the worst elements in the race are made common knowledge. In many localities we are known and judged by those members of the race who are frequenters of police courts.

White Americans need to become better acquainted with colored Americans. They need to come into closer touch with the progressive, home-building, education-seeking elements of the Negro race; to come into closer sympathy with their aspirations and struggles. This they can accomplish in a large measure by reading Negro publications.

Let Us Have the Truth

August 24, 1918

On Monday morning all of the New York dailies carried accounts of a "riot" at Camp Merritt, N.J. The reports all varied in length and as to facts. Some stated that the affair had resulted in the death of one white soldier and five or six colored soldiers; others stated that only one or two men were killed.

From most of the papers the impression to be gleaned from headlines and the articles following was that some colored soldier had for some unknown reason whipped out a razor and slashed a white soldier, thus starting the trouble. The World alone of all the papers on Monday morning gave another version of the affair, a version which it said was most probably the true one.

According to this version, there was an argument between a colored soldier and a Southern white soldier at the YMCA hut; the white soldier objecting to the colored man's presence. The argument resulted in an altercation in which the white man was cut with a knife or a razor. There was then a general fight, and the white military guard that was called out fired into the colored troops, killing and wounding a number; just how many, nobody has been able to find out.

There is one thing of which we feel absolutely certain; and it is that no Negro soldier went out of his way to pick a fuss and a fight with a white soldier. Whenever there is trouble of this kind between Negroes and whites, it will be found in nine hundred and ninety-nine times out of a thousand that the trouble was in some way provoked by the whites. Neither North or South do Negroes go among white men to make trouble.

Even if a Negro wanted to do it, the means by which he could start trouble are limited, he would have to start right out with a fight. But the means by which a prejudiced white man can start trouble are many. He can do it by using one little word.

When the truth about the Camp Merritt affair is known, we are sure it will show that some white soldier—and a Southern one at that—started the whole thing. It would be wisdom on the part of the War Department to put no colored soldiers in camps where there are Southern white soldiers.

The only way to stop these rumors is to turn on the light and give the public the truth. If it was the fault of the colored soldiers that this thing occurred, The Age will, nevertheless, welcome the truth; but we are willing to wager that the trouble began otherwise.

The Stories of Negro Life in the *Saturday Evening Post*

April 5, 1919

The writer has received a number of letters complaining about a series of stories of Negro life running in the Saturday Evening Post. The complaints about these stories were that they were caricatures of life among colored people and that some of them were downright misrepresentations of the race. Some of those who wrote me felt that the stories were intended as direct insults.

It is a good many years since I have been a reader of the Saturday Evening Post, so I had not read any of these stories. Not that the Saturday Evening Post is not good reading of its kind, but in my crowded days I do not have time for that kind. When I have a train trip before me I often like to give myself over to reading merely for diversion, but at such times I do not bother with any of the half-way stuff; I go to the other extreme. On my train trips I love to read Smart Set or Life of The Parisian or to pick up some very foolish book like "Dere Mabel."

Having a trip to make a few days ago, and remembering the complaints about the stories in the Saturday Evening Post, I stopped at the newsstand and bought a copy. I was first of all completely overwhelmed by the magazine itself, 165 pages, equal to a book of 600 pages, first class typography, splendid illustrations, excellent paper, expensive advertisements, and a mass of reading matter which must interest a vast number of people all for five cents. It seemed too much for the money.

The number which I bought contained one of the stories of Negro life. It was entitled "Painless Extraction." I have not read any of the other stories in this series, so I do not know what their general tone has been but "Painless Extraction" in spite of the fact that it has a corking good plot which is well worked out is not true to life.

This story purports to deal with life among the best classes of colored people. The characters are a leading and wealthy physician, a properous dentist, the physician's wife, the dentist's sweetheart, an efficient trained nurse and a manager of a successful business, yet the author makes these people talk like a group of ignorant Negro cotton field hands down in darkest Alabama. In fact, he makes them do things to the English language that many an ignorant cotton field hand would never be guilty of.

Either the author of these stories does not know the best classes of colored people well enough to write about them or he thinks that the impossible dialect which he has invented—for no Negroes on earth speak the dialect he writes—is necessary to give color to his work. What he has done in "Painless Extraction" is to spoil a clever piece of work by unpardonable blemish. It makes his work as absurd and untrue to life as if he had written about cotton field hands and made them talk like people in polite society.

There was another objection: the artist who illustrated the story evidently intended his pictures to be caricatures. The illustrations are no more true to life than the speech which the author puts into the mouths of his characters. He must have gotten his ideas of Negro types from the poster advertisements of minstrel shows.

The Saturday Evening Post evidently pays high prices for the material that goes into its pages, therefore it ought to be careful to see that it is getting the real thing, even in its stories of Negro life.

I can understand why a great many colored people have objected to these stories; they do misrepresent the race. I suggest that colored readers everywhere of the Saturday Evening Post drop the editor a line and tell him their objections and their reasons for them.

If this does not move them to stop burlesquing the race, then more drastic steps should be taken.

Reaping the Whirlwind

August 2, 1919

Last week we had race riots in the National Capital. If those riots were traced back to any one cause, that cause would be found to be the sort of mob violence propaganda which was carried on by the Washington newspapers for weeks before the riots occured.

These newspapers kept reports of "attacks on white women" before the public daily. And there had been several cases of attacks on women. The first of these was an attack on colored girls by white men. These two girls boarded a street car and were the only passengers in the car when it reached the end of the line. The conductor and the motorman preceded to lock both doors and assault the girls; they did not entirely succeed, but they are both now under arrest. There had been three cases of attacks on white women but in all three of these cases the suspect was one and the same man, and he was under arrest.

Now the newspapers of Washington were not chiefly concerned with the fact that either white or colored women had been assaulted in the District of Columbia; what they were chiefly concerned with was an attempt to make the public believe that there was more crime in Washington with Prohibition than there was when the city was wet, and to convict the Police Department of inefficiency. They had a grudge against the heads of the Police Department and they were endeavoring to influence the discussion on Prohibition then going on in Congress.

And so, unmindful of the fact that they were playing with fire; no, worse than fire, dynamite, they went on "playing up" big the news of attacks on white women; for this not only fitted into their plan to defeat Prohibition legislation and discredit the Police Department, but it made splendid news; everybody bought the papers to read about the "attacks."

They played with fire until they lit the train of dynamite leading to the magazine, then they found they couldn't put it out. The service men loafing around Washington took the matter into their own hands and began to avenge these "attacks on white women." And they did it by mobbing innocent and unoffending colored people on the streets and by taking them off street cars and beating them. The common cry was, "There goes one" and the Negro who was sighted had to run for his life.

This kept up to two days and nights, and it was jolly good fun for the service men and those who joined with them. It was also good stuff for the newspapers and they "played it up" big. One newspaper thought that the whole affair ought to be made to go bigger, so on the third morning the Washington Post came out in an account of the way in which service men were chasing colored people through the streets. The account was headed: "SCORES ARE INJURED IN MORE RACE RIOTS SOLDIERS AND SAILORS ATTACK

162

IN DOZENS OF MELEES PENNSYLVANIA AVENUE THE SCENE OF MOST FIGHT-
ING. BEYOND CONTROL OF POLICE." In the body of the account the following paragraphs were printed:

> "MOBILIZATION FOR TO-NIGHT"
>
> It was learned that a mobilization of every available service man stationed in
> or near Washington or on leave here has been ordered for to-morrow evening
> near the Knights of Columbus but, on Pennsylvania Avenue, between Sev-
> enth and Eighth streets.
>
> The hour of assembly is 9 o'clock, and the purpose is a "clean-up" that
> will cause the events of the last two evenings to pale into insignificance.
>
> Whether official cognizance of this assemblage and its intent will bring
> about its forestalling cannot be told.

Then what neither the Washington newspapers nor the Police Department or the Federal authorities seemed to have any idea of happened. The
Negroes, after having been chased and beaten for two days and receiving
no protection from District or Federal authorities, undertook their own protection from District or Federal authorities. And they did protect themselves.
And they not only protected themselves, but they saved the National Capital
from becoming the scene of a shameful and bloody massacre. For if the
mobbing of colored people had gone on unchecked and it was only the self-
defensive action of black men that checked it—Washington would have been
another and worse East St. Louis.

The writer went to Washington while the riots were on; and while there
he made it his business to call on the editors of the three leading newspapers
and to impress upon them their responsibility in the whole matter. Since his
return to New York the writer has been visiting the editors of the great
metropolitan dailies telling them the same thing. It is in the power of the
newspapers of the United States to inflame or suppress mob violence against
the Negro, and they must realize and assume their responsibility.

Not only the newspapers of Washington, but the newspapers of many
other communities have been sowing the wind, and these other communities, like Washington, will reap the whirlwind.

Report of the Department of Justice on the Radical Negro Press

November 29, 1919

In response to a resolution introduced in the Senate by Senator Miles Poindexter of Washington, Attorney General Palmer filed a report on radical propaganda in the United States and what the Department was doing to suppress it. A part of Mr. Palmer's report was devoted to "radicalism and sedition" among Negroes, as reflected in their publications. That portion of the Attorney General's report, as printed in last Sunday's New York "Times," opens as follows:

> At this time there can no longer be any question of a well-concerted movement among a certain class of Negro leaders of thought and action to constitute themselves a determined and persistent source of a radical opposition to the Government, and to the establishment rule of law and order.

That statement is both misleading and inaccurate. It is misleading to say that there is a well-concerted movement among a certain class of Negro leaders of thought and action to constitute themselves a determined and persistent source of radical opposition to the Government. The use of the word "Government" would be correct in a discussion of European politics; because in Europe the political party that is in control is termed "the Government." And in Europe the party that is out of power is, naturally, always opposed to the party that is in power; so the party that is out is always opposed to "the Government."

But that meaning of the term does not apply in America. To be opposed to the Government would mean in this country to be opposed to the duly constituted sovereignty. The term used in this country to denote the political party in power is "the Administration," and to be opposed to the Administration is one of the prerogatives of American citizenship. It is safe to say that to-day more than half of the citizenship in the United States is opposed to the Administration.

So when the word "Government" is used in the statement quoted above it is inaccurate more than misleading. There is no movement among Negroes of any class in opposition to the duly constituted sovereignty of the United States. But on the other hand, Negroes of every class, not only leaders of thought and action but the masses of the race, are opposed to the Administration. And they are going to use all the strength at their command to help put that Administration out of power. There is nothing seditious about that. To go over the reasons why they are opposed to this Administration would be a work of supererogation.

When the report says that these Negro leaders are in opposition to the "establishment rule of law and order," it states an inaccuracy; and it is difficult to use mild a word as "inaccuracy." If opposition to LYNCHING, DISFRANCHISEMENT, JIM CROWISM, INEQUALITY IN EDUCATIONAL ADVANTAGES, INEQUALITY IN INDUSTRIAL OPPORTUNITY, if opposition to these be opposition to the established rule of law and order, then radical Negro leaders are guilty of the charge of sedition made against them.

The object of the whole fight being made by radical Negro leaders is for the establishment and maintenance of the rule of law and order; is for the impartial interpretation and enforcement of the laws of the land and the Constitution of the nation.

But we judge that all of this nobody knows better than the Department of Justice.

Negro Publications in Danger

January 31, 1920

The Graham Sedition bill is now in Congress. There is one section of this bill which threatens the very existence of colored newspapers and magazines. The section is Section 6, which in part reads as follows:

> Sec. 6. That every book, magazine, newspaper, document, handbill, poster, or written, pictorial, or printed matter, memorandum, sign symbol, or communication of any form . . . wherein and whereby appeal is made to racial prejudice the intended or probable result of which appeal is to cause rioting or resort to force and violence within the United States or any place subject to the jurisdiction thereof, is hereby declared to be non-mailable, and the same shall not be deposited in any post office for mailing or be conveyed in the mails delivered from any post office or by any letter carrier.

It can be clearly seen that if this section of the Graham bill becomes a law it will be possible to construe and interpret it in such a manner that would bar from the mails every Negro newspaper and magazine published in the country today.

The Negro is opposed to appeals to racial prejudice; indeed, one of the reasons for the existence of the Negro press is to fight appeals to racial prejudice but if this section of the Graham bill becomes a law, the Negro press can be denied the right to voice the legitimate protest of the race against wrong and injustice. Under such a section the mere printing of the facts and data about lynching might make a publication nonmailable.

The bill is now in the hands of the Rules Committee of the House. This committee is composed of: Philip P. Campbell, Kansas; Bertrand H. Snell, New York; Edward W. Pou, North Carolina; Simeon D. Fess, Ohio; Aaron S. Kreider, Pennsylvania; Porter H. Dale, Vermont; William A. Rodenberg, Illinois; Einis J. Garrett, Tennessee; James Cantrell, Kentucky; Daniel J. Riordan, New York.

All pressure possible should be brought to bear on this committee and upon all members of Congress who are amenable to the expressed opinion of free and independent constituencies. The entire colored and white constituencies in all the politically free states should be appealed to at once to take immediate steps to urge upon their representatives in Congress, both Republican and Democratic, to vote against this section unless it is amended to exclude any and all agitation or propaganda for the enforcement of existing laws by constitutional methods.

For many months the South has been trying to devise plans by which the so-called radical Negro publications could be kept out of that section of the country. In this bill we see the plan perfected. The South is deluded with the idea that the Negroes there would all be happy and contented if they were not stirred up by meddlesome Northern Negroes.

If this section passes, no Negro newspaper that carries a protest against wrong and injustice to the race will be allowed to go through the mails. This will virtually kill the circulation of every worth while publication of the race in the country, at least through the South. Every Negro periodical should do all in its power to help kill this bill.

The Graham Sedition Bill

February 7, 1920

The Graham Sedition bill with its iniquitous section aimed against the Negro press of the country is dead. It was killed by the prompt action taken by the American Federation of Labor, the National Association for the Advancement of Colored People, the Society of Friends, and the several liberal minded individuals who appeared before the House Committee on Rules to oppose the measure.

The Rules Committee after the hearing stated that it would not favorably report the bill but declared that it was convinced that a sedition law of some sort should be passed, and a new sedition bill is being drafted. The new bill will be a compromise between the Graham and Davey measures. The new bill will evidently be shorter and not so drastic as the former one; it is also likely that the language will not be so inclusive; this will, of course, make it a harder measure to oppose successfully.

We are not in favor of any kind of sedition legislation, because we consider it both unnecessary and dangerous. Unnecessary because there is already sufficient law on the statute books for the protection of the Government, and dangerous because any sedition bill that Congress may pass is more than likely to be construed and interpreted by judges and courts in a manner that will eventually abridge the constitutional rights of the people to free speech and free assembly.

The members of the House Rules Committee admitted that there was plenty of law to deal with conspiracy against Government, but stated that the Attorney General claimed there was no law whereby the authorities could deal with an individual who advocated the forcible overthrow of the United States. That is to say, if a soap boxer got up on a street corner and advocated the overthrow of the United States by physical force there is no existing law by which the Government can protect itself against him.

Of course it is difficult for anyone with the slightest sense of humor to believe seriously that the United States stood in any danger from the said individual soap boxer. However, if Congress proposes a law dealing exclusively with attempts to overthrow the Government by physical force, very few will be found to take exceptions to it. But such a law should contemplate only overt acts, and not opinions.

The menace of the Graham bill was that it was not aimed exclusively against attempts to overthrow the United States by physical force. It was so framed that it could be interpreted for the purpose of preventing strikes, for the purpose of breaking up radical organizations of all kinds, and for the purpose of preventing the circulation of progressive Negro publications in the South.

As to the purpose last mentioned above we still need to be on our guard. The Graham bill is dead, but the determination of certain forces to stop progressive and radical Negro publications from circulating among the colored people of the South is not dead. The new sedition bill must be carefully scanned, and if a Negro press joker is found in it the race must summon all the power it can to kill it.

The Victory and the *New York World*

June 2, 1923

The victory of the New York "World" in its fight against conditions prevailing in the Florida convict camps is not only an important achievement but it is almost unprecedented.

There have been so many fruitless exposés on the part of newspapers and magazines that they have become commonplace. Indeed, the public has become accustomed to shudder for a few days over startling revelations and then forget all about them, feeling that after all nothing will be done. This same sort of thing was felt when the "World" made this revelation about the Tabert case and the conditions existing under the convict lease system of Florida. But a definite result has been accomplished.

The "World" timed its exposé just before the opening of the Florida Legislature and under the glaring light of publicity which the "World" centered upon Florida, the Legislature was forced to act. Conditions were investigated, and finally, by special act, the system of leasing prisoners to private corporations was abolished, and by another statute, the practice of shipping prisoners was also abolished.

There is probability that other Southern States where the convict lease system and the practice of the lash are in existence will follow the example set by Florida.

The achievement of the "World" is a significant illustration of what can be done by agitation and publicity.

There was some unwillingness on the part of the Legislature to take proper action, but the people of the State of Florida were unable to bear the shame and humiliation which the facts published in the "World" placed upon them, and therefore, sufficient pressure of public opinion was brought to bear upon the Legislature to compel it to act.

Too much credit cannot be given to the New York "World" for this great service to humanity.

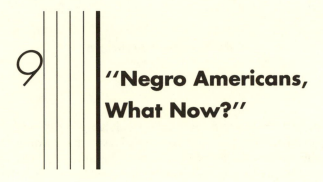

"Negro Americans,
What Now?"

*The American Negro has more at stake in present world
crisis than any other group in this country; is it not then
something in the nature of a crime for colored men when
they get together to waste their entire time in foolishness?*
James Weldon Johnson, "Cut Out the Comedy"
(May 3, 1917)

Johnson told his readers that they were living in a serious age—the most serious in the history of the
world—and it was rapidly approaching its most
critical point. Believing that there were too many non-
sensical activities occurring within the black community, he emphasized the need for African-Americans to
better utilize their spare time. In the following editorials, he contended that there was a need for serious
discussion and debate by blacks on the contemporary
issues and the effects that these issues might have on
their lives.

Ruffianism in Harlem

April 29, 1915

We, as a race, are less to be excused for indulging in ruffianism than any other group in this country; and for the simple reason that we ourselves are so often made the victims of ruffianism we should do nothing that sanctions it.

There are some colored boys and men in Harlem who think it is a great thing to see how tough they can be. They are not only a public nuisance, but they are a detriment to the race.

It is mean business to jump on a lone Italian peddler and beat him and break up his stand. It is also mean business for a crowd of colored men to stand around and encourage by laughter, such actions.

It leaves little room for us to protest against the mob violence of which we are so often victims if we go about practicing the same sort of thing upon other people on a smaller scale.

It is the duty of colored men to do all they can to discourage acts of ruffianism on the part of those of the race in Harlem who think it is a mark of distinction to be tough.

Cut Out the Comedy

May 3, 1917

We know a very sensible colored man who often makes the remark that the Negro is laughing about the very things he ought to be crying over. There is a lot of truth in the remark. To a number of Negroes, a number far too large for the good of the race, everything is funny, life is one great big joke.

There are too many "comedians" in the race. There is too much story telling and loud laughing. Take any average group of colored men, not ignorant men, but men of fair intelligence, and what are they talking about? Generally a lot of nonsense. They are laughing loud about something that "Bill" said or something that "Jim" did or over some story old or new.

There is a place in life for story telling and laughter, but the place is small, especially in this day and time. With thoughtful people, people who understand the meaning of present day life, story telling and laughter are merely momentary relaxations from the stern realities. Too often, where two or three or a half dozen of us are gathered, we make them the main business.

This is a serious age, the most serious in the history of the world, and it is rapidly approaching its most critical point. Men everywhere are thinking and discussing. On the streets, on the cars, on the trains, wherever they get together, intelligent men are expressing to each other their interest in what is happening and what is going to happen. The American Negro has more at stake in the present world crisis than any other group in this country; is it not then something in the nature of a crime for colored men when they get together to waste their entire time in foolishness?

The world is to-day being made over. Old traditions, old ideas, old conventions, old governments, old civilizations are at this moment being broken up and melted down in the crucible of this great war. And they are all to be shaped and moulded anew. The question comes, is the American Negro going to rise to the opportunity of taking a hand in helping to shape and mould them for the good of his own future? The opportunity is here, but it is going to require serious thought and wise action to take advantage of it. And it can't be done by "comedians."

The demand of the hour is for earnestness of words and of thoughts and of actions. Colored men and women everywhere should be concerned with what effect the tremendous forces now at work may have on us as a race. For this effect is going to be great one way or the other. When this crisis is over and the world again settles down, the Negro is going to be either much better off or much worse off. Which it will be depends largely upon what steps he himself now takes.

If the American Negro fully realized the significance of passing events, he would drop the grin and set his jaws and clench his teeth with the determination of gaining from the present upheaval every rightful advantage that he possibly can.

Let every thoughtful colored man and woman make a study of what is now transpiring; let them read what is being written on this great world crisis by students and thinkers—every newspaper and magazine offers the opportunity, and the public libraries are filled with books on the subject; let them when they get together exchange ideas and discuss the probable effects that will come to us as a race; let them try to find the best ways and means of making those effects advantageous. In a word, let us be serious. Let us, for the present at least, cut out the comedy.

Following Up "The Negro and the Jew"

February 2, 1918

Last week we had something to say about the Negro and the Jew. We traced certain similarities between the two races and also some of the differences, and we pointed out that the lessons for the Negro to be learned from the differences were more important than those to be learned from the similarities. We showed that prejudice against Jews does not spring from any idea of his inferiority and also how and why the Jews can act as a unit, while the Negroes seem not able to do so. Let us now consider at least one other point of difference.

The Negro does not possess the same sense about money that the Jew possesses. Do not misunderstand this to mean that the Negro does not know how to make money like the Jew—although that is in a very large measure true—for conditions being taken into consideration, he is fast learning the trick. But the mere making of money is aside from the point, for history proves that there may exist a race of rich slaves as well as a race of poor freemen.

The point we are driving at is that the Negro begs and pleads and strives for his rights but has not yet realized that rights also cost money. Let there be a question of rights also cost money. Let there be a question of rights for the Jews, and they will raise a hundred thousand dollars, five hundred thousand dollars, a million dollars, if necessary, to help fight; while Negroes, generally speaking, seem to think that their rights are coming from somewhere out of the skies.

It is no excuse to say that Negroes do not make or possess so much money as the Jews; our numbers are so much larger, and pennies from us would amount to considerable sums. The colored people of New York City could raise ten thousand dollars by contributing ten cents each. Yet there are instances on record where legal cases in which were involved interests of the race had to be dropped because the colored people of the city or county or state would not or did not raise a few hundred or a few thousand dollars to fight them through.

We repeat that another difference between the two races is that the Negro does not yet realize that rights also cost money.

The Imitative Negro

September 21, 1918

Imitation in itself is not a bad characteristic; it depends upon what you imitate. It is largely through imitation that civilization has been spread. It was because the barbarians imitated that civilization of Greece and Rome that north and central Europe is now civilized. Not that they are much better off for it, but at any rate they are civilized.

It is because the Negro is such a good imitator that he has acquired western civilization so fast. I have seen the British West Indian in London, and he is as English as a lord. I have seen the French West Indian in Paris, and he is as French as a marquis. I do not doubt that the Negro would make a perfectly good Chinese with the exception of the pigtail; and he is fast overcoming that difficulty. It is this ability to imitate and assimilate that has made it possible for the Negro in the United States to outdistance the American Indian in the race. The Indian, in spite of his advantages and opportunities, remains an Indian. The Negro, is spite of his handicaps and obstacles has become an American. The Negro is an American in language, customs, mode of thought and religion. The Indian is still just about as much of a savage as the law allows him to be.

But the dangers that go with the ability to imitate are equal to the benefits. For one who finds it easy to imitate good things, finds it just as easy, often easier, to imitate bad things. It is this point that the Negro's facile gift has worked him woe; he has picked up the bad as well as the good. After all, the Indian is an awe inspiring sight; a sight that somehow inspires a certain sort of respect. He absolutely disdains to learn or copy either what the white man calls good or bad, but remains himself.

The dangers of the ability to imitate was impressed on the writer's mind when he saw the other night a crowd of young colored hoodlums ranging the streets of Harlem, breaking up the straw hats of passers-by, even going into shops to attack men. Where did they get the idea? If it was a custom that had come down to them from their African ancestors, it would demand some respect, even if it was heathenish; but, no, it is something they only recently learned from white men. And who are the white men they learned it from?

For years the members of the Stock Exchange have indulged in the sport of breaking up the hat of any members who dared to appear on the floor of the Exchange arrayed in a hat of straw on the 15th of September. It was a sort of a good-natured game with these busy men; and it is likely that if any man whose hat was broken took the matter seriously, the hat breaker would willingly buy him a new one. Young, white hoodlums caught the idea from the Stock Exchange brokers, and then the young, colored hoodlums caught it from the white ones. The practice has almost gone out of vogue among the white hoodlums, and it is doubtful that it is practiced any more in the Stock Exchange, most likely not since the country entered the war; but it is still being followed by the young colored ruffians of Harlem. And they carry it on more viciously than it has ever been carried on by the whites. They do not do the thing in a spirit of fun; they are ready to attack and injure any man who tried to protect his property.

We do not know what a judge would rule, but we are of the opinion that a man who went to the extent of doing some serious bodily harm to one of these scamps would not have to pay much of a penalty.

173

When we imitate the virtues of other people, we evoke admiration. When we imitate the vices, we evoke contempt.

One of the things a law and order league could attempt in Harlem, would be to break up this practice among these young gangsters.

Two | *New York Age* **Political Editorials**

10 Politicians

Statesmen of the "Coal Blaze" breed should, down in the depths of their hearts, love the Negro, no matter how they outwardly revile him; for how could they ever become or remain "statesmen" if they did not have the Negro to revile?

James Weldon Johnson, "The Extinguishment of 'Coal Blaze'"
(November 12, 1914)

"When men in office are opposed to the Negro, and show it in their interpretation and execution of the law and in the moulding of sentiment, it matters very little to the colored voter what their other policies may be," Johnson proclaimed.[1] In other words, it was more vital that African-Americans knew and understood how a political candidate felt about them than to know what the candidate thought about a particular issue such as the tariff. Because of the race problem, blacks were not in a position to make political decisions based on local and national concerns or the policies set by candidates and their parties. It was regrettable, Johnson believed, that African-Americans in casting their ballots were forced to be guided by such a narrow consideration. Consequently, the penetrating issue before his people was that of their salvation. Johnson, too, was mainly guided by this premise in his roles as editor and race leader. Many of the following editorials were written to oppose or defend the policies and principles of a politician or some other political measure. These

177

editorials, Johnson admitted, were biased in nature and were written to influence the reader.

African-Americans had an unyielding faith in constitutional guarantees that caused them to persist in going to the polls. Southern whites on the other hand proclaimed loudly that constitutional rights for blacks were subversive, involving the overthrow of white supremacy.

In the following editorials, you will note Johnson's superb ability in making race prejudice such a contradictory and ridiculous thing. When he jabs his perceived enemies with the truth, it is difficult to see how they would not be compelled to see the folly in race prejudice.

The Candidate Who Squares
Up to Requirements

October 15, 1914

It is [now], and will be for some time to come, more important to the colored voter to know what a candidate's attitude is toward the Negro than to know how he stands on questions affecting the general public. It is more important for him to know how a candidate feels regarding the doctrine of the equal rights of men than to know what he thinks about the tariff. The colored voter is more concerned about a candidate's uprightness of soul and bigness of heart than about correctness of his political and economic views. When men in office are opposed to the Negro, and show it in their interpretation and execution of the law and in the moulding of sentiment, it matters very little to the colored voter what their other policies may be.

That we are compelled to be governed by such considerations is regrettable, but it is nevertheless, true. Like other citizens, we ought to be in a position to be guided in making our political decisions solely by the large local and national issues before us and the policies of the various parties and candidates regarding them; but the fact is, at present, that the greatest issue before the Negro is his own salvation.

By what must the colored voter be guided in settling upon a candidate? He must be guided either by the candidate's outspoken sentiments on the doctrine of human rights as it affects the Negro or by his record on the same. It may seem a narrow position to take, but in this mode of arriving at a decision there is never any danger of choosing an inferior candidate; for whenever a man, in the face of opinion in this country can rise to the height of believing in fair play and treatment for the Negro, when he has the courage to express that conviction and the nerve to carry it into practice, we may be doubly sure that he is the kind of man best fitted for any high trust.

The above being true, the colored voters of New York will be in no doubt as to which of the gubernatorial candidates in the coming elections should receive their support.

Charles S. Whitman is the only one among them that squares up to our *special* requirement for a candidate. He does not come before us with untested sentiments but with an established record.

The first fact in Mr. Whitman's record, as it directly appeals to the colored voter, is that he is a Republican of Republican ancestry. It is a sad thought that the term Republican has lost some of its ancient magical charm; nevertheless, it is still prima facie evidence of good will toward us. A candidate bearing any other brand is always justly open to suspicion.

His immediate appointment, after his election in 1909, of Mr. Cornelius W. McDougald as an Assistant District Attorney proves that Mr. Whitman not only believes that the Negro should be protected before the law, but also that he is entitled to representation and participation in the administration of the government. Nor can it be said that this appointment was in payment of any political debt, for Mr. Whitman's election was all along a conceded certainty on which the entire colored vote had little or no effect; and the appointee was a young man fresh from his studies, who, up to that time had not had the opportunity to render political service.

But had the appointment been made solely in payment of a political debt—and political debts, like all others, should be paid—credit would still be due to the man who had the integrity to pay it.

It is well known that for many years the clubbing of colored men under arrest was a popular diversion of the police of this city. Various ineffective orders by various officials had been issued, but it was not until Mr. Whitman rigorously prosecuted three policemen for assault that the outrageous custom was completely stopped.

However, it was in the Lyric Theatre case that he struck at a deep-rooted wrong against the Negro which is of so long standing that it has come to be regarded as right. It was in this case that he showed supreme moral outrage, for he was treading on forbidden ground.

A colored gentleman and lady holding orchestra tickets for a performance at the Lyric Theatre were refused their seats. The usual procedure heretofore has been for the injured party to swallow his treatment or go to the expense of a civil suit in which he might be awarded damages of one dollar as balm for his wounded feelings. In this instance, complaint was made to the District Attorney's office. Mr. Whitman at once had the assistant treasurer of the theatre arrested, charged with a violation of the Civil Rights Bill, tried and convicted. In this case, he tackled the most inflated bugaboo and at the same time, the most humiliating wrong connected with the entire race question, the idea that a colored person, no matter how well dressed or behaved, may be debarred with impunity from places of public accommodation and entertainment. It is a ticklish point, and a man of less courage would have avoided touching it. And it is a point that can be finally settled only by a realization being brought to prejudiced people that the law will not tolerate any such discrimination. Mr. Whitman took the only effective step toward bringing that realization—a criminal prosecution.

These are some of the facts which indicate how the man stands on the question of the greatest importance to us, the question of equal rights for all citizens.

Then there is the man himself, clean cut, clear-eyed, firm-jawed, active and vigorous, a born fighter; this would make him a valuable champion for us, even if he only decided to let us alone, to do us no harm; but he is not a mere neutral, his record shows that he will fight for the principle that a Negro has equal rights before the law with other citizens, and this makes his championship invaluable.

Looking over the entire field, Charles S. Whitman presents himself as the only candidate for Governor who squares up to the colored voter's requirements, the only one who has a special claim on the support of the Negro.

The Importance of Electing Whitman

October 29, 1914

It is important that the colored voters of New York do all in their power for the election of Charles S. Whitman for Governor.

He is, secondly, a liberal-minded man, who has the bravery to put his convictions into practice. That he believes the Negro should be accorded the same consideration that all other citizens receive; that he believes the Negro has a right not only to the protection of the government, but also to participation in it; and that he is not afraid to take an open and avowed stand on these propositions is already proven by his record.

In the third place, the election of Whitman and the Republican ticket will throw New York into the Republican column and lead to the restoration of the Grand Old Party of 1916.

By this time, colored men ought to know what it means to us to have a friendly administration in power in Washington.

The Extinguishment of "Coal Blaze"

November 12, 1914

It seems that "Coal Blaze," the one time red hot Governor of South Carolina, has at last been extinguished. He of the fiery words and sulphurous breath had hoped to heat things up in the United States Senate; now, all of that patriotic fervor of his to save his state and the nation by damning the Negro will have to smoulder on his heaving breast.

That leads me to say that statesmen of the "Coal Blaze" breed should, down in the depths of their hearts, love the Negro, no matter how they outwardly revile him; for how could they ever become or remain "statesmen" if they did not have the Negro to revile?

President Wilson's "New Freedom" and the Negro

November 19, 1914

When a man gets mad or drunk, he blurts out the truth; that is, the truth which he would not utter under normal conditions. President Wilson got mad at the delegation from the Equal Rights League, that had an audience with him last week, and he blurted out the truth, the truth about how he really feels toward the Negro.

The country now knows what his innermost sentiments are. There may have been other Presidents who held the same sort of sentiments; but Mr. Wilson bears the discreditable distinction of being the first President of the United States, since Emancipation, who openly condoned and vindicated prejudice against the Negro.

In effect, the President dismissed the delegation summarily. It was given out from the White House that the audience terminated as it did because the spokesman of the delegation lost his temper and became insolent and offensive in his remarks. Anyone who will carefully read the reports of the incident can see that it was really the President who lost his temper and that it was only the President who made any remark that could be termed offensive. And he lost his temper because he did not like being told the truth about a disagreeable subject. If Mr. Wilson's heart and his brain had been on the right side on this question, he could have patiently listened to whatever was said.

The general charge of "insolence" savors too much of a false standard of dignity; or worse, it smacks just a bit of a despatch that might be received from any Southern community at any time, which reads, "Negro lynched: cause, insolence to white man."

The President is quoted as saying that he had not been addressed in such a manner since he entered the White House. We are prepared to believe that is true; but, what could he expect under the circumstances?

Could he expect men making a plea for fundamental justice for their own race to indulge in the polished, dispassionate and soulless phrases to which he himself is given? Could he expect them to talk as though they were discussing an appointment to some fourth-class post-office?

We do not know what Mr. Trotter said, but it is certain, if he had in any way overstepped the bounds of propriety, the facts would have been clearly set forth in the newspaper reports.

No man with any sense of fairness can justify the President's segregation policy. It is wrong in general, because it is contrary to law, because it is contrary to the spirit of democracy and Christianity, because it is contrary to enlightened humanitarian thought. It is wrong in particular, because it is contrary to what has been the common practice for fifty years, and because it is enforced against a class of colored people that furnish no reason for it. The colored clerks in the Departments are all men and women of education and no small degree of culture. In fact, it is not an overdrawn statement to say that, in educational equipment, the colored department clerks average above the white clerks in the same grade; for, whereas a colored college graduate must seek such a position, the white university man can go into unlimited higher vocations open to him.

As Negroes, we resent the President's attitude and action. As an integral part of the republic, we are mortified to see the head of the nation make himself an apologist for discrimination between citizens on the basis of color.

The President has preached "The New Freedom," he had raised his voice against religious prejudice, he has used the influence of the United States, backed up by the power of its army and navy, in the interest of the landless peons of Mexico; but not one word had he uttered for fair play to the ten million Negroes in this country; not one word of hope or encouragement has he thrown out to them; but whenever he had used his great influence, it had been against them and for their humiliation.

Mr. Wilson, the men who waited upon you did not go to ask any favors; neither did they go to have a Sunday School lecture read to them from a primary catechism; nor to be patted on the head and told to be "good little niggers and run home"; no, those men went as citizens of the United States to you as the Chief Magistrate of the nation to ask that you investigate and correct an unwarranted wrong that had been put upon their race of self-respect and placed upon it an official government badge of inferiority; that is what they went to ask, and it vexes you, it makes you angry, they shall not be allowed another audience. Great God! what can be this Democratic Administration's conception of Democracy.

In this whole matter, Mr. Wilson's attitude, while not in keeping with his position as President of this great nation, is, at least, explainable by what we know of him. But it is incomprehensible where those members of the delegation and other colored men who voted for Wilson two years ago ever got the idea that he would act differently from the way in which he has acted. What single deed or utterance in his whole life has there ever been that could be so construed or twisted as to give them the faintest hope that Mr. Wilson would prove a second Lincoln? or even a second-rate Lincoln?

It is perhaps, after all, a good thing that the incident happened as it did. If Mr. Wilson had listened to the delegation, and made some cautious and perfunctory remarks about "looking into the matter, etc.," nobody would ever have known that the Equal Rights committee had waited upon him and, most probably, nothing would ever have been done.

As it is, the attention of the country has been focused upon this wrong, and the judgment of the American people, which at bottom stands for fair play, will call a halt on this retrocession to ante-bellum tenets, and blot out this reproach on our national government.

183

To the Administration and all who stand against the Negro in this country for a fair and equal chance—you had as well take notice now as later. The Negro question will never be settled until it is settled right. You may evade, you may postpone, you may circumvent, but it will ever spring up to confront and confound you.

Do not delude yourselves with the thought that we are so weak that life and spirit can be crushed out of us, that we can eventually be ground down and reduced to nothing. We are of a race that has never despaired or died; other races may wither before you, other races may come and pass away, but we are of a Race Eternal, we are of the Mother of Races.

We are ten million loyal citizens of this republic; we have helped to till its soil and we have helped to fight its battles; whatever share of national duty, however humble it may have been, that has fallen to our hands we have striven faithfully to perform a larger and nobler share of that duty—what more can you require?

We ask no more than an equal chance; but that much we demand.

The President's Message

December 17, 1914

The most striking effect of the President's message is the strengthening of the opinion that he will not face a disagreeable position; he will ignore it or coin a poetic phrase to cover it.

There is not one word in his message about the relations of this Government to conditions in Mexico; although the most vital steps taken by the present Administration were those taken with or against that republic. The Wilson policy of "watchful waiting" was a blunder and a failure, it is an unpleasant subject for the President, so he is silent on it, he ignores it.

He meets the present agitation for an investigation of the military preparedness of the United States with phrases that he no doubt learned to frame at Princeton. Beautiful phrases but, nevertheless, nothing but phrases where stern facts and figures were wanted.

What bearing upon the question whether the United States is or is not adequately prepared for its defense have such phrases as "We are at peace with all the world." "Dread of the power of any other nation we are incapable of." "We are the champions of peace and concord." "We much depend in every time of national peril, in the future as in the past, not upon a standing army, nor yet upon a reserve army, but upon a citizenry trained and accustomed to arms."

Fine phrases, all of them, but for practical purposes they rank very little above Bryan's Chautauqua phrase, "and the sun would go down on a million men in arms." They mean nothing to people who want to know how many soldiers we have, how many men in the navy, how many rifles and rounds of amunition, and how many men we could equip and put into the field within a certain time if necessity demanded.

Military preparedness is an unpleasant subject to the President, so he does not meet it squarely; instead, he goes up into the clouds and in rainbow tints he paints glittering gems of thought.

Woman suffrage is an unpleasant subject to the President, so when a delegation of women called on him some months ago he dodged the whole question by stating that he could express no opinion on a subject which had not been considered in the platform on which he had been elected; he, however, did not hesitate, in direct opposition to the Democratic platform, to force the repeal of the Panama Canal tolls. When the women asked some rather pointed questions he dismissed them by declaring that "he would not be heckled."

Of course segregation of Negroes in the Departments at Washington is a very disagreeable subject to the President, so when the Equal Rights delegation called on him he did not complain of mere heckling, but declared himself insulted and summarily dismissed the delegation.

As we said, the President's message goes to confirm the opinion that he will not squarely meet a question which places him in an unpleasant position. He will ignore it or paint the glittering gems of thoughts on the clouds or plainly show his annoyance.

Bryan and His Million Men

December 17, 1914

In his speech before the Baltimore Bar Association last week Secretary Bryan defended the anti-defense policy of the President in the following words:

> But I never fought beside a braver man than he who to-day occupies the White House. It is not that he himself lacks courage or that he doubts the courage of his people that he does not want this country to arm itself. The President knows that if this country needed a million men and needed them in a day, the call could go out at sunrise and the sun would go down on a million men in arms.

Was any such rhetorical tommy-rot ever before uttered by a Cabinet officer on a serious question? There is not the least doubt if the President called for a million men that a million men would at once answer the call, but military experts agree that it would require not less than six months to mobilize, equip and train an army of a million men.

Mr. Bryan must be dreaming of the days when at the sound of the tocsin each man would grab his flint-lock musket from the wall and rush to the front. In this day of scientific warfare, a million men, untrained and unequipped, no matter how brave and willing they might be, could accomplish absolutely nothing.

It took the Government a couple of months to mobilize and equip an army of less than 250,000 men for the Spanish-American war; and even then the job was poorly done. The arms furnished to the volunteers were for the greater part antiquated; and, due to poor sanitary conditions, the majority of the losses for the entire war ocurred in the concentration camps in the United States, among the soldiers who never got a chance to see the front.

Without advocating military preparedness or the reverse, we merely wish to call attention to the fact that we have a man in the position of Secretary of State who with serious intent gives public utterance to such a piece of sentimenal buncombe, "and the sun would go down on a million men in arms."

Ex-Attorney General Wickersham to Our Defense

December 17, 1914

Last week the Southern Society of New York gave its twenty-ninth annual dinner at the Waldorf-Astoria. Now the Southern Society has other purposes beside that of dining annually and listening to speeches eulogizing the "lost cause" and extolling Southern chivalry and heroism at the expense of those virtues as possessed by people in other sections of the country. It has serious purposes, and one of them is to keep the New York Negro in his place. This organization has for years carried on a systematic propaganda of fomenting and spreading prejudice against colored people in this city.

By using its influence to secure places for Southern writers on the great dailies here, it at one time threatened to turn almost the whole New York press bitterly against us. For a while it published an anti-Negro pamphlet which was distributed in the seats of the theatres; its members have made it a business to register an objection to the presence of Negroes in hotels, restaurants and places of amusement, and in various other ways it has striven to keep alive a prejudice which would naturally subside in a city so cosmopolitan as New York. Of course, there are fair-minded, generous people who belong to the Southern Society, who are affiliated with it for purely social purposes, but find that, in no way, effects these aims of the organization.

At these annual dinners it is a settled custom to have some speaker from the South who runs the whole gamut of sub-tropical oratory. This year it was the Honorable Skelton Williams, United States Comptroller of Currency. Among other things he said:

> All other issues have appeared to us light and negligible when white supremacy was threatened. Happily such fears are now no more to be regarded than as a frightful dream. Our constitutional convention in the different States have so limited and safeguarded the right of suffrage in an effort to secure an enlightened electorate, that Negro rule has ceased to be a menace.
>
> Long ago we determined that the Negro should never be our master; that we would work with him and help him and let him help and work with us, but that, as a social and political equal, the best interests of both races and of the country demanded stern, final and definite prohibition. The dignity, welfare and prosperity of the two races of the entire country are and will be promoted by the policy of strict segregation.

Ex-Attorney General Wickersham was present and spoke. In the course of this speech he addressed the following remarks to the Comptroller. Read them carefully:

> I do not believe that this problem will ever be solved by the total disfranchisement for all time of 10,000,000 of our citizens. No people can thrive and advance if, side by side and working with them, are 10,000,000 who are disfranchised from all voice in government.
>
> God knows that this is a difficult problem and God knows it will be solved, but it cannot be solved by denying to any, be he black or yellow or red, the right of a voice in making the laws by which he shall be governed and in the choice of the men who shall govern him.
>
> Believe me, this problem is not solved by the method you offer.

Mr. Williams is not a Southern rough neck. He does not belong to the class that would lead a lynching bee. He is a gentleman of education, wealth and refinement. He is, in fact, one of the bluest blooded of Virginia aristocrats, and might well be said to represent what is highest and best in Southern thought.

What then is the deeper meaning of these words coming from him? The meaning is none other than this, that it is the avowed purpose and determination of the Southern people, regardless of what a negligible minority among them may think, to force the Negro in this country into a permanently secondary civil and political status. That is the thing we have got to face, and that is the thing we have got to fight. Any other song they may sing to us is a mere lullaby. Are we prepared or preparing to meet this inevitable struggle or are we going to drop into that recognized and accepted secondary place?

As Mr. Williams' words sound the note of Southern sentiment of to-day so do Mr. Wickersham's words seem to belong to a past generation. At this time, when so many of those who are our best friends are scarcely more than mitigators, his words ring out with truth and courage like those of Garrison, Phillips and Sumner.

And Mr. Wickersham deserves to rank in our regard along with the fearless, outspoken men who fought our cause in the years gone by; fought it because they knew in doing so they were fighting the battle of justice and human rights. Nor is this the first time he has spoken and taken action in our behalf. We have not forgotten the stand which he took with William H. Lewis against the American Bar Association.

We are indeed fortunate in having a man of Mr. Wickersham's calibre as a friend. He has not only a high and broad sense of human rights, but he has the moral courage to express what he thinks. And let no one think it did not require fine fearlessness to say what he did as a guest of the Southern Society of New York.

In this connection we again have occasion to express our thanks to the New York "World." It was the only paper in New York which came to our attention that gave a full account of the parts of these two speeches which touched on the Negro.

It appears that the "World" has taken a stand for us even in advance of our old and staunch friend, "The Evening Post."

In this column we reproduce a strong editorial from the "Globe" on Mr. Wickersham's speech. The "Globe" has several times recently spoken out in behalf of our rights.

The most surprising incident in this whole affair is, according to the reports, that Mr. Williams' speech was received in silence while the members of the society several times interrupted Mr. Wickersham with applause.

Perhaps with a few more men like the Ex-Attorney General to address them at their annual dinners, even the Southern Society of New York may be brought to see the light.

President Wilson's Transformation

January 14, 1915

The most remarkable thing about President Wilson's Jackson Day speech is the wonderful transformation which it indicates. He is no longer the austere political scholar, the detached historian viewing with cold and impartial eye the passing show. He has received a baptism of love for his fellow man.

He is animated with a desire to rub elbows with the common people, his heart goes out to them. He gives indications that he would like to be known as a "good mixer." Various surmises at the reasons for this change might be given, but let it suffice merely to hope that some portion of this milk of human kindness will be bestowed upon the ten million colored citizens of this country. There was even a change in the manner in which the President expressed himself. His accustomed dignity and elegance of expression was overshadowed by the introduction of a colloquial, not to say slangy, style. It may be that he was trying to make his language harmonize with the popular conception of Andrew Jackson's character or, perhaps, it was a bid to become known as "Woody" Wilson.

The speech would have been stronger if some things in it had been left unsaid. For example, the following words said in defense of the Administration's Mexican policy:

> It is none of my business and it is none of your business how long they take in determining it. It is none of my business and it is none of your business how they go about the business. The country is theirs. The government is theirs. The liberty, if they can get it, and God speed them in getting it, is theirs. And so far as my influence goes while I am President nobody shall interfere with them.

These words are simply amazing when we recall the many recent steps of interference taken by the Wilson Administration in the internal affairs of Mexico; more vital steps than have been taken by any other Administration since the Mexican war.

The Democrats are somewhat divided on what will be the effects of the President's Jackson Day speech. The Republicans are united in the opinion that it will not strengthen the President or his party.

Governor Slaton on Lynching

January 29, 1915

Governor Slaton of Georgia has chafed considerable under the editorial criticism in the Northern newspapers regarding the lynching at Monticello. In a telegram to the New York "World" he resents their term "uncivilized" being applied to Georgia and Georgians. He goes on to state that lawlessness is not confined to Georgia or to the South—which is true—and he promises to do all in his power to bring to justice those guilty of this latest crime against law.

We believe the Governor is in earnest, but why did he need to say, "Of course, the provocation was great?" We have yet to hear a Southern man speak out for justice and rights to the Negro without offering some sort of apology to prejudiced Southern opinion.

Washington and Lincoln

February 22, 1915

By a curious coincidence, the birthdays of the two Americans who are the greatest historic characters of the nation fall but ten days apart. This fact cannot fail to bring up each year a more or less direct comparison between Washington and Lincoln. It does not take a keen observer to note that Washington suffers by the comparison. The estimate of Lincoln's greatness has steadily increased, while that of Washington has remained the same—if it has not diminished.

Robert Ingersoll expressed more truth than wit when he said "Washington has become a steel engraving."

As the years go by, Washington's figure recedes, he becomes more misty and cold; on the other hand, Lincoln looms up larger, closer and warmer. The character of Lincoln to-day stirs the nation as that of no other patriot.

What was the essential difference between these two men, both of them so supremely great? Why is Washington little more than a massive monument, impressive but cold; while Lincoln is a living force, a force that can raise us to a state of exultation that is almost religious?

Lincoln was the possessor of love. He was not only wise and just and true and brave, but he had boundless love for his fellowman. It is this in Lincoln that draws men closer to him, it is this in him that thrills men's hearts, it is this in him that takes him out from the ranks of the mere heroes of the world and places him among the saviours of mankind.

190

History fails to record any man so near perfect and, at the same time, so completely human as Abraham Lincoln.

22 Caliber Statesmen

February 22, 1915

Won't some member of the Senate or the House offer a resoluton to gag the Negrophobes in Congress? One week, a bill is introduced to exclude absolutely from the country all immigrants of African descent, regardless of qualifications. The next week, a bill is introduced making the intermarriage of blacks and whites a crime. And now, before we can recover from these two blows aimed at us, here comes the favorable return of a bill for the separation of the races on street cars and all other public conveyances in the District of Columbia.

What can be the conception of public duty of these men who are the instigators of this tireless attack upon us? What can be the size of their souls? As small as their minds must be can't they find some other subject to occupy them? Can't they devote their meager ability toward an effort to straighten out the mess into which the Democratic party has put the whole country? Or can't they, at least, sit still in Congress and listen to men who have something to offer for the general welfare of the nation, and then try to vote intelligently?

Some men with a 22 caliber brain and a heart the size and softness of a hickory nut get into Congress. He gets there because there is such a thing as race prejudice. Were it not for race prejudice this same man would be, at best, a $700 a year country lawyer. In Congress he finds himself entirely outclassed by men of breadth and depth; and he realizes that there is only one way by which he can attract publicity and convince the people back home that he is doing something to save the country, and that is by introducing some bill against the unoffending and long-suffering Negro. Perhaps he does not expect the bill to pass, but he feels that he has discharged his moral duty; and made a record which again entitles him to the votes of his patriotic constituency.

The trouble with this breed of "statesmen" is that they were born more than fifty years too late; for it is more than fifty years since the occupation of slave driver and slave catcher went out of existence.

If the brains and hearts of these men were right, they could not help but see and feel that the best interests of their communities lie in the fair and humane consideration of the race question. They have a great opportunity. More than that, they have an awful responsibility; for largely upon what they now say and do depend the future peace, happiness and security of their own posterity.

If these men cannot rise to a comprehension of the great general problems before the country; if they have nothing to contribute toward the great general welfare of the nation; then, for the love of Mike (pardon the slang), let them keep still.

Florida Politics

June 15, 1916

According to the estimates of the recent primary election in Florida, Governor Trammell, of that state, has been elected to the United States Senate to succeed Senator Bryan.

In this election, the paramount issue was anti-Catholicism. Some three years ago Senator Bryan had one of his personal friends who is a Roman Catholic appointed to the postmastership at Jacksonville, and it was around this appointment that the fight against him was chiefly made: Governor Trammell being his principal opponent. Here we have an explanation of the Governor's action several weeks ago in ordering the arrest of two Catholic sisters of charity in St. Augustine, on the ground of violating a law which was considered a dead letter.

Trammell took that action to appeal to the anti-Catholic element which was fighting Bryan; for if the motive had been merely to enforce the law, he could have ordered the arrest of some of the white teachers in one of the schools at Jacksonville maintained by Northern philanthropy, but that would not have had just the political effect that was desired.

However, the arrest of two sisters of charity for teaching colored children in a religious school caused such a sensation that the Governor felt called upon to put up some sort of defense for his action, and this is how he did it. In some of his printed campaign matter the following statement was made:

> A few have attacked him (Governor Trammell) because he took a firm stand for the enforcement of the law prohibiting white teachers from teaching (in) Negro schools, but the hosts of Democrats who believe in white supremacy approve his stand.

And so, whatever might be the issue, the Negro still remains the "bogeyman," the buffer, the football of Southern politics.

Hughes the Nominee

June 15, 1916

The nomination of Charles Evans Hughes means victory for the Republican party. We know of no other man who could have been named who would have made the defeat of Woodrow Wilson and the Democratic party more certain. There are several Republican leaders who could defeat Wilson, but, as we say, none of them could make that defeat more of a certainty than Hughes.

Among the other candidates for the nomination there were men of equal ability and character, but none of them could approach Justice Hughes in availability. He was the only Republican of presidential size who had not been forced to take sides in the bitter fight of 1912, and hence, he was the only man who, as the nominee, could assure harmony between the two wings of the party. Nor can he be criticized for having kept out of the fight for his position made it impossible for him to have done otherwise.

In Mr. Hughes, the Republican party has a candidate of the highest order. His ability and character are beyond discussion; and, besides, he holds the confidence of the people. In his telegram of acceptance he states his position on the great issues with a force and clearness and comprehensiveness which, considering its brevity, make the communication nothing short of a miracle in thought or expression. No better platform on which to go before the American people will be needed than the one laid down by Justice Hughes in his message of acceptance.

As to the preeminence of his qualifications for the presidency of the United States, there can be question; but colored men all over the country have been asking during the past few weeks. "How does Hughes stand toward the Negro?" They concede that unlike President Wilson, he is a man absolutely free from prejudice, but they point out that as Governor of New York he did nothing to indicate special interest in the Negro. They feel that what the race needs in a president is not only mere absence of prejudice, but sympathetic interest. And they have been wondering if Charles E. Hughes has or will develop this sort of interest. In our opinion fears upon this point are needless.

As Governor of New York, Mr. Hughes was scarcely called upon to consider the Negro race with regard to its peculiar civic status; but as a member of the Supreme Court, he has been called upon to do so. Let us see what has been his attitude on the bench.

Justice Hughes has been on the right side of every question which has come before the Court regarding the rights of the Negro. In his first year on the bench he announced the decision of the Court which held as unconstitutional an Alabama statute sanctioning peonage. Furthermore, it was

Justice Hughes who wrote the decision holding the Oklahoma Jim Crow law unconstitutional. In fact, the series of Supreme Court decisions favorable to the Negro began with Justice Hughes' presence on the bench, the Alabama peonage decision being the first.

Charles Evans Hughes will be the next President of the United States, and it is our belief that by his acts and words he will stand not for the fair rights, but also for the fair consideration of colored American citizens. His record on the Supreme Court is the foundation of our belief.

Wake Up Colored Men! Wake Up!

November 2, 1916

Do colored men fully realize that the coming election brings with it a crisis in the history of the race? Do they fully realize what the election of Woodrow Wilson will mean for us as a people? If, in his first term Woodrow Wilson has gone so far in his Negro policy, what are we to expect if he receives the endorsement of the country for a second term?

Do colored men fully realize what the race has lost in the past three and a half years? It has lost the national political status which it has been fifty years in winning. Do colored men fully realize what would happen in four more years under Woodrow Wilson? The race would practically lose its national citizenship.

What then is the duty of colored men who vote in the states where their votes are counted and count for something? It is their duty not only to vote for Charles E. Hughes, but to do all in their power to help defeat Woodrow Wilson.

We repeat that nothing is farther from our choice than to have to take up this issue. We should prefer, as simple American citizens, to consider only the general issues that affect the general welfare. But this issue is forced upon us, and we can do nothing less than accept it. Nevertheless, in taking up this issue, we are not guilty of any hyphenism. We are not seeking the advantage of any outside power at the expense of the United States. We are simply seeking, as Americans of undivided loyalty, to maintain our status and rights as citizens. If we do not succeed in doing that, all other issues will be of no importance to us.

We know there is no danger that colored men will vote for Woodrow Wilson—no self-respecting Negro can do that—but there is danger that, either through negligence or apathy, many may not vote at all. That is why we say, "Wake up, colored men! Wake up!" This is no time for negligence or apathy. We are facing a crisis in the history of the race.

For once, let us show that we have our own vital interests at heart. Let us work and sacrifice, if necessary, to protect those interests. Let every colored man in all the free states cast his vote for Charles E. Hughes and the Republican party, the only party, whatever might be its shortcomings, that stands between us and political annihilation. Let him cast that vote early. If it means a sacrifice of time and money to cast that vote, let him make the sacrifice gladly, for he is voting not only for himself, but for his children.

Let every colored man in the free states who has the future of the race at heart, make himself an agent to get out the negligent and apathetic colored vote. Let him not be satisfied with casting his own vote, but let him make it his duty to see that others do not neglect to vote.

Finally, let every colored man in the free states vote not only the national Republican ticket, but also the state Republican ticket. Whatever other party he may have heretofore affiliated with in local politics, let him this time vote the Republican ticket from top to bottom.

Let us remember that we hold the only political protection for our brethren in the South. Let us not forget that their fate is largely in our hands. Let us remember that a vote cast for Democratic state government in New York is a vote cast for Democratic oppression throughout the South.

Vote unitedly for Republicanism. Vote to defeat the Democrats.

Make it your business to vote STRAIGHT REPUBLICAN TICKET on Tuesday, November 7. Vote Early and Avoid the Rush.

Vote against the Democratic Party and DEFEAT WILSON.

Our Double Loss

December 7, 1916

We, as a race, have been so busy lamenting the fact that Mr. Hughes was defeated for the presidency, that we have overlooked the fact that we have also lost him from the Supreme Bench. When Mr. Hughes was nominated we pointed out that his record as a member of the Supreme Court was a guarantee that on the race question he would be absolutely fair. That he would also be sympathetic, we did not know; but we were absolutely sure that he would be fair. We then pointed out that the series of favorable decisions on the Negro recently made by the Court began with the presence of Justice Hughes on the bench. The first of these decisions was the Alabama Peonage Case, and that was handed down during Mr. Hughes' first year as a justice, and was written by him. The other favorable decisions followed in more or less rapid succession. Before this series of decisions, the Supreme Court had been through all its history consistently unfavorable toward the

195

Negro and his rights. Mr. Hughes may not have been the sole cause of this reversal of attitude, but there can be no doubt that he had a great deal to do with it.

Now, as a result of the election, we have Mr. Wilson in the presidential chair and Mr. Hughes off the Supreme Bench; so our loss is a double loss.

Theodore Roosevelt Speaks

July 12, 1917

For three years the American Negro has been listening to a flow of high sounding words about democracy and humanity, coming from the highest authority in the land; all the while the truth being forced upon him by facts that the speaker of these words, consciously or unconsciously, did not include black men in either his "democracy" or his "humanity."

The American Negro has seen the whole nation stirred to action over atrocities in Belgium and Serbia and Armenia; while seemingly nothing could be done or even said about atrocities in Waco and Gainesville and Abbeville and Memphis and West St. Louis.

The American Negro sees the nation go forth as the champion of oppressed peoples in other lands; and his bewilderment gives way to a feeling of contempt for the civilization and the religion that can clothe themselves in such hypocrisy.

These feelings have been growing stronger through the past three or four years, and reached their greatest intensity after the burnt human sacrifice at Memphis and the massacre at East St. Louis; while the empty words about making the world safe for democracy were still echoing through the land.

And thus the American Negro stood, straining to hear words of sincerity. They have come. Come from the lips of Theodore Roosevelt, our champion of old. With all his tremendous might and power he struck a blow at hypocrisy. He held the mirror up to the face of the nation so that it could see itself through the eyes of truth. He also shed a new light across our sky and shed a new hope in our hearts.

Harding Starts Well

November 13, 1920

President-elect Harding has started well. His moderate and restrained utterances on the morning after his election made a good impression on the country. He said that the overwhelming vote by which he was elected did not make him feel exultant but humble. The country will also think the better of him for declining the offer made by the Navy Department to put the Mayflower and a battleship at his disposal for his visit to the Panama Canal. In this he showed good sense and good taste, for aside from the extravagant waste involved in having a battleship take him on a vacation jaunt there would be the sort of ostentatious display which never has fit in well with American ideas.

It appears also that he is doing all he can to avoid the conference at the Mexican border suggested by the President of Mexico. In doing so Mr. Harding states that he does not wish to put himself in a position that might in any way embarrass the present Administration. Of course, this is not only good diplomacy, it is also good politics. If Mr. Harding can keep up the impression he has formed since his election he will have comparatively easy sailing through his term of office.

At the same time President Wilson is displaying poor judgment and bad taste. He has lost an opportunity of retrieving some of his popularity with the people by not sending a generous message of congratulations to the President-elect. By the omission of this simple act he will strengthen many of the harsh criticisms that have already been made of him. His offer of the Mayflower and a battleship through the Navy Department does not cover up the omission. The message of congratulations should have preceded or accompanied the offer. Indeed, the offer, in the absence of the message of congratulations, does not constitute a courtesy but almost the opposite.

Bryan on the Negro Question

March 31, 1923

Some weeks ago William Jennings Bryan made a speech in Washington at a dinner of the Southern Society. He spoke on the political policy practiced in the South regarding the Negro and the franchise, and he made the declaration that the South was handling this whole question in the wisest and in the only practical way.

In a recent issue of the New York "Times" Mr. Bryan, whose statements had been commented upon and criticised very widely throughout the northern part of the country, published a statement in which he amplified the views he had expressed at the dinner of the Southern Society. The article in the "Times," from every point of view, is unworthy of the reputation which Mr. Bryan has as a statesman and a man of brains.

Mr. Bryan begins by juggling terms and definitions in an attempt to cause that solid statement in the Declaration of Independence about all men being created equal to vanish into thin air. That statement in the Declaration of Independence has produced more sophistry, perhaps, than any equal number of words ever set down. Volumes have been written to place into the clear and unequivocal words of the Declaration of Independence meanings that were never intended. It ought to be a waste of time to point out that the mind or minds capable of conceiving the Declaration of Independence had sense enough to know that all men are not equal either physically, or intellectually, or even morally; and the Declaration of Independence clears up the whole question by stating specifically upon what grounds all men are equal.

Mr. Bryan dismisses the Declaration of Independence with a gesture that places it among matters purely academic and declares that the question in the South is, which race shall control the government and make the laws under which both shall live. In making such a statement arguing from it, Mr. Bryan does nothing more than set up a straw man. The question as to which race shall control the government is not the question, and probably never will be the question, in the South. Even if every Negro in the South were indiscriminately and in a wholesale manner given the right to vote and exercised the right, it would not be a question of which race would control the government. The Negroes are only one-third the population of the South and one-tenth the population of the United States, and with less wealth, less training, and less organization, how would the question of their controlling either the South or the nation ever arise?

Mr. Bryan continues further with a wholly specious argument. He says:

> Suppose for the sake of argument that no limitations were placed upon suffrage and that the blacks, voting in mass(e) for officials of their own color, took charge of the Government and made laws for both blacks and whites; is there any white man who believes that the laws made under these circumstances would be better for both or administered with more fairness than now?

But why suppose such a thing? There is not the slightest reason to believe that if Negroes were given the right to vote in the South the blacks would vote en masse for officials of their own color. Negroes in New York are given the unlimited right to vote and they vote not only for white as well as black candidates but vote very largely for Democratic as well as Republican candidates.

Such statements by Mr. Bryan merely beg the question and make it difficult to believe that he is sincere.

In the matter of equality of suffrage in the South, what is it that the Negro demands? Is he demanding that he be given the unlimited right to vote and that he be sustained in the exercise of that right, regardless of other considerations? Not at all. All that the Negro demands is that he be given the right as an American citizen to vote under the identical qualifications required of other citizens. He cares not how high those qualifications are made—whether they include the ability to read and write, or the possession of five hundred dollars, or a knowledge of the Einstein Theory—just so long as those requirements are impartially demanded of white men and black men.

Mr. Bryan's assumption that if the Negroes in the South voted the laws of the South would not be so good as they are and that this civilization would suffer, is one that is more than open to question. The policy which Mr. Bryan stands for, that is, for the so-called purity of the ballot in the South and the reservation of it to white men only, has been tried for the past forty years; and what are the results? Does the South stand above any other section in the country where any men who meet the qualifications are allowed to vote? Not at all. Of all the sections of the country the South stands at the bottom intellectually, morally, and politically. Intellectually it is a desert, morally and socially it bears the distinction of being the only part of the civilized, maybe even the uncivilized world, where a human being may be burned alive at the stake. Politically it is rotten, and that goes for white men as well as black, for not only are black men disfranchised but white men dare not express their honest political opinions or act in accordance with them.

Let Mr. Bryan meet the issue squarely. He says in his statement that he does not believe it is right for ignorant unqualified black men to make laws for white men. Does he believe it is right for ignorant, unqualified white men to make laws for black men? Let him answer this question: Does he believe that the black man in the South who meets all of the requirements of citizenship should be denied the vote; and the white man who cannot measure up to such requirements be allowed the vote? We will then know just where Mr. Bryan stands. From the sophistries in his statement in the "Times" we cannot tell.

It is never a very nice thing to impugn any man's motives, but, interpreting Mr. Bryan's remarks on the subject of Negro suffrage in the light of his career as a politician, we are led to believe that he is simply issuing another "Bryan policy" which he hopes will attract votes that will give him the nomination for the presidency if not the office.

199

Domestic Politics

Of course, there are those who will think that any brain which is small enough to occupy itself with devising a law to make white people ride in one end of a street car and colored people in the other end is too small to comprehend, much less to grapple with the great national questions which are now pressing for an answer.

James Weldon Johnson, "Early On the Job"
(December 23, 1915)

"The basic spirit of America is democracy, and though that spirit is often thwarted it is constantly struggling forward and will finally prevail," Johnson wrote.[1] His *New York Age* editorials are a testament to his belief in this nation's democratic principle. As a civil rights advocate and editor, he worked effectively and arduously in pursuit of the freedom guaranteed African-Americans based on this nation's Constitution.

In 1914 when he joined the staff of the *Age*, he was a supporter and oftentimes a defender of the Republican Party. He contended that as long as the Democratic Party was under the influence of men who openly proclaimed that they had no interest in seeing African-Americans obtain their rights, it would be sheer folly for blacks to align themselves with that party. Until 1922, Johnson was a supporter of the Republican Party. He told his readers that the Republican Party had been the only bulwark that had stood between African-Americans and annihilation, civil and politi-

201

cal.[2] In December 1922 when the Dyer Antilynching Bill failed in the senate, Johnson, who had worked assiduously for the passage of the bill, became disillusioned with the Republican Party. He stated that blacks had made the antilynching bill the price of their Republican political support. "No Negro voter in the future can in national elections support either the Democratic or Republican party. To do so, would be to write himself down as an ass,"[3] he noted.

The notion of a third party became appealing to Johnson. A strong third party, he wrote in his column, would not only go far toward working out the political salvation of the country at large but it could prove a very direct means through which blacks could work out their own political salvation.[4]

The Lost Sheep

November 19, 1914

One by one, and two by two, they are coming back to the fold. Some sort of a fold is, after all, better than being left on the bare mountain side, exposed to the cold bleak winds and without a single blade of grass in sight.

Reading back, we see that the heading of this article, "The Lost Sheep," is especially applicable to the colored men who rushed from the Republican off into the Democratic party and are now more than anxious to rush back. It is certain that they got lost, and it is no less certain that they were sheep. They used just about the amount of judgment, foresight and common sense that you would expect from sheep.

Their chief claim and excuse is that the Negro's political salvation lies in his casting an independent vote. Perhaps, it does; most surely, it will; but it is doubly certain that his salvation does not lie in casting his vote for and with the men who are determined that he shall not be saved.

As long as the Democratic party is in the control and under the direction of men who not only make no effort to see that the Negro gets the rights of equal citizenship, but who absolutely deny that he should have those rights, it is the sheerest folly for us to think of allying ourselves with that party.

Common sense, more than sentiment, dictates that the Negro should cast his vote with the Republican party, because that party at present, guarantees him more than any other existing party that has any chance of gaining governmental control.

When there comes forth another great party—not conceived in slavery and nurtured on prejudice—another great party that stands on a higher and broader platform of human rights than the Republican party, then it will be sensible independence for us to transfer our support.

The error of our "lost sheep" may be due, in some degree, to a misconception of independence. Independence, in itself, is not a cardinal virtue. A man may be independent and, at the same time, be a fool or a villain. All the virtue there is in independence depends upon how, when and where it is asserted. Assuredly, there is no virtue in the independence that leads a Negro to support the present brand of Democracy.

They are coming back. How shall we receive them? Perhaps it is here incumbent upon us to rise to the magnanimous height of making more joy over the one that was lost than over the ninety and nine that went not astray.

The Supreme Court Again Dodges

December 3, 1914

Although a majority of the United States Supreme Court expressed the opinion that the Oklahoma "Jim Crow" law proviso permitting railroads to furnish sleeping, dining and chair car accommodations to white people only was unconstitutional, the Court nevertheless, failed to issue a decree declaring the law to be unconstitutional. This action is entirely in accord with the position which the Supreme Court has always taken upon questions involving the rights of the Negro. In every such case the Court evades the issue by dodging behind some technical error in the previous proceedings.

A law was passed in Oklahoma which contained what became known as the "luxury" clause. This clause permitted the railroads of the state to provide Pullman accommodations for white people only. Five colored men brought suit to obtain an injunction restraining the railroads from enforcing this law. The case was carried to the Oklahoma Federal Court, which declared the law to be constitutional.

The case was passed upon this week by the United States Supreme Court. A majority of that Court expressed the opinion that the law was unconstitutional, but refused to issue a decree declaring it so or to grant an injunction restraining the railroads from enforcing it. The Supreme Court simply affirmed the dismissal of the case by the Oklahoma Federal Court; and, so, the law stands just as it was before the suit was brought.

It will be hard for the layman to understand why, after a majority of the Justices expressed the opinion that the law was unconstitutional, the Court did not issue a decree to that effect.

The reason given by the Court for not passing on the constitutionality of the law was that the five Negroes who brought the suit had not shown that they had applied to the railroads for accommodations under the law or that the railroads had notified them that accommodations would be refused them.

A decision of that sort is enough to make a man feel that there is something wrong with legal procedure in this country; and that the sentiment of contempt for courts, which has been so constantly growing in the last decade is founded in reason.

It is true that legal procedure in the United States runs to the letter rather than to the spirit of the law; it makes a fetish of technicalities.

Here was a case in which the majority of the Court held that the petitioners were right, that what they sought remedy against was wrong; and yet, they decided in favor of the wrong because those who were in the right had neglected to dot an "i" or cross a "t."

After fighting a long and costly suit through to the highest court of the land, it is more than discouraging to be thrown out on purely technical grounds. The only comfort to be gained is the fact that a majority of the Court expressed the opinion that the law was unconstitutional. However, the law stands just as when it was passed, and the only remedy is to bring another suit in strict conformity with the letter of the law.

It is interesting to note that four of the Justices, who agreed with the majority of the Court in affirming the action of the lower court, expressed no opinion on the constitutionality of the law. They are Chief Justice White of Louisiana; Justice Holmes of Massachusetts; Justice Lamar of Georgia; and Justice McReynolds of Tennessee.

Negro Exclusion Amendment Defeated

January 14, 1915

The unexpected has happened. The amendment excluding immigrants of the "African or black race" which the Senate tacked on the Immigration bill was defeated in the House by a vote of 252 to 75. This action leaves the law of 1870 as it stood, making persons of African nativity or descent eligible to admission as aliens with all the rights of possible citizenship. All of the Republicans and 157 Democrats voted against the amendment; the 75 votes in favor of it all came from the Democratic side.

It is gratifying to see that the fight against the amendment was led by Representative Burnett, a Southern Democrat representing the State of Alabama and joint author of the bill. Mr. Burnett not only pleaded that the amendment would defeat the main bill but that it would be an unwarranted reflection upon the millions of Americans of African descent. It takes no stretch of the imagination to connect the influence of Dr. Booker T. Washington with the stand taken by the Representative from Alabama.

Mr. Mann, the Republican leader, rose high above politics. He is opposed to the Immigration bill, and although he knew the passage of the exclusion amendment would imperil the passage of the bill he nevertheless, said "although it is a temptation to the opponents of this bill to vote for this amendment and thus kill the bill, I shall not stultify myself by doing this injustice to the colored race."

It gives us renewed hope and encouragement to have such words uttered in Congress.

It is reported that Representative Eagle of Texas and Quinn of Mississippi frequently used the word "nigger" in the course of their remarks. The only comment their action deserves is that men who can narrow themselves down to such a contemptible compass cannot, by any possibility, stretch themselves to a comprehension of great national questions.

"A Vigilance Committee"

July 15, 1915

The idea now being advanced by the Southwestern Christian Advocate to have a Vigilance Committee at Washington, with a salaried superintendent in charge, to watch legislation affecting the race, is a good one.

The reasons in favor of such a plan are many. For one, it has been some time since there has been a member of the race to represent us in the National Government; another, our ancient friends who fought our battles in Congress are nearly all dead, and the majority of those who are still alive have become quite silent; but most important, that element in the country which is antagonistic to our best interests is now in the ascendency in the councils of the nation; so there is constant danger that our welfare will not only be neglected, but that it will be assailed.

There is no doubt that a Vigilance Committee, composed of honest, intelligent and loyal men—or men and women—headed by an energetic and capable superintendent, could both do us a lot of good and help us to avert a lot of harm. The good work possible for such a committee far outweighs any objections that could be brought against its organization and maintenance. It would have a splendid effect upon Congress for that body to know that this Vigilance Committee, having behind it the united support of the ten million Negroes of the country, was listening to every word uttered and watching every action taken that affected the race.

But here comes the rub. What about the support, especially financial? The advocate figures out that $10,000 a year, contributed by our leading church and fraternal organizations will do it. But will it be possible to collect $10,000 a year in voluntary contributions from these organizations? From the results of many attempts along more or less similar lines, we would judge that it cannot be done. We say it should be done, and we do not say it can't be done, but we confess that it admits of considerable doubt.

The difficulty would arise in securing continued voluntary contributions from various organizations. Whenever an organization felt the pinch of its own needs it would also be apt to feel that it could not afford its contribution. Perhaps, a surer plan would be a nation wide organization for the specific purpose. Or, as was suggested in these columns a few weeks ago, a race organization composed of the existing fraternal organizations welded into a permanent, independent alliance.

However, the idea places before us something so good and so necessary that an earnest effort should be made to devise some plan for carrying it out.

Hurtful Helpfulness

July 15, 1915

Very often a good cause is hurt more by a foolish friend than by a wise enemy. In this manner, the cause of international peace is injured by the new organization headed by Rev. John Haynes Holmes. The Rev. Mr. Holmes is a very able man, and one who could do a great deal to create a sentiment for world peace, but he allows his enthusiasm for the cause to lead him to an extreme where few sensible people will follow him.

This new organization pledges its members not to enlist nor to approve of the enlistment of anybody else "for any military or naval service." This is a perfect application of the old phrase "too much of a good thing." Peace is a good thing, but such an organization would give us peace beyond endurance.

The members of this new society pledge themselves not to enlist either in the army or navy, in case of war with some other nation; whom then do they expect, in such an event, to protect them, their wives, their children and their property? Such a pledge is nothing less than indirect treason.

This new propaganda is founded upon the theory of non-resistance, a theory to which no self-respecting man can subscribe. Non-resistance does not guarantee peace. The non-resistant may decline to fight, but that does not stop the other fellow from jumping on him. The non-resistant is not only continually jumped on, and jumped on because of his non-resistance, but he undergoes a feeling of self-degradation and contempt on the part of others that far outweighs any virtuous satisfaction he may get from refusing to fight.

It is a mere hallucination to imagine, in a world where struggle is the law, that any individual, race or nation can exist, much less progress, unless it is able and willing to struggle, to struggle in physical conflict if it becomes necessary.

Such a movement as the one headed by the Rev. Mr. Holmes is hurtful to the cause of peace.

The kind of help given a few days ago to the cause of woman suffrage by ex-Secretary Bryan was of the same hurtful variety. In a recent speech advocating votes for women, Mr. Bryan advanced the argument that women were as much entitled to the vote as men because there were more women in the churches and less women in the jails than men.

This is as foolish as the idiotic arguments against woman suffrage; and more damaging, because it is advanced by a friend of the cause. Any analytical mind can discover why there are more women in churches and less in jails than there are men; and the same mind can clearly see that they are reasons which have nothing to do with the merits of the question. Men are generally deprived of the vote for going to jail, but they are not given the vote for staying out. Church attendance is no reason for being given the right of franchise; an atheist is entitled to the right to vote.

The question of votes for women and also votes for colored men is based on the sound proposition that the right to govern should be derived from the consent of the individual governed; that consent expressed by the ballot. It is in accord with Lincoln's maxim that no man is good enough to govern another man without that other man's consent. The governed individuals of a state are entitled to the right to express their consent as to how they shall be governed, regardless of color, sex, wealth or even education.

Any limitation upon universal suffrage, except the obvious ones of infancy and lunacy, are simply assumptions by aristocrats or plutocrats or some other breed of "crats," in a greater or less degree, of the divine right to rule.

We are not surprised at Mr. Bryan for advancing such a childish argument for we have long realized that he would reach the limit of his natural powers as the superintendent of a large Sunday School. Actions like his and the Rev. Mr. Holmes makes us repeat, "Lord, save us from our foolish friends."

Capital Punishment

August 5, 1915

The trial and execution of Becker has demonstrated at least one thing, and that is the evil effect that capital punishment may have upon a community. For several weeks the city of New York was in an unhealthy state of mind over his fate. This was due principally to the manner in which the local daily papers handle such cases. Column after column was printed giving in detail each effort pro and con, the sorrow of the grief-stricken wife was laid bare, even the minute workings of the mind of the doomed man were exhibited to the public; so that when the fateful hour arrived a great many people felt as though it was an intimate acquaintance being sent to his death.

There was a time in England and this country when people could witness a public execution without receiving such an impression as Becker's death gave, but our civilization is becoming too high-keyed and too tense for such exhibitions.

It seems certain that one of two things must soon be done in the interest of public morals and decency; either the newspapers must discontinue their present manner of handling notorious cases or capital punishment must be abolished.

Early on the Job

December 23, 1915

On the opening day of Congress, Mr. Clark, a representative from Florida introduced his customary bill. When we say "his customary bill," it is hardly necessary to tell the regular readers of The Age what the bill is about. For those who are not regular readers of The Age we say that it is a bill to require all transportation companies, firms and persons within the District of Columbia to provide separate accommodations for the white and Negro races and to prescribe punishments and penalties for violating its provisions, and to provide for its enforcement.

The bill provides that within four months after the passage of the Act each and every transportation company, firm, or person operating cars, vessels, or vehicles of any character on regular routes of travel within the District of Columbia for the conveyance of passengers for hire shall provide separate and distinct accommodations for the conveyance of white and Negro passengers.

The bill provides that any company, firm or person operating means for the transportation of passengers and that fail to comply with the provisions of the Act shall be liable to a penalty of $500 a day, the same to be recovered in any court of competent jurisdiction at the suit of any passenger, one-half to go to the person bringing the suit and the remaining half to the District of Columbia. Further, that representatives or agents of companies, firms, or persons which violate the Act shall be deemed guilty of misdemeanor and subject to a fine of $500 to $1,000 or imprisonment in the District jail for three to six months, or both. Further, that any person who shall enter or be in any compartment or section of any vehicle not designated or set apart for persons of his or her race, and who shall fail or refuse to vacate, shall be deemed guilty of a misdemeanor and subject to a fine of $100, or imprisonment for thirty days, or both. Further, that conductors, motormen, and persons in charge of vehicles are empowered with police to enforce the Act.

This is the same old bill, the introduction of which has become a habit with Congressman Clark. He would undoubtedly feel that he had not done his duty, that he had not earned his salary, that he could not again look his constituents squarely in the face if he failed to introduce this bill making it a crime for white and colored people to ride in the same street car in and about the capital city of the nation. Here is an example of misdirected zeal and industry and perseverance that is truly pitiable. Who knows what laws and counsels for the good of the nation and the glory of Florida might not germinate in and emanate from the dome of the Honorable Mr. Clark if he did not make this one bill the chief and sole object of his thoughts and labors? Who knows but that in this time of international turmoil, when our own country is trembling dangerously near the brink, when there is dissension within and without and the national heart is disquieted, when there is such urgent need for the highest and best patriotism and statesmanship, who knows, we ask, but that in Mr. Clark's cranium might be hatched the clear, calm and wise judgments for which the whole country is breathlessly—and we may add hopelessly—waiting, were it not for the fact that the gray matter contained in the aforesaid cranium is a raging, seething, tempestuous, tumultuous mass, rendered so by the sight of colored and white citizens riding in the same street car in the nation's capital? Who knows but that Mr. Clark's voice might be heard calling to the diverging elements of the nation, inspiring the unity which the country dreamed it was realizing, before "hyphenates" became an American word, were it not that all of its wind-power is being used up in preaching the separation of white and colored citizens, even in the street cars of the capital of this great democracy?

Of course, there are those who will think that any brain which is small enough to occupy itself with devising a law to make white people ride in one end of a street car and colored people in the other end is too small to comprehend, much less to grapple with the great national questions which are now pressing for an answer. We must admit that this argument seems to be beyond contradictions; so, perhaps after all Mr. Clark is going his mental limit.

Why the Difference?

February 3, 1916

The nomination of Louis D. Brandeis to be an Associate Justice of the Supreme Court caused a sensation; and there are indications that his confirmation will meet with some opposition. Most likely he will be confirmed, but he is sure to come in for a great deal of discussion.

In the opinion of many this action of President Wilson bears all the marks of a political stroke. Perhaps it may so prove; but if Mr. Wilson had in mind the advancement of his political chances, he would in our humble opinion, have made a far more effective stroke had he named ex-President Taft.

But we have no intention of discussing the Brandeis nomination from a political point of view. We do not believe the appointment will add greatly to the President's popularity, so we let it go at that. However, we were struck by the following, clipped from the Washington despatch to the New York Sun:

> A telegram was received to-day at the office of the Committee on Judiciary of the Senate as follows:

"We protest to the end and resent vigorously the appointment of the Jew to the United States Supreme Court bench. We American gentiles feel bitter and will no longer support the President. Where he gained one Jew he will lose 10,000 gentiles. It is a disgrace and a shame.
"SOUTHERN GENTILE DEMOCRATS"

Mr. Brandeis is not the first Jew to be appointed to high office in this country. Jews have held important places in our diplomatic service; and President Roosevelt appointed a Jew to a place in his cabinet. Of course, a place on the bench of the Supreme Court is higher and more important than any diplomatic or cabinet position, and the Brandeis appointment will therefore be a greater shock to people of anti-Semitic sentiments than any they have yet experienced. It may not be necessary to add that persons in this country who have anti-Semitic sentiments are numerous.

Nevertheless, in spite of the number of people who hate Jews, in spite of the telegram reproduced above,—and the Senate will receive others like it—anybody who supposes that any fight will be made on the ground of Brandeis being a Jew will be disappointed. In fact, the telegram from "Southern Gentile Democrats" and any other attempts which may be made to raise a racial issue against Mr. Brandeis will only serve to strengthen his hand. The reason is simple; any senator who would have opposed the nomination on other grounds will now refrain from doing so for fear of being accused of fighting Brandeis on account of race. In a word, there is not a single senator with any regard for his political future who would dare to let it be known or even suspicioned that he would oppose the confirmation of Mr. Brandeis because he is a Jew. And that brings us down to what we started to say.

There is parallel between the condition of the Jewish race and of the Negro race which is often remarkably striking. They are both the victims of prejudice and persecution. In many parts of the world this prejudice is stronger against Jews than against Negroes. Even in the United States there are a great many people who have a stronger antipathy to the Jew than to the Negro. So eminent a man as the late Professor Shaler of Harvard University, in his book, "Neighbors," confessed that although he was a Southerner by birth and in sentiments his personal dislike of Jews was much stronger than of Negroes. He went so far as to say that he knew Negroes of whom he was extremely fond, but that all Jewish persons, for some unexplainable reason, were positively repulsive to him.

Again, in this country, both Jews and Negroes are forced to maintain their separate and distinct racial identity; though the reasons for it may differ.

Now, although there is so close a parallel between the two races, there is also the widest sort of a divergence; as the Brandeis case shows. This case does not cause us to ask why a Negro should not be named for a place in the Supreme Court, but it does cause us to ask another question.

There are, perhaps, twelve million Negroes in the United States and about two million Jews. Both races are separate groups within the nation. Both are the objects of race hatred. We might carry the analogy farther, but this is sufficient to prompt the question, "How is it that any Negrophobe in Congress need have no fear in introducing laws against the colored citizens of this country and no hesitancy in using the vilest and most insulting language concerning the whole race; while no Congressman with an equally bitter prejudice against Jews would dare to breathe his sentiments in public, much less introduce anti-Jewish laws or insult the race?"

We protest against injustice as well as do the Jews. Our vote in the states where it is counted is larger than the Jewish vote in the entire country. Why is it then that anybody can kick and insult twelve million of one prescribed race, while nobody dares open his mouth publicly against two million of another race that also suffers proscription? Why is it that prejudice in the one case can run the limit and beyond, while in the other case, no matter how strong and bitter it may be, it must restrain itself?

When you weigh the whole matter up and down and look it through and through you will find this to be the one answer that stands out big and clear: the twelve million Negroes in this country are, comparatively speaking, paupers; while the two million Jews have a controlling interest in the finances of the nation.

There is no doubt about it; we may accomplish what we will but, until we make ourselves felt as a financial element in the country, they are not going to stop kicking our dog around.

The writer does not intend to say that the possession of wealth by the Negro will bring an end to prejudice. It has not done so in the case of the Jews; a Jew-baiter hates a rich Jew, perhaps, worse that he does a poor one. But the possession of wealth by the Negro, as a race will do this much, it will make presidents, senators, congressmen and all politicians, as well as business men and people in general, very particular about how and when they express or show their prejudice. And that is the main thing we are striving for. We should, of course, be glad to have everybody like us, but whether they like us or not, our demand is for them to "treat us right." If we must make a choice, we should rather be disliked and treated as men and citizens, than loved and treated without consideration.

In this material world and in this most material country in the world, it is an idle dream for the Negro to hope to be able to demand full consideration until he is able to back up that demand with the power of money. The intellectual development of the race must be coupled with corresponding financial development. In our present condition we can demand nothing, we must beg for all we get.

Any member of Congress who wishes to do so can stand in the national legislative halls and vilify and insult twelve million Negro citizens of the

Republic, and he can do it with impunity; but it is an extremely dangerous thing for any man in public life to breathe one word against two million Jews, or even to let it be known that he has anti-Jewish sentiments.

Vote the Republican State Ticket

October 12, 1916

There are a number of New York colored men who feel and say that it will be advantageous for the Negro in this state to vote nationally with a Republican, and, for state and local officers to vote with the Democrats. We wish to say with all the emphasis we can put into our words that it will not be advantageous to do any such thing.

No good, sufficient and far-reaching reason that would embrace the colored people of any locality or state or of the nation can be given why a colored man should vote the Democratic ticket.

To vote the Democrat ticket in this state because Democracy here is not so antagonistic toward us as it is in some other sections of the country, or even because it throws us a few crumbs from the feast, when we must, at the same time, remember that the New York Democracy is a strong and undivided part of the national Democracy; and that the national Democracy stands for "keeping the Negro down"; to so vote is nothing less than to barter our weapons of defense for a bauble, nothing less than to sell our less fortunate brethren into bondage. A Democratic vote cast in New York is an endorsement and strengthening of Democratic practices in Mississippi.

So long as there is a Solid South which stands for Negro oppression, for Negro disfranchisement, for the elimination of the Negro from all share and participation in the government; so long as that Solid South is the guiding influence in the Democratic party; just so long must there be a solid Negro vote opposing it; just so long the Negro cannot afford to vote the Democratic ticket in either a state or national election, thereby giving aid and support to the great common enemy.

We say to colored men of New York state and all the other free and enlightened states, turn to the history, the ethics, the aims and the accomplishments of the two chief political parties and compare them. Now cancel, if you will, the debt of emancipation, cancel debt of enfranchisement, cancel the debt due to the fact that the Republican party has been the only bulwark that has stood between us and annihilation, civil and political; charge that this bulwark has not always withstood attack, but admit that it has even been the only bulwark; blot out, if you will, the whole account and if you feel that the Republican party has done little for us tell, in the name of God, what are we to expect from Democracy?

The vital interests of the race hang upon the outcome of this presidential election as they have hung upon no other in thirty years. The Administration of Woodrow Wilson has robbed the Negro of every vestige of national political rights. Four more years of Woodrow Wilson would practically rob the Negro of every vestige of national citizenship. We say then to colored men that, notwithstanding what may be the attitude of the local Democracy, they cannot afford to do the least thing that will strengthen the national Democracy.

Let the colored men in New York and in all of the civilized states vote the state as well as the national Republican ticket.

Under the Dome of the Capitol

May 3, 1917

The writer was present last week when Mr. Moorfield Storey argued the Louisville Segregation Ordinance Case for the National Association for the Advancement of Colored People before the United States Supreme Court at Washington. There were fifteen or twenty representative colored men at the hearing. We should like to have been possessed of the power to sound the inmost thoughts of these colored men and of the white people present and of the Justices on the bench while the two lawyers who pled the case for the other side were talking. The writer for himself must confess that at times he experienced a strange sensation while listening to the Negro discussed before this highest tribunal in the land as something just outside of American citizenship; indeed, as something just below humanity.

Both the lawyers for the other side appeared to be able men and doubtless the reasons they gave were the best that could be given to bolster up and excuse so bad a law, so undemocratic, so unconstitutional a law. But one not familiar with the case might have thought that they were pleading to have the homes of the white people of the South protected from wild beasts or against the presence of lepers. And as we sat there we wondered how far the presence of so many respectable and intelligent colored men would go to offset such an argument.

At two o'clock Chief Justice White announced a recess of thirty minutes. The writer and two other American citizens, one colored and the other white, went down in the basement to the public lunch room to get something to eat. We were met by an employee who told us we could not be served. When asked why, he informed us that Senator Overman (of North Carolina), on becoming chairman of the committee that has charge of the Capitol grounds, issued an order that no colored person should be served in either of the lunch rooms.

This, under the very dome of the Capitol of the greatest democracy in the world! It was a thing to arouse all the hates and furies and put murder in a man's heart.

We went across to the Congressional Library and were served just as any other American citizens. The man who is responsible for the rules that govern the Library building is from the civilized state of Massachusetts.

At two-thirty we returned to the Court and heard Mr. Storey's strong plea for right and justice and humanity, and the writer felt that the better and greater part of this nation does stand for right and justice, and will ultimately see that right and justice are done. The Overmans and Vardamans and the others of their ilk who are now in high places will not and cannot dominate long. They are riding now just as their predecessors did in the fifties, and they are going to fall just the same.

The basic spirit of America is democracy, and though that spirit is often thwarted it is constantly struggling forward and will finally prevail. When the opposing forces were at the height of their strength, the better part of this nation arose and struck down slavery. The better part of this nation changed the organic law of the land and made us citizens. And the better part of this nation is going to see that we are given full and equal justice.

The Overmans and the Vardamans and all like them will pass away, the great spirit of democracy will live and press forward forever. It only remains for us to try to keep pace with it, and we shall surely come into our own. That is my faith.

The Japanese Question in California

July 12, 1919

Senator Phelan of California comes out in the press this week in a most gloomy prediction for his state. He foresees in the increase of the birth rate of Japanese there the complete overwhelming of the white race. He bases his gloomy predictions on the conditions which allow Japanese women to come into California as the wives of Japanese men already living there. One of the stipulations in the gentleman's agreement between Japan and the United States was that Japan would allow no more of her laborers to come to this country. The wives of laborers were, however, excepted; as a result large numbers of Japanese women have been steadily coming in as wives of the laborers already here.

It is against these women that Senator Phelan raises his warning. He says they not only work as laborers, but are giving birth to large families and thereby increasing the Japanese population, in spite of immigration restrictions. He says:

These women work in the fields as laborers and so circumvent the agreement, and then they give birth to children and thus defeat the purpose of the agreement by increasing the horde of non-assimilable aliens who are crowding the white men and women off the land. If this is not checked now, it means the end of the white race in California, the subversion of American institutions and the end of our Western civilization. The fight is on. On which side do you stand?

The feeling against the Japanese on the Pacific Coast is almost entirely economic. But it is not, as some might suppose, because the Japanese work for less wages than the whites and so reduce the standards of living; it is because the Japanese work harder and longer than the whites, because they can make money where the whites fail, because they set too hard a pace in work for the whites to follow.

The Japanese have gotten on the land, and certain products of the land on the Pacific Coast are wholly in their control. They almost completely control the trunk farm products and the berry products of that whole region. They work on the land longer hours, they cultivate it more painstakingly, and they get better results from it than the whites. The white man does not want to work that hard. He wants some time to ride around in his Ford and to socialize. As a result he can't stand the competition, and he is being driven off the land. From this arises the prejudice against the Japanese on the Coast. We could wish that that was the cause of prejudice against Negroes in the South.

The Japanese are fast coming into possession of the land in California and other Pacific States. In the public markets of Seattle the finest vegetable and fruit stalls are owned by Japanese; and they have white men and women working for them. These Japanese are getting possession of the land and they are making money, and their money is being invested in business. If they keep it up for a generation longer, they will be in a position to defy Senator Phelan and all others like him.

It is an eye-opener to all colored men to see what the Japanese have done on the Pacific Coast, in spite of prejudice and laws against them. One can ride for miles and miles and see nothing but Japanese at work on the land. One can arrive at a station and see car after car being loaded with berries; and all of the loading, all of the shipping, all of the clerking, all of the handling both of the berries and money being done by Japanese.

Nevertheless, we think that Senator Phelan's forecast is too dark. We do not think that Japanese thrift will mean the "end of the white race in California and the subversion of American institutions and Western civilization." The Japanese are not trying to overthrow anything in California; they are only asking to be let alone to extract the best living they can out of the soil by their own labor.

If industry and thrift on the part of the Japanese workers mean the end of the white race in California—well, let it end; for the truth would be that it had already reached the point of decay and rot if it could not stand the fair competition of hard work, industry and energy expended on the soil.

The IWW Body in Congress

August 30, 1919

For a good many months some people in the United States have been trying to explain the new spirit of the Negro by attributing it to Bolshevik or Socialist, or IWW propaganda. When the United States entered the war the birth of this new spirit was noticed; it was then attributed to pro-German propaganda. Of course with German propaganda dead it had to be attributed to some other cause.

There are two reasons for this course of action; one is founded in utter blindness and the other in sheer craftiness. One is founded in the lack of, according to the Negro, the traits and aspirations which are common to human nature everywhere; and the other is founded in an effort to couple up the new spirit of the Negro with some movement which is so unpopular that it can be crushed and killed in the effort to destroy the movement.

We think that the main reason is in craft. For while there may be some people who fail to realize that the Negro reacts to certain stimuli in the same manner as other human beings, who fail to realize that he does of his own volition aspire to freedom and liberty and justice, these people must be very few. A man does not need to know psychology, he needs to know only a little history to understand the absurdity of such an opinion.

But there are a great many people who are crafty enough to know that if this new spirit of the Negro can be hitched up to some movement against which a great national prejudice has already been built, they will have the sanction of patriotism and all the other virtues in their efforts to crush and kill it.

In the early days of the war, the red rag in the face of the nation was pro-Germanism; anything under the sun could be done in the name of anti-pro-Germanism and receive the approval of the multitude. The writer, of course, has never killed anybody; but he could not prevent the thought occurring to him during that period that if he was forced to do such a distasteful job the best defense he could possibly offer would be to accuse his victim of pro-Germanism.

Pro-Germanism did not last long enough to afford full opportunity to crush and kill the new spirit of the Negro; so the effort is now being made to couple it with what is, if anything, more unpopular. Through the press

217

the words, "Socialism" and "Bolshevism" and the initials "IWW" have been given such meanings that the American people shudder when they hear them. They do not stop to make any inquiry into their meanings, they simply shudder. These terms have about the same effect upon the average American that the words "Ku Klux" had on a colored child fifty years ago.

The crafty ones know that if they can hitch the new spirit of the Negro up with these terms, they have a club that they can use with tremendous effect. So the Honorable Mr. Byrnes of South Carolina has brought the matter upon the floor of Congress. In substantiation of his statements he read various "radical" statements and opinions from Negro publications. Well, at any rate, he has given Congress some material for thought, material which perhaps it would never have received had it not been for the gentleman from the Palmetto State.

The strange thing about the matter is that most of these "radical" statements and opinions which the South Carolina Representative read on the floor of the House were not radical at all; much less were they seditious. Their general tenor was a demand for protection of life and property, an equal chance to work and an equal opportunity to vote. As for sedition, there was no expressed or unexpressed wish for the overthrow of government, or separateness from existing government; there was, on the other hand, the demand for fuller oneness with government. To none of these things should a member of Congress or any other good American citizen object. Perhaps the statements which seemed particularly alarming to the statesman from South Carolina were the ones declaring that if neither the city, county, state or Federal government would protect the Negro's life against mobs, he would do it himself. But his alarm was uncalled for; all he needed to do was to help secure protection for the Negro's life against mobs, at least in South Carolina.

How many Negroes in the United States are interesting themselves to find out something about the principles of Socialism and of the IWW we do not know. We do know, however, that the number is comparatively small. Of course, there are some; the race could lay no claim to intelligence if there were not. But the great mass of the race know little or nothing of the principles of Socialism; they do not know whether "Bolshevik" applies to a new theory of government or is it the name of a new European country; they do not know what initials, "IWW" stand for,—and yet these same masses are discontented, they know they are unjustly treated, and they are determined to secure something nearer like justice for themselves and their children.

And it is in these masses, these discontented masses, that the new spirit of the Negro breathes and lives.

The "Jim Crow" Car in Congress

September 13, 1919

Last week Congressman Madden of Illinois went before the House Interstate and Foreign Commerce Committee and urged the abolition of the "Jim Crow" car in interstate railroad traffic. This he did in support of a bill which he has introduced requiring "equal and identical rights, accommodations and privileges" for both races on railway trains. Mr. Madden declared that the Government has no right to draft its citizens in defense of the flag and at the same time say to them that their rights are inferior to those of other citizens of the United States. He added that Chinese and Japanese are allowed to ride on trains on equal conditions with the whites.

Representative Rayburn of Texas and Sanders of Louisiana, members of the committee, answered Mr. Madden by stating that the Negroes of the South did not want to ride in the cars with the white people.

Mr. Rayburn said: "You want to force the Negroes to ride in the cars with the white people, when the Negroes themselves would rather ride in separate cars than be mixed up with white people."

Mr. Sanders said: "We of the South contend that the Negro prefers separate accommodations."

Both Mr. Rayburn and Mr. Sanders hold the egotistic position of the Southern white man on this matter; that is, that with colored people who protest against the "Jim Crow" car it is a question of riding with white people. It is not a question of riding with white people, it is a question of paying equal fare for inferior accommodations, and of having to submit to the humiliation of being compelled to ride in this inferior place which is designated for them and no one else. To say that the white people are compelled to ride in the first class car is only to play with words.

Many people in the North make the same mistake regarding hotel accommodations. They think that a colored man in going to a white hotel is seeking to be with white people. The truth of the matter is he is looking for something to eat and a decent place to sleep. This whole idea is only a demonstration of the supreme egotism of the white man. He thinks to himself that the Negro looks up to him as a paragon, as the one thing to be desired and to be near. In truth, the Negro often looks down on him as the most damnable hypocrite, scoundrel and savage that the world ever knew.

The greatest illumination is shed on the mind of Mr. Sanders of Louisiana by his use of the phrase, "Our Negroes down South." Mr. Sanders is here using the phrase in just about the same sense as it was used by the slaveholders of Louisiana before the Civil War.

Sooner or later the Government must face this question of discrimination on the railroads which it is operating. And if the Government ceases to operate the railroads, the Supreme Court of the United States must face the question, at least, as it applies to interstate traffic.

We wish more power to Mr. Madden of Illinois.

The Faults in Our Courts of Law

November 15, 1919

Time and again the plea has been made that one of the main causes of mob law and lynching is found in the technical delays which are possible under the procedure which regulates practice in our courts. It has been claimed that the people, when they see a criminal taking advantage of this and that technicality with the purpose of delaying punishment indefinitely or escaping it altogether, become impatient and take the law into their own hands.

There is no doubt that there are times when what seems to be an unfair advantage is taken of the method of procedure in this country; but it should be remembered that the delays which sometimes stand in the way of swift execution of the law and of which the people are often so impatient are not imperfections, they were expressly provided for. The law and the procedure in the courts are based on the maxim that it is better for ten guilty men to go free than for one innocent man to be punished. This maxim is especially adhered to when a man's life is at stake.

The possibility of delays in our courts may be a fault and one that needs to be remedied; but it is not so serious a fault as another which is very common in the courts of the South; that is, the power which twelve men have to render a verdict not in accordance with the fact and which is very often exercised when the just verdict would be one against a white man and for a Negro.

A despatch from Knoxville, Tennessee, states that Judge Nelson in that city has issued an order by which the twelve men who served as jurors in the race riot cases last August, freeing fourteen white men and entering mistrials as to five others, are debarred from serving as jurors in his court so long as he is the presiding officer. In entering the order he said, "The verdict of the jury in the said cases was wholly unwarranted by the facts."

Such a thing has often happened, but seldom has a judge had the courage to say and do what Judge Nelson said and did. Mere delays appear to be an inconsequential fault in a procedure which allows twelve men to violate their oaths and deliberately bring in a verdict contrary to the facts.

Those who are anxious for a reform in the way law is dealt out in our courts would do well to consider what happened in Judge Nelson's court.

Report of the Justice Department on Sedition among Negroes

December 20, 1919

We have a copy of the report of the Department of Justice on Radicalism and Sedition Among the Negroes as Reflected in Their Publications." The report occupies twenty-seven pages of the report of the investigation against "Persons Advising Anarchy, Sedition, and the Forcible Overthrow of the Government."

The pages devoted to the Negro come at the end of the report; and, judging from what was the evident purpose of the report, these pages make the most ludicrous anticlimax that could be imagined. We don't know how good a case the report makes out against the people discussed in the first one hundred and sixty pages, for we have not yet had the time to read that portion; but we are prepared to say that if it doesn't make out a better case than it makes out against the Negro, the Department of Justice has wasted a good deal of time and a considerable amount of Uncle Sam's cash.

If any jury of fair minded persons can find in the twenty-seven pages devoted to the Negro anything which justifies those pages being made a part of a report against "persons advising anarchy, sedition, and the forcible overthrow of the Government," the writer will agree to eat a bundle of these reports without taking water.

Whoever got out the report filled it with extracts of both prose and poetry from the radical Negro press. But what do all of these extracts amount to when boiled down? They amount to a demand not for anarchy, not for the overthrow of the Government, but to a demand for the strict and impartial enforcement of law, and to an expression of the determination of the Negro to defend himself when and where the law refuses or fails to protect him against the mob. Indeed, the main note running through all the quotations from the Negro publications mentioned in the report is a demand for law and order, but law and order based on the recognition of the equal rights of every American citizen.

Of course, the chief thing in these radical periodicals on which the accusing finger rests is the open or implied endorsement of the action of Negroes who in the recent "race riots" defended themselves and protected their homes against the mobs because the law refused or failed to protect them. Well, what about it? Can any sane man say that these Negroes did not act within their legal and moral rights? More than that, can any sane man say that these Negroes did not perform what was their obvious duty? Will any white man say that white men would not have been expected to act likewise under like conditions?

Let those who are holding up their hands in holy horror at the mere thought of lawlessness on the part of Negroes stop and consider that in not one of these outbreaks were Negroes the original aggressors. All of the "race riots" which occurred last summer were started by lawless white men. Then let the holy horror against lawlessness be directed against white mobbists and not against Negroes defending their lives and their homes when the law shows itself unable or unwilling to do so.

There are gentle friends of the Negro who greatly deplore any indication on his part to oppose with physical force mob violence and community lawlessness. They feel that it will arouse still more bitter sentiment against himself, and what is worse, a great many of him might get killed, for he is so far outnumbered. These friends should not expect the Negro to submit to wholesale murder for the sake of increasing his reputation for gentleness and patience. If they do, they are expecting too much from the present-day Negro. As for getting killed—that does not strike much terror to the heart of the Negro now; thousands of Negroes died in France for what has been for them a dream, if not a lie; so the thought of dying in defense of their own lives and property does not impart any great dread; they reason that if they are threatened with death by wholesale murder, it is better to meet it by facing the mob than to meet it by being shot in the back while running or by having their houses burned down over their heads.

Let a little of this investigation into lawlessness and this indignation against lawlessness be directed against the degenerate, blood-lusting white men who make up the mobs to whom the lynching and murdering of Negroes is a pastime, a Roman holiday sport.

If the Department of Justice wants to do a job of investigating worth doing, let it not stop at the open and just discontent expressed in the Negro press over the wrongs and injustices suffered by black American citizens; let it get at the grounds and reason for that discontent. And if it wants any assistance on the job, the Negro press will gladly give it.

As it is, the department has done only about one-third of what it ought to do. The third that it has done makes out no case of "sedition" against the Negro; it simply shows that the Negro has just grounds for complaint at this treatment in this country, and has sense enough to know it and sense enough to say it in a clear, intelligent and forcible way. Indeed, it seems that this latter is what shocks the writer of the report more than anything else. He is a man who has evidently, like many others, been asleep on the Negro; he has been thinking of the Negro in terms of twenty or thirty years ago; all at once he is called on to read a number of Negro publications, and he is amazed, overwhelmed, dumbfounded, to find that the Negro knows what he wants, knows what he is to reproduce its statement of principles.

But, after all, this report of the Department of Justice is not so bad. So far as we know, it is the most effective step yet taken to let the whole country know just what the Negro is discontented about, to let it know what the Negro of to-day is thinking. The American Negro could wish for nothing better than that the Department of Justice would put a copy of this report in the hands of every man, woman and child in the United States.

Enforcing the Eighteenth Amendment

February 28, 1920

Senator Warren stated last week that it will cost $50,000,000 a year to keep the country dry; that is, to enforce the Eighteenth Amendment. The Senator made this statement on the introduction by him of a bill "for enforcement of the national prohibition act by establishing government warehouses," which provides for the segregation and safeguarding of all liquor until it can be bottled and sold for medicinal and similar purposes. The bill was prepared at the Treasury Department; so the sum mentioned is an estimate and not a guess.

In our opinion even the great sum of FIFTY MILLION DOLLARS will not be adequate for the continued and effective enforcement of the Eighteenth Amendment. As time goes on and the force of superintendents, inspectors and spies is enlarged and perfected for doing this almost impossible job, it will be found that more money is needed.

Now since Congress has demonstrated that machinery can be provided by the Federal Government for the enforcement of one amendment to the Constitution, why should it not provide for the same purpose regarding other amendments which are equally mandatory?

The old excuse for not providing machinery for the enforcement of the Fourteenth and Fifteenth Amendments has been that it would necessitate an unconstitutional interference with the rights of the States. The excuse is a lame one, for Congress is given the right to provide for the enforcement of these amendments.

But now comes the Eighteenth Amendment and knocks the whole theory of interference with States' rights in the head; for in enforcing this amendment not only are States' rights interfered with but county rights, city rights and individual rights.

In enforcing this amendment, the Federal Government will have the right to put a spy on the trail of the individual citizen to see that he does not transfer a half-pint of whiskey from his home to his office. The old theory of States' rights no longer stands in the way of providing means and machinery for the enforcement of the Fourteenth and Fifteenth Amendments.

A New Third Party

March 25, 1922

To anyone who is a student of politics in the United States it is plain that the political salvation of the country depends in a very large measure upon the existence of a third party. Of course, "third" parties are always in existence. A citizen never realizes how many "third" parties are always in existence. A citizen never realizes how many "third" parties there are until he goes into the booth to vote at a presidential election. The average voter is then always amazed to find out how many men are running for the President on tickets of various denominations. But so far as the political salvation of the country is to be worked out by a third party, it must be worked out through a third party which is strong enough to defeat either of the major parties if not to win.

The Progressive movement was the last third party bade fair to succeed; but the Progressive movement died before its founder died, and hopes for a real third party must turn in another direction. There are no present indications that the Socialist Party will be the realization of those hopes. The Prohibition Party which once loomed on the horizon, has been definitely put out of business by the Prohibition Amendment. Just before the last presidential campaign an effort was made to form a third party that would be a factor through a coalition of the political labor elements and the Committee of Forty-eight, but the coalition did not succeed. At the time it looked as though we were going to have a labor party in the United States that would somewhat correspond to the labor party in England.

There is now an effort on foot, backed by some of those who were in the movement to organize the Labor Party, to form a third party to be known as the Liberal Party. We hope that it will succeed. At any rate, this movement starts with one advantage at least over its immediate predecessor, and that is in the name chosen for the party. The name, Labor Party, is better suited to England than to the United States in the face of fact that England is a monarchy and the United States a so-called democracy; because in England all persons who earn their livelihood, either through labor with the hands or the head, are eligible members of the Labor Party. We doubt whether writers and artists and scientists, etc., in the United States would, at least at present, feel that their place was in the ranks of the "Labor Party." But the name, "Liberal Party," would have a peculiar appeal for just such men as well as a general appeal to what is more strictly known as the working classes.

A strong third party in the United States would not only go far toward working out the political salvation of the country at large but it could prove a very direct means through which the Negro could work out his own particular political salvation.

As the Negro is now situated, politically, he is the victim of a sort of gentlemen's agreement between the two parties. One openly declares and says that it does not want him while the other accepts him but privately agrees to reduce what it does for him down to the lowest minimum. With a third party in the field which is a real political factor, the Negro can actually make his weight felt.

The tentative program of the Liberal Party says that it will be liberal in its principles as well as in its name. We hope that it will succeed.

The Supreme Court Reverses Itself

March 21, 1923

The far-reaching importance of the decision by the United States Supreme Court in the Arkansas cases has not been fully realized, we fear. Indeed, when the decision was first rendered it was taken only as another victory in the fight to save the lives of the Arkansas peonage victims. But the comments of various prominent lawyers are now making it plain that the Supreme Court not only reversed the lower court in these cases but even reversed itself.

Mr. Louis Marshall, the eminent lawyer who was counsel for Leo Frank, has come out in a letter in which he says that the Supreme Court in the Arkansas cases has adopted a principle which he contended for and which the Court refused to adopt in the Leo Frank case. The principle for which Mr. Marshall contended was that a man did not have a trial by due process of law, in accordance with his constitutional guarantees merely because he was tried in a duly constituted court if that court was not free to function.

The Supreme Court refused to subscribe to that principle in the Frank case; but in the Arkansas cases Mr. Moorfield Storey, who argued the cases, won decision which is based upon this principle. Mr. Marshall, in the statement he has made, says:

> The stone that the builders rejected now becomes the chief of the corner. . . . Due process of law now means not merely a right to be heard before a court but it must be before a court that is not paralyzed by mob domination.

So it can be that this decision reaches far beyond the impending facts of the Arkansas peons. It extends not only to colored but to white men. However, it is especially important for Negroes because it makes possible a contest in any case in which it can be shown that the decision of a court was influenced by a mob.

Lloyd George on Prohibition

July 7, 1923

The seizure of the liquor stores on certain foreign ships in the Port of New York last week caused considerable local and British excitement. United States officials went aboard a British ship and broke the seals of the liquor stores which had been placed there by British customs officers. These seals were intended to show that the liquor was not to be opened in the United States but was to be used on the homeward trip after the ship had passed the three-mile limit.

Naturally, there was a good deal of excitement in England over this incident and there was a good deal of hot air expanded over it. Mr. Lloyd George made an utterance of remarkably cool common sense. He counselled the English people not to get excited over the seizure of the liquor in New York harbor and declared that America was not only well within her rights but that the English people ought to extend a certain measure of sympathy to her in her difficulties. He said, "America is making a very bold experiment to deal with probably the greatest curse of modern civilization. She has tried many experiments but they have been only comparative successes. She has made the decision, with a courage that characterizes that great people, to try the prohibition experiment; one that has never been on this earth before. Let us give her a fair chance."

We are by no means frantic about prohibition, nor are we entirely sure that it will bring in the millennium that was promised, but we are absolutely in sympathy with the effort to give it a fair trial. It has been claimed that alcoholic drink has been the cause of the majority of human woes and sufferings. If that is true, it is right to abolish it or to restrict it to the lowest point possible. The United States is making this experiment and the experiment ought to be a fair one. If the experiment is fairly made and it is found that the abolishment of alcoholic drink does measurably increase human health and happiness and well-being, the whole world will eventually adopt the policy adopted by America. If, on the other hand, prohibition fairly tried fails to bring any of these advantages in any degree, the world will not bother with it and America will finally discredit it; but, we repeat, it ought to be given an absolutely fair trial.

12 International Politics

For a great part of the world the word "democracy" is a fetish. But the American Negro has been disillusioned. He knows from experience that a despised people can be deprived of their rights, oppressed and down trodden in a democracy just as effectually as under the worst form of autocracy.

James Weldon Johnson, "Russian Democracy and the Jews"
(March 22, 1917)

In 1917 the United States entered World War I under the slogan, "Make the World Safe for Democracy." Even though Johnson understood the confusion and contradiction of such an objective, he nevertheless encouraged his readers to support the nation's effort against Germany. Johnson told his readers that America's hypocrisy was apparent in the international community by condoning lynching and oppression within the borders of the United States on the one hand, and calling for democracy in Germany on the other.

In 1920, James Weldon Johnson represented the NAACP in an investigation of possible wrongdoing and abuses in the American Occupation of Haiti that had begun in 1915. Any documentation of corruption or military abuse by the American military could discredit President Wilson whom Johnson intensely disliked. In Johnson's final report on the Haitian situation, the problem comprised three distinct forces: the financial, personified by the National City Bank of New York; the military, characterized by their physical and mental abuse of Haitian natives; and the American advisors with their expensive automobiles and jewelry, all paid for out of the Haitian treasury.[1]

These editorials signal Johnson's interest in cultural, economic, and political issues affecting the African diaspora. They reflect an early recognition on his part of the living connection between African-American lives and the black presence in the international community, especially the United States' role in furthering racial ideologies and neocolonial interference in Latin America and the West Indies.

The After Results of the Great War

October 15, 1914

When the first shock of the great war passed, thoughtful minds all over the world began to speculate upon what the after results will be. In most parts of the world they are speculating upon the political results; upon what changes will be made in the map of Europe, upon what territory will be given to or taken from this or that nation and upon what new alliances will be formed. In the United States, true to our national genius, we are speculating upon what it will mean to us in dollars and cents.

We colored Americans might well interest ourselves in speculating upon what this war will finally mean for those engaged in it who are racially and nationally in positions similar to our own.

It is quite probable that Russia will not forget the Jews, who are fighting so valiantly in her ranks; nor that England will fail to remember the much needed assistance being given by her native Indian regiments. France is already the only one among the great nations which has reached that high plane of civilization on which a man is judged by merit and not by color, but even she will receive a new baptism of the spirit of "Liberty, Equality and Brotherhood" through the brave and brilliant conduct of her black troops from North and West Africa.

No one can foretell what the outcome will be; but, perhaps, after all, the oppressed peoples will come out of this titanic struggle as the only real victors.

The Administration's Mexican Policy

October 29, 1914

If it were not for the great war in Europe the attention of this country would be more keenly centered upon the blunder of the Administration at Washington with regard to our relations with Mexico. The Democratic press is loud in declaring that had it not been for President Wilson's misnamed policy of "watchful waiting" we should have been at war with our neighboring republic. The truth of the matter is, it was the President's policy that came very near involving us in war with that country.

First came the diplomatic mistake of refusing to recognize Huerta. Then the foolish demand that he get down and out—a demand that could not be enforced; then the raising of the embargo against the shipment of arms and ammunition to the rebels; then the sending of a great fleet to Vera Cruz—out of this last act arose the embarrassing "salute the flag" incident. Either of these steps, if taken with a strong nation, would have brought on war. War was avoided only on account of Mexico's weakness.

Ever since the Spanish-American war and our acquisition of certain territory from Spain, the influence of the United States in Latin-American affairs has been greatly widened, and the several Republican Administrations have been dealing successfully with just such problems as that which arose in Mexico. These problems were successfully dealt with because long experience had given to the Republican party a corps of trained men, who knew how to handle such questions.

The great trouble with the Democratic foreign policy is that the party has very few men who have had the practice. The ludicrous mistakes made by so many of the lately appointed diplomats illustrate this fact.

In this matter of foreign policy, at least, the Democrats would have done well to have followed in the footsteps of the Republicans; and anyhow, until they had learned the ropes.

Once More Haiti

October 29, 1914

Haiti is again in the throes of a revolution, and we are once more compelled to feelings of regret at the thought that the only real independent Negro state in the world has not yet achieved stable government.

However, the condition in Mexico stops the ever ready critics from pointing their fingers and declaring that the stage of affairs in the Island Republic is due to the innate incapacity of the Negro for self-government.

The fact is revolutions occur in Haiti, for the same reasons that they occur in Venezuela, Colombia, Nicaragua, Honduras, Guatemala and Mexico; and in none of the latter countries is there any considerable Negro element with the possible exception of Honduras.

The writer will some time give in these columns his opinion as to the causes of revolutions in Latin-American countries, and how those causes apply to Haiti.

The Art of Living

April 29, 1915

The Latin, both of Europe and South America, has often raised the question as to whether the people of England, Germany and the United States know how to live. If those who have studied Latin life, either in Latin countries or through Latin literature, will consider they will find that this is not an idle question.

That place in the sun which Germany wants for herself collectively, every Latin by instinct claims for himself individually, and he would know how to fill it, being well versed in banking. Odious to such a temperament must be the heavy mind of the Teutons, their pedantry and meddlesomeness, their sentimental idealism, their emphatic pathos, their grotesque taste, all does not need so much apparatus, it would crush his genius. He loves his case, and he feels that the victory of Germany would increase everywhere that irrational tension from which the modern world is suffering. It is not only the foolish ruinous armaments that he deprecates, but the pressure on everybody of aimless tasks and struggles, the foolish romantic will making so many damnable faces and arousing so many damnable passions. He knows better how to live.

The knowledge of the art of living is best exemplified in France and the ignorance of it is best exemplified in the United States. In this country everything is always at high tension and everybody is always on the dead run, and to what purpose? Is our well-being and happiness thereby increased?

We boast a great deal about our American hustle. A Frenchman has very aptly described hustle as doing a thing badly while making a fuss over it. At any rate, they do most things better in France and with less noise about it.

And one Frenchman suggests the story of another Frenchman who while in New York visited a business friend in his office downtown. The New Yorker was glad to see the Frenchman and invited him to take dinner at his home. After the office was closed they started up town. The New Yorker rushed his friend into a subway local; at the Grand Central station he rushed him out and into an express; at 72nd St. he rushed him out of the express into another local. When they arrived at the house they sat around and chatted for half an hour until dinner was served. After dinner they sat and smoked and talked. Then the Frenchman asked the question. "Why did we have to take the train to get here?" His host replied, "Well, you see, we saved three minutes." The Frenchman questioned again, "And, what are we going to do with them?" The American's further reply is not recorded.

The American people are the victims of hustle even when they are off duty. They hustle even when they are pleasuring. Baseball with the thermometer at 90 in the shade, and fox-trotting all night are fair examples.

When it comes to the real art of living, of getting the greatest happiness, contentment and well-being out of life to the development, cultivation and satisfaction of both mind and body, the Teutonic and the so-called Anglo-Saxon peoples have much to learn from the Latins.

20th Century Civilization

May 13, 1915

The horrors of the European war have steadily mounted up until they have reached the tragic climax of the destruction of the Lusitania. A great merchant ship, filled with non-combatants, carrying women and children, sent to the bottom without a moment's warning. No deed ever committed by Barbary Pirates could exceed this act of inhuman brutality.

It is useless for the German Government to seek to justify itself. It is a principle of international law, so well known as never to be questioned, that a merchant vessel, even when carrying contraband of war, cannot be destroyed without notice and without regard for the safety of crew and passengers.

A merchant vessel captured by the enemy is a legal prize, and may be taken into a port controlled by the enemy. If the enemy finds this impracticable or inconvenient, he may destroy the vessel, after making arrangements for the safety of crew and passengers; but there is nothing in the usages of war to justify the instant sinking of such a ship.

There is no extenuation, much less justification, in the fact that warning was given; in fact, warning makes the deed appear more atrocious because it shows that it was premeditated and afterwards executed with full knowledge of what was being done. It is as though a black hand should send out a letter of warning and afterwards step out from a dark corner and stab his victim in the back.

When two armed ships meet and engage in battle, if one of them is destroyed it is a matter of glory for the other; these are the conditions of a fair fight; this cannot be said of the sinking of the Lusitania. Because Germany has not the sea power necessary to blockade an enemy's ports and capture his merchant vessels, she is not justified in using methods of assassination.

What is the truth that rises naked from out all the savagery and brutality of this war? It is the fact that twentieth century civilization, the so-called white man's civilization, is nothing more than a thin veneer, and underneath this thin veneer is the same cruel barbarism that Caesar found two thousand years ago.

The U.S. and Germany

May 13, 1915

The sinking of the Lusitania brings about a crisis such as the United States Government has not faced since the first shot was fired on Fort Sumpter, not excepting the blowing up of the Maine.

The destruction of the Maine in the harbor of Havana precipitated the Spanish-American war; but the thought of going to war with Spain never for a moment caused this country any degree of uneasiness; the war with Spain was little more than practice for the army, experience for the militia and a holiday for the Rough Riders. On the other hand, the barest possibility of the United States becoming involved in the present world conflagration is enough to make the most militaristic of fire eaters pause and take thought.

Feeling is tense, but the country is not hysterical, it is patiently waiting to see what the President will say. The President in his speech in Philadelphia last Monday night sounded the note on which his policy will be based; he will undoubtedly strive to maintain peace at any price. This course will be gratifying to a great many timid souls, but to many others, who do not in the least desire war, it will be disappointing and distasteful.

There are many whose desire and prayer are that there be no war, yet they do not wish to see the nation take a stand that is cowardly and ignoble. There are many who feel that the United States should take no active part in this war, but still that there rests upon this Government a certain moral obligation to make strong and open protest against what is brutal and inhuman beyond the general demands of warfare.

That there is some such moral obligation it is difficult to deny. We cannot completely throw off this obligation by saying that the affairs of England or France or Russia are no concern of ours. To pass along the street and see a bully beating an old woman imposes the moral duty to interfere. We cannot shirk that duty by saying that the old woman is not our mother or our aunt or our grandmother.

Yet, what are we going to do about it? In these days of "scraps of paper," broken treaties and neutrality violations, words of protest seem nothing more than an idle waste of time and effort. Still, it appears, there is no action that we can take. If we should go so far as to declare war against Germany, how could we carry the declaration into effect? It would be impossible to attack her with our navy; if such a thing were possible, the British navy would have done it long ago. The effect of an army that we could add to the allied forces on the western battle front would be absolutely infinitesimal. Perhaps the only practical thing we could do would be to join in the allied attack on the Dardanelles.

But there is another element in the problem. If our so-called German-American citizens have been so obstreperous and vindictive because this Government has not openly sided with Germany in the present struggle, what would be their attitude, what would be their course of action if this country were actually at war with their beloved Fatherland? There are said to be some 20,000,000 of them in the United States, and under present conditions they do constitute a problem. A problem more serious than the Negro problem.

And it is ever to the credit of the Negro that a problem of this kind—a problem of disloyalty and treason—he has never created.

The Diplomatic Muddle

February 24, 1916

Our State Department is certainly in a diplomatic muddle. The Lusitania question was reaching some sort of a settlement; although there is little doubt that the note the Administration was about to accept from Germany would have been a distinct disappointment to the country. For days there was delay during which the attempt was being made to prepare the country for a backdrop from "strict accountability." Then came Root's great speech, which made the acceptance of Germany's note impossible. If Root's speech had been made a day later it is probable that the Lusitania incident would have been closed.

The Administration, in search for an excuse for rejecting the German note, seized upon an order issued some days previously by the Imperial Government to the effect that German submarines would sink all armed merchantmen of the allies after March 1. Our government set up that it could not go into a settlement of the Lusitania case unless Germany withdrew or modified its order to sink armed merchant vessels of the enemy. But this stand has served to increase the Administration's embarrassment; for, previous to the new German submarine order, our State Department addressed a note to the entente allies to the end of having merchant vessels disarmed and indicating that the United States would change its attitude regarding such ships carrying armament and hold them as auxiliary vessels of war.

Now, strange as it may seem, the very reason given by the Administration for rejecting Germany's final note on the Lusitania Incident; that is, the new German submarine order holding armed merchantmen as auxiliary vessels of war is in exact harmony with our State Department's note to the entente allies on the same subject. In a word, we are disagreeing with Germany for backing up something which we ourselves proposed.

The country knows that the Department of State and no Administration has had such crises to meet since Lincoln was president; nevertheless, the country cannot overlook the mistakes which are being made.

Russian Democracy and the Jews

March 22, 1917

One of the first effects in this city of the news of the Russian revolution was the rejoicing of the Jews on the East Side. They almost entirely suspended business, and spent the day congratulating each other and expressing their joy to the extent of dancing in the streets. If anyone has a reason to be jubilant over recent events in Russia, it is the Jewish people; because they are the ones who have suffered most under the old regime. And it is the American Negro who can best appreciate the reason for this joy, because we are the only other people who have a deep understanding of what the Jews in Russia have suffered. And the conditions which give us this deep understanding enable us not only to estimate the present joy, but also to foresee the future disappointments.

For a great part of the world the word "democracy" is a fetish. But the American Negro has been disillusioned. He knows from experience that a despised people can be deprived of their rights, oppressed and down trodden in a democracy just as effectually as under the worst form of autocracy.

The Jews have much to rejoice over, but if they believe that the change of government in Russia is going to mean an immediate end of all their troubles as a race in that country, they are doomed to disappointment. The Russian Government will hardly go farther for the Jews than the United States Government will hardly go farther for the Negroes. In this country the organic law of the land was amended and changed so as to confer on the Negro all the rights of American citizenship; and ever since that time, courts and legislature and congresses and even presidents have winked at and connived at those rights being taken away.

The greatest thing that the American Negro gained as a result of the Civil War and the amendments to the Constitution was the right to contend for his rights. And that is the position in which he now finds himself, merely endowed with the right to claim the rights of American citizenship and to fight for them. If he goes to sleep on what is written for him in the Constitution, he will wake up some day to find himself a virtual serf or truer still, he will never wake up.

In our opinion, the case of the Russian Jews will be similar. The government will probably confer on them the full rights of citizenship, but so long as they continue as a separate race against whom there is general prejudice, they will find that the Russian people will take every opportunity to deprive them of those rights and the Russian Government will look on while it is done.

We feel that the Jews in Russia will now get the right to fight for their rights, and that it will be a hard stubborn fight, a fight from which the American Negro may learn a great deal.

As Others See Us

April 26, 1917

Elsewhere we reproduce from the Philadelphia "Public Ledger" a despatch from Berlin which quotes Dr. Ludwig Haas, a prominent member of the German Reichstag, as making some very plain statements of his opinion about the United States and the Administration. He sarcastically refers to the wish of the United States to see democracy established in Germany and to the lynching and oppression of Negroes within the borders of the United States.

Unfortunately the United States cannot answer him back. Unfortunately the United States is in the position of preaching one thing and practicing another. How long will it be before the great American Democracy does away with this double standard? How long will it be before the United States makes itself invulnerable to such attacks as the one hurled by Dr. Haas?

As Others See Us

August 23, 1919

The following paragraph from an editorial in the Philadelphia Public Ledger is significant:

There is no way of knowing what is said in Russia or India or Germany or Mexico of the recent outbreaks in this country. But it is easy to imagine that similar reports from abroad would get a lot of complacent Americans to talking of "peoples unfit for self-government." We should have jingoes bellowing from the housetops for the fleet and for armies of invasion.

What does America think that other nations ought to think about her after the mobbing of Negroes in the streets of Washington and Chicago? Does she think that the opinion which she has of Bolshevik Russia has any justification for being worse than the opinion which Bolshevik Russia has of her? In truth, America's opinion in the matter should be influenced by the fact that nobody in this country can be quite sure of what is transpiring in Russia, while every American citizen knows what took place in Washington and Chicago.

Moreover, if the stories which we hear about mob violence in Russia are true, it is also true that the violence is being directed against those who are considered to be conspiring or acting against the authority of the existing government; but in Washington and Chicago the mobs beat and killed loyal and unoffending American citizens.

We can make a pretty fair guess as to what is being said in Russia and India and Germany of the recent outbreaks in this country; and as for Mexico and all the rest of Latin-America, we know definitely what is being said.

Several years ago we gave in this column an explanation as to why Latin-America dislikes the United States. Americans generally and most of the officials at Washington seem to be puzzled by the fact that in spite of the Monroe Doctrine which is supposed to be the great safeguard of the independence of the Latin-American republics, and in spite of other demonstrations of patronizing friendship on the part of the country, America fails to be moved to any display of genuine gratitude, and even shows the opposite feeling whenever it is not unsafe to do so.

This attitude of Latin-America is based almost entirely on the way in which the Negro is treated in the United States. Latin-Americans realize that they are not white people in the North American sense, and many of them who may not have realized it have had the realization forced upon them on a visit to this country. Thousands of wealthy and cultured Latin-Americans have visited the United States and have been treated like colored people. And not only this, but the American has carried his prejudices with him into Latin-American countries.

The distrust and the dislike which the people of Mexico and the rest of Latin-America have for the United States will be strengthened by the occurrences at Washington and Chicago; and we know quite definitely what they are saying about those outbreaks.

The Peace Treaty

July 5, 1919

The peace treaty has been signed; and so the long war is a peace settlement that would be some guarantee of permanent peace; the treaty that has just been signed is the same as the treaties technically closed for a while at least. But it is not the treaty that by which wars have been settled in the past, except that in some respects it is worse.

In this settlement, the main source of all the international trouble between the great nations has not been touched, and that is the African question. There stands Africa, as she was before, exploited, robbed and oppressed; and just as surely as she is treated unjustly will she come up again to confuse and confound the nations.

The most outstanding failure of the whole peace conference is the individual failure of Woodrow Wilson. It was he who more than any other single influence brought the world to hope for and expect a new order of things. It was he who by speech and pen spread the doctrine of the new democracy and humanity, and scarcely one of the things which he preached so eloquently has been included in the terms of peace.

To read the speeches of President Wilson, and especially his Fourteen Points, and then consider what has been the outcome of the conference at Paris is almost to lose hope in anything like a better day.

President Wilson had a great opportunity. He failed. Just why, in our opinion, he failed we shall state at a later time.

Failure of the Peace Treaty

November 29, 1919

The Senate failed to give its consent to the Peace Treaty. We have no regrets to express. When the terms of the treaty were first made public we gave our opinion on it. From the general view we could not see that it gave any promise of stopping war; and from the particular view we could not see any benefits that would come from it to the darker peoples of the world.

The truth is, the treaty was not framed to meet and embrace the spirit that was in the hearts of the peoples of the world at the end of the war. It was a very little improvement on treaties that have been made all through the ages; in some respect it was worse than many.

Even so, Mr. Wilson might have been able to force it through if he had used a small bit of the political sagacity with which he used to be credited. But the methods he used for bringing about what was called a universal measure were the most narrow and partisan imaginable.

It is likely that the President will again submit the treaty in December, but it is unlikely that it will have any better fate unless the Administration accepts the reservations in whole or in part which were passed by the Senate.

The result is a severe blow to Mr. Wilson's pride. He had put himself before Europe as the voice of America. The fact is, the American people are and have all along been apathetic about the whole business. Everything that has happened since the war has been a disillusionment of the high hopes with which they fought, and they place the League of Nations together with the other illusions.

The Irish Question Again to the Front

December 27, 1919

The attempt on the life of Lord French has brought the eternal Irish question again to a climax of the most dramatic intensity. This question simply will not [die]. The Irish patriots simply will not let the conscience of England and of the world go to sleep on their question. We say the conscience of the world, because Ireland has become a world question.

The Irish question is a test before the world of the sincerity of the British Government. How much of it did England mean when she proclaimed during the war that she was fighting so that the smaller peoples might have self determination? How much did any of the nations mean? Of course, they didn't mean for it to apply to themselves at all. England did not mean it for Ireland or for Egypt or for India; France did not mean it for her colonial possessions; the United States did not mean it for her colonial possessions or even for her millions of colored citizens within the States. All of these powers meant that the right of self determination was to be applied only to the smaller peoples who were under German domination. England, France and Italy meant that the smaller peoples under German domination should be freed, and not for the sake of freedom, but for the specific purpose of creating a number of little buffer states that would stand between Entente Allies and German power.

And yet, even though everybody with any sense has long since known that the powers when they talked about self determination during the war were merely talking buncombe, it is just as well to have the truth of the matter demonstrated. That is exactly what is being done by the Irish question.

239

The British Parliament has passed the Irish Home Rule bill. This bill provides for sectional legislatures for Ireland; that is two legislatures, one in the North for Prostestant Ireland, ar.d one in the South for Catholic Ireland; the two legislatures to be linked up by a council, and to be eventually merged by their own action. The powers of the Irish legislatures include everything except the right to tax on incomes and excess profits, except the control of the high courts, and except the control of the army and navy. Except for these things, Ireland will have home rule. Sounds a little like a joke, doesn't it?

It is not likely that the Irish patriots will accept anything short of an independent government with all their rights belonging thereto. At any rate, the Irish are to be admired for the way in which they have kept up the fight for what they believe to be their just rights; they have not allowed England to go to sleep on the question, and England will have to settle it some day or another, and settle it right. There is a lesson for the Negro in the United States.

Disarmament

July 9, 1921

In spite of the fact that England and Japan have both intimated strongly their willingness to enter into a conference to consider disarmament, the United States, which according to all the circumstances ought to be the leader in such a movement is hanging back. But what it is that actually keeps the United States from taking the lead in this matter has not yet been made known.

The arguments thus far which have been publicly advanced against it would not convince any person of ordinary common sense. There are those who are warning that the United States cannot afford to disarm while other nations remain armed. Nobody of whom we have heard, either in this country or England or Japan, has ever proposed such absurd action.

The proposal is that the United States call a conference of England and Japan and herself to consider the imitation of armaments. There, of course, is no reason why all the other military nations should not be included in this conference. If they propose that such a conference should be held and the limitation of armaments be fixed proportionately, neither the United States nor any other nation would be placed at any disadvantage beyond which it now is.

Such a course would not only lessen the danger of war because if the nations were unarmed they would be less likely to jump into a scrap; but it would go further than any other step which could be taken now to readjust and ameliorate the economic condition of the world.

General Jan Smuts, Premier of the Union of South Africa, a man who has proved himself to be a statesman of the broadest vision and highest ideals, made a profound impression before the Imperial Conference recently held in London when he spoke on this question. General Smuts declared that if England persists in trying to stagger along under the load of military and naval armaments, she is doomed. There may be reasons why the United States should not take what is not only the spiritual, but the common sense leadership in this matter, but those reasons have not yet been made known.

The War-Making Power

July 9, 1921

The American Federation of Labor has had up for discussion a resolution which, if adopted, will be revolutionary in its effects. The resolution contemplates withdrawing from Congress the power to declare war and placing it in the hands of the people by constitutional amendment.

The proposed resolution provides that a declaration of war must have the approval of the majority of the voters of the country, and that all those voting in favor of the declaration of war must be compelled to take up the active prosecution of the same before those voted against the declaration.

This modification of the proposed resolution makes doubtful whether or not the Federation is in earnest or not, because it is highly improbable that any amendment to the Constitution containing such a proviso could be adopted. The fundamental policy of this country is government by a majority, so if the majority of the people voted for war the minority would, according to that policy, become a part of the majority, that is, so far as practical results go.

But the main idea of the resolution is a good one and might have a chance of being put through. It is likely that it would stand as good a chance of adoption as prohibition. Furthermore, it is in accord with common sense. One of the tragedies of history has always been that of peoples and nations being forced into wars concerning which they had to fight and pay for.

There is little doubt if the making of wars were taken out of the hands of Government and placed in the hands of the people very few wars would be declared, and practically none would be fought.

Bernard Shaw on the United States

August 27, 1921

Some months ago we had the pleasure of reprinting in these columns a letter received from Bernard Shaw, the great English dramatist. It was a letter in which he expressed his opinion about lynching and lynchers. It was, of course, in the Shawian vein.

There is now going the rounds of the press another letter by Mr. Shaw. This letter is in reply to one written him by Mr. Oswald Garrison Villard. There have often been rumors that Mr. Shaw intended to make a visit to the United States. These rumors took on such definite sound within the last few weeks that Mr. Villard wrote Mr. Shaw as follows:

> My Dear Mr. Shaw: I understand a number of friends are writing to you and urging you to come to the United States. May I say how gratified we of the Nation would be should you come to us?
> Yours sincerely,
> Oswald Garrison Villard,
> Editor

In reply to Mr. Villard's letter, Mr. Shaw wrote as follows:

> Dear Mr. Villard: This conspiracy has been going on for years. I have no intention of either going to prison with Debs or taking my wife to Texas, where the Ku Klux Klan snatches white women out of hotel verandas and tars and feathers them. If I were dependent on martyrdom for a reputation, which happily I am not, I could go to Ireland. It is a less dangerous place, but then the voyage is shorter and much cheaper.
>
> You are right in your impression that a number of persons are urging me to come to the United States. But why on earth do you call them my friends? G. Bernard Shaw.

This letter of Mr. Shaw's is what we might call "rich." We hope it will go all over the country, for it carries a sting that is wholesome, a sting which will be felt by even the most toughskinned, red-necked mob leader and lyncher in the country.

Shaw has an art which it would be a blessing if more writers, specially colored writers, in this country had, and that is the art of beating down with ridicule the thing which is not at all affected by any reason or argument or justice or right. We know of no writer, white or black, in the United States, with the possible exception of H. L. Mencken, who comes anywhere near Shaw in wielding this powerful weapon, for it is more a weapon than an art. In this country where hundreds of colored and white writers, too,

242

rave against the South, H. L. Mencken gets under the skin by ridicule. And so if there were more writers who instead of railing against the unrighteousness of lynching and other evidences of race hatred, would hold up to view the lyncher as he really is, a blood-thirsty degenerate criminal, there would be fewer men to make any defense whatsoever of what is now in some sections regarded as a pastime.

The last paragraph of Mr. Shaw's letter bites deeper than anything else. He says to Mr. Villard: "You are right in your impression that a number of persons are urging me to come to the United States. But why on earth do you call them my friends?" This is too good to be wasted. We hope every southern newspaper will see it.

Gandhi a Prisoner

March 25, 1922

The British Government in India has finally come to grips with non-cooperationists by arresting, trying and convicting Gandhi, the leader of the movement. Gandhi was arrested on charges of sedition. The Standard Dictionary defines "sedition" as follows:

> language or conduct directed against public order and the tranquility of the state; disorder or commotion in a state, not reaching the point of insurrection; also the stirring up of such disorder, tending toward treason, but lacking an overt act.

Gandhi advocated non-cooperation with the government. No doubt the preaching of such a doctrine practically falls under sedition. Gandhi has been sentenced to six years in prison without labor. Through the whole trial he maintained the role which his followers have ascribed to him, that of a prophet and saint. He did not try to exculpate himself. He declared that he was not sorry for what he had done and that if he were released he would continue to do the same things. He has called upon his followers to abstain from violence but to continue to carry out the program of non-cooperation which he has laid down.

It remains to be seen what the effect of Gandhi's arrest will be upon the movement launched by him. The indications are that the movement will be strengthened, that Gandhi will be more of a power in prison than out. But what should interest observers more than anything else is what will be the final result. It will be of absorbing interest to know whether the means and methods advocated by Gandhi can be as effective as the methods of violence used by the Irish. If they are, it will mean a new hope for independence and self-determination on the part of those peoples and groups who are prohibited the possession of the implements of force. If non-cooperation brings the British to their knees in Africa, nor is there any reason why it should not bring the white man to his knees in the South.

Diplomatic Preparedness

April 22, 1922

At the Disarmament Conference in Washington the best all round prepared delegation was the Japanese and that preparation consisted largely in its linguistic abilities. The diplomatic game is largely one of the ability to talk with and to understand not only all that is said but all that is meant. In this the Japanese were preeminent. In addition to their own language they spoke and understood English, French, Italian and Chinese. This undoubtedly had much to do with Japan's great diplomatic successes at the Conference.

Now comes word that the Russians are the best prepared delegates linguistically at the Genoa Conference. George Tchitcherin, the head of the delegation, speaks three languages fluently. Two other members of the delegation are said to speak English fluently. It is admitted that this gives the Russians an immense advantage over their colleagues in committees and on the Conference floor, as the latter are compelled to rely on interpreters. It will be interesting to watch and see if Russia can score at Genoa a similar diplomatic success to the one which Japan scored at Washington.

A Remarkable Little Book

February 10, 1923

For some time we have been planning to take up where we left off our talk about books. We now take up the subject again and consider a book which has just been published in London. It is entitled, *The Black Man's Place in South Africa*. Its author is Peter Nielsen. Mr. Nielsen is a white man who has lived in South Africa and occupied official positions there [for] thirty years.

In his brief preface Mr. Nielsen states that he has "studied the ways and thoughts of the natives of Africa on the spot, not through interpreters, but at first hand, through the medium of their own speech which I profess to know as well as the natives themselves."

The book is not a book of descriptions either of the country or of the customs of the natives. It is rather a discussion first of the innate qualities and capabilities of the Negroes of South Africa and secondly, of their present and future civil and social status in that country.

Mr. Nielsen opens his little book—the volume comprises only one hundred and fifty pages—by answering the question, "Is the African native equal to the European in mental and moral capacity, or is he not?" which he declares to be the crux of the whole situation. He goes about answering this question in a logical and scientific manner. First he takes up some of the well known physical comparisons such as prognatism, orthognatism, hairiness of body and lack of hairiness, odors, thickness and capacities of skulls, etc. Mr. Nielsen says conclusively that these differences, many of which are obvious, do not indicate any inferiority on the part of the Negro; in fact, many of them would indicate the opposite.

For example, much ado has been made about the statistics on cranial capacity but not much has been said about the fact that the cranial capacity of the Esquimaux is greater than that of most of the civilized peoples of Europe. We do not need to be told that so far the Esquimaux have done nothing to startle the world in any kind of mental achievement.

Mr. Nielsen next takes up a comparison of the mind of the African native with that of the white man. After considering all of the arguments pro and con, he arrives at the very proper conclusion that the differences are not so important as they might appear. He makes the rather enlightening statement that all men think in the same way but not always the same things.

The author says, "The difference between the mind of the philosopher and the ploughboy is one not of kind, not even of degree, but of content. The things that occupy the mind of the peasant farmer are not the same that fill the mind of the university don, but if the respective environments of the two types had been reversed the professor might have thought about manure and the farmer about metaphysics."

In another paragraph Mr. Nielsen makes the same statement in a still more striking manner. He says, "In his thinking about things he knows the black man comes to the same conclusion as the white man when he thinks about the same things." And he goes on to say that the reason why the native of South Africa does not think about electricity and differential calculus is because he does not know about those things, but if he did know about them and was called upon to think about them, he would do so in the same way that the white man does.

Mr. Nielsen in his little book points out that the average native in South Africa is called upon in meeting and overcoming the conditions of his environment, to display as much mental ingenuity and ability as the average workman in an industrial city in Europe.

The author completely disposes of the "Nordic" theory lately revived and made popular in this country by Madison Grant and Lothrop Stoddard. The Nordic theory, in a word, is that early in the beginning an inherently superior race of blond Europeans left their lairs in the north from time to time to harass and conquer essentially inferior peoples in the south. They mixed with these inferior peoples of the south and thereby succeeded in rearing those mighty civilizations which flourished around the borders of the Mediterranean Sea in past ages. This Nordic theory further claims that those mighty civilizations waned and declined when the "blue" blood of blonde invaders became absorbed and lost in the inferior streams.

Mr. Nielsen very aptly says that apart from any satisfactory evidence in history to back this theory, it is unsatisfactory in that it does not explain why these super-blonde men failed to establish within their own original habitats any of the great cultures which they are supposed to have imposed upon inferior peoples far to the south. This writer asked the question in a book which he published some ten years ago, if civilization originated with what we now call white men, why was not its first seat in the German forests rather than up the valley of the Nile?

Altogether, Mr. Nielsen has written a book in which he produces convincing argument of the physical, mental and moral equality of the South African natives compared with the whites. He ends his little book with a pessimistic note, however. He does not see how the two races can live together in South Africa unless the result be amalgamation. This he believes at all costs should be averted. His plan is for physical segregation, that is, parts of South Africa to be given over to the natives and other parts to the whites. He sees no other way out. Of course, there is another way. The time may not be very far off when the South African natives themselves will dictate the method of the solution.

Three | New York Age Literary Editorials

13 Literature and Poetry

We have often heard the prophecy that we as a race are to furnish the great American poets, musicians and artists of the future. There is every reason for this prophecy to come true. . . .

James Weldon Johnson, "A Poetry Corner"
(January 7, 1915)

Johnson told his readers that "although there is no single recipe to be followed for making a race great, there is a single standard by which the greatness of a race can be measured. The greatness of a race may be measured by the literature it has produced."[1]

The common denominator in thinking about African-Americans had been primarily shown in stereotypes, which, for the most part, had been constructed through the literary process. Johnson believed that just as these stereotypes were shaped, propagated, and bolstered by the literary process they could be smashed as well by similar means. This challenge, he extolled, should be met by a group of writers reared by the race. As precursor, participant, and historian of the Harlem Renaissance, James Weldon Johnson had as much to do with the growth and recognition of this new literary movement as anyone.[2] And he used his column to further that movement with his interpretations of music, poetry, and literature. A "Poetry Corner" was introduced in his column where he published new poets and reviewed poetry in general. He also published some important writings during this period. In 1922, Johnson brought together some of the works of the outstanding contemporary black writers for his volume *The Book of American Negro Poetry*. This work attracted attention to the cultural and literary value of black writers in American life.

Anthology of Magazine Verse
and Other Books

January 7, 1915

Mr. William Stanley Braithewaite has issued the "Anthology of Magazine Verse for 1914." The book contains the full text of the seventy-seven poems which Mr. Braithewaite judges to be the best of all those published in the leading American periodicals during 1914. Mr. Braithewaite's stamp of approval on the poems included in the "Anthology" will be accepted by editors, critics and lovers of poetry in both this country and England, because his word is authoritative.

Those who may be interested in the article, "A Poetry Corner," cannot do better than secure a copy of this book. From it can be gained a clear idea of the trend and form of contemporary poetry, a knowledge of what the poets of to-day are thinking and writing about and the manner in which they are doing it.

But, we started out to say that not one person in a thousand who sees Mr. Braithewaite's name and who knows that he is recognized here and abroad as the highest critical authoritative on poetry in the United States, knows that he is a colored man. We should be ashamed to make a guess at the proportion of Negroes that never heard his name.

This brings us to consider one of the most discouraging phases of our condition—this applies to the intelligent Negroes—and that is the almost absolute indifference to books and makers of books. Not only to books in general, but books in particular.

There are white people writing books to prove that the Negro is naturally an inferior and that he should not be allowed even to aspire to equal citizenship in this country. And we regret to say that to a large number of people they do prove it. There are other white people and men of our own race who are writing books in the Negro's defense. And, yet, the mass of even intelligent colored people do not know what is being said against them or for them. The great books that have been written by Dr. Washington, Dr. Du Bois, Professor Kelly Miller, Charles W. Chestnutt and others should have been bought and read by not less than 250,000 Negroes, perhaps by 500,000. If an intelligent foreigner, familiar with our conditions, in this country, was told that not 50,000 Negroes (of course, this figure is too large), out of the 10,000,000 had bought these books he would be apt to say that a race which showed such a lack of interest in its own welfare did not deserve any better treatment than it received.

A short time ago the writer met a colored man of intelligence and sufficient means who had delayed for two years reading a book by a Negro author, a book that he was anxious to read, because he had not yet found anyone who could lend it to him.

How many who read this article have read any of the following books on the race question lately published:

Out of the House of Bondage	By Kelly Miller
A Study of Boston Negroes	By John Daniels
Race Orthodoxy in the South	By Thomas P. Bailey
In Black and White	By L. H. Hammond
Democracy and Race Friction	By John M. Macklin.

There is another book which ought to be in the possession of every colored professional and business man and woman in the country; it is the "Negro Year Book 1914–1915" edited by Mr. Monroe N. Work of Tuskegee.

A Poetry Corner

January 7, 1915

The charge is sometimes made that nobody reads poetry now, but everybody writes it. This a bright epigram, but, as with all epigrams, it contains only a flash of truth.

It is true that never in the history of literature has there been so large and general an output of poetry as there is now, nor has the average of the general output ever before been so high. Perhaps, there are no poets of the first magnitude writing—we must leave that judgment to posterity—but the great mass of verse being printed in books and periodicals is far above mediocrity.

We have often heard the prophecy that we as a race are to furnish the great American poets, musicians and artists of the future. There is every reason for this prophecy to come true; we are more richly endowed for such a work than the white race. We have more heart, more soul; we are more responsive to emotional vibrations; we have a larger share of the gifts of laughter, music and song; in a word, we are less material and we are, by nature, more artistic than white people.

But although poets are born, they have to be made afterwards. That is, to write acceptable poetry, one needs to be born with a discriminating sense of beauty and rhythm, and with a brain capable of conceiving interesting, if not original, thoughts and ideas. This much means having the necessary tools; but a working use of the tools must be acquired, the trade must be studied and learned.

Now suppose some of us have these natural tools for making poetry; what is the first step to be considered in learning to use them? The first step to be considered is the material upon which we are to work. That material is the English language. The English language is the material which is to be moulded and chiseled and polished into thought forms of beauty. Here is where workmanship counts, and good workmanship is all important. You may have the most divinely inspired thoughts, but if you do not know the English language you cannot write poetry—at least English poetry.

Learning to use the English language to the extent of making it the expression of poetry is no light task. You must not only have a large vocabulary and know the ordinary meanings of words, but you must know their different degrees of force and weight and their different shades of color and tone. Moreover, you must learn to sense that subtler meaning which words in certain combinations have, a meaning which is beyond definition.

All of this, perhaps, sounds pedantic, but there are practical means of acquiring this necessary knowledge. Two books are indispensable, an unabridged dictionary and a book of synonyms. (Fernald's Synonyms is best for the beginner, as it gives the correct usage for prepositions.)

After the above, it seems almost needless to say that the trade mark of mediocre poets is the constant use of worn out phrases and rhymes. No writer can expect to attract attention by coupling "night in June" with "silvery moon," or "stars above" with "lady love," and perhaps, making it worse by adding "turtle dove."

But no one who has poetic talent should continue to mar his work by such patent faults. By the study and practice indicated above you can succeed in writing acceptable poetry; that is, if you are born a poet. And, conversely, even if you are born a poet you can never give yourself adequate expression until you master the language.

That there is a great deal of poetic talent in the Negro race is shown by the mail which comes to the office of "The Age." Most of the verses sent in are extremely crude, but we feel that there is enough talent manifested to warrant encouragement.

"The Age" will therefore establish a "Poetry Corner" for those who are ambitious to write poetry. We hope gradually to raise the standard of acceptance until to be published in the "Poetry Corner" will carry some distinction. If, through this means, only one, out of the many who will make the attempt, should be encouraged and aided toward reaching a high degree of excellence the space would be far more than paid for.

Manuscripts should be plainly written or typewritten on one side of the paper, and addressed to the editor of this column. Unpublished poems will not be returned, so contributors should keep copies of their work.

Shakespeare

April 20, 1915

Sunday, April the twenty-third, will be the three hundredth anniversary of the death of Shakespeare. Notwithstanding the terrible period through which the world is now passing, English speaking people everywhere will celebrate the event, and every civilized nation will be cognizant of it.

In any catalog of human greatness Shakespeare and his work stand at the top. To-day, three hundred years after his death, his fame is greater than it ever was, and is constantly increasing. Nor is it confined to his own land and tongue; the Germans claim that they understand and appreciate him better than the English do.

The great poet is for all time; he lives while other great names become but memories. Take the great trinity in war, Alexander, Caesar and Napoleon, and see how they shrink into littleness before the great trinity in poetry, Homer, Dante and Shakespeare. Above the great soldier, the great statesman, the great scholar or the great inventor, the great poet still stands typifying the highest achievement possible to the human intellect.

So great is Shakespeare that he excites as much wonder as admiration. We find it impossible to believe that he knew how well he wrote. The marvel has led some people to doubt that he wrote at all. These people hold that what we call Shakespeare must have been written by some learned man, such as Lord Bacon, and not by an actor named Shakespeare who "had small Latin and less Greek." They base their claim upon the fact that in Bacon's time it was beneath the dignity of a gentleman to be known as a playwright; so Bacon wrote the plays in Shakespeare's name. But in Bacon's time it was a great honor to be a poet; and it is plain that the same hand which wrote the Shakespeare plays also wrote the Shakespeare sonnets and poems. Then why did not Bacon put his name to the sonnets and poems? The whole theory is absurd.

What is the secret of Shakespeare's greatness? It is nothing less than sheer magic. He is the great magician with words. He blends words and ideas in such wonderful music that he plays upon every emotion of the human heart, from the tenderest to the fiercest.

Take this picture of moonlight:

> How sweet the moonlight sleeps upon this bask!
> Here will we sit and let the sounds of music
> Creep in our ears; soft stillness and the night
> Become the touches of sweet harmony.
> Sit, Jessica. Look how the floor of heaven
> Is thick inlaid with patines of bright gold;
> There's not the smallest orb which thou behold'st

But in his motion like an angel sings,
Still quiring to the young-eyed cherubims;
Such harmony is in immortal souls;
But whilst this muddy vesture of decay
Doth grossly close it in, we cannot hear it.

Or take this cry of remorse from "Macbeth":

Can'st thou not minister to a mind diseased;
Pluck from the memory of a rooted sorrow;
Raze out the written troubles of the brain;
And, with some sweet oblivious antidote,
Cleanse the stuff'd bosom of that perilous stuff,
Which weighs upon the heart?

Note the wonderful imagery in these two brief lines from "Romeo and Juliet," describing the breaking of day:

Night's candles are burnt out, and jocund day
Stands tiptoe on the misty mountain tops.

Listen to the marital trumpeting in the following lines from "Henry V":

O for a Muse of fire, that would ascend
The brightest heaven of invention,
A kingdom for a stage, Prince to act,
And monarchs to behold the swelling scene!
Then should the warlike Harry, like himself,
Assume the port of Mars and at his heels,
Leash'd in like hounds, should famine, sword and fire
Crouch for employment.

Such passages could be multiplied indefinitely, each rivalling the others in beauty, but these are sufficient for the purpose. In what lies the enchantment in these passages? Is it in what they teach or in what they preach? No, it is in their bewitching music. Music that charms the mind and the senses.

One explanation of Shakespeare's wizardy in the use of words is that he wrote when the language was new, when he could take words and use them in any sense he saw fit. There is much in this explanation. Any manner in which Shakespeare used a word seems natural to us, even if it does sound quaint. Take for example the last word, "employment" in the quotation above from "Henry V." But now the language is set and the words are old; for a modern writer to use it arbitrarily would simply be to brand himself as eccentric.

255

Now, everybody knows about Shakespeare; but how many know him, how many read him? No English speaking person can rightfully claim to be cultured who is not in some degree familiar with Shakespeare. But aside from the question of culture, the immense delight and pleasure which his works afford should be an inducement to everyone to read them. He is the one English poet who never grows old. The same play, the same poem, the same passage may be read over time after time, and it will never fail to reveal new beauties.

Let those who do not know Shakespeare begin on this three hundredth anniversary of his death, and make the reading of his works a habit. You will be more than repaid.

About Poetry and Poetry Makers

December 16, 1915

We have not lost our interest in poets or poetry because the "Poetry Corner" has been filled only at intervals during the past month or so. In fact, we are more feverishly on the outlook for acceptable verse than we were when the "Corner" was first established. Each time we pick up a letter addressed to the Editor of the "Poetry Corner" our heart flutters with delightful anticipation; but sad to say, it is seldom that we experience realization.

The death of Dr. Washington brought us a flood of poetic contributions but, excepting a very few, they were below mediocrity. Many of the contributors appeared to be in the class with those versifiers who write the "in memoriams" which traditionally end with some trite line as this:

> May our loved one sweetly rest
> Peacefully on Jesus's breast.

We do not say this for the purpose of ridicule, but to emphasize again the fact that lines chopped off in regular and rhymed, do not necessarily constitute poetry. We take the time and space to say something more on this subject because we believe there is a great deal of poetic talent in the race; talent which if encouraged and developed will some day give to America its greatest poets. It was for the purpose of helping to develop this talent that "The Poetry Corner" in "The Age" was started; but this can be done only by demanding that those verses which are published shall reach or surpass a certain standard of excellence.

Poetic talent is a gift, but poetic talent alone will not enable any one to write acceptable poetry; study is necessary. A poet needs to learn his trade, to get the mastery of his tools, just the same as an artist or sculptor or a musician. It is necessary for him to obtain, at least, a fair mastery over the language in which he writes. He must know words and what they mean and how they are used. He must also know something about the mechanism of verse; that is, he must know something about rhythm and metre and tone, color and rhyme.

Among those who send in contributions to "The Poetry Corner" there are many who have only a shallow knowledge of the English language and no knowledge at all of the mechanism of verse, yet who show that they possess some degree of poetic talent. There are others who show a fair knowledge of the language, but who know only a little of the mechanism of verse. We have before us a contribution written with some degree of thought and skill; but the author hopelessly marred his effort by falling into the common error of mistaking assonance for rhyme; for example, he makes "gone" rhyme with "own, "fact" with "back," "incomplete" with sweep," "here" with "care," and "home" with "sun."

Then there are other contributors to "The Poetry Corner" who have poetic talent and ideas coupled with a knowledge of the English language above the average and a familiarity with the mechanism of verse, who, not-withstanding, fall short of effectiveness in their efforts. They thus fall short because they are trying to write in the past rather than in the present. They are trying to reproduce something like what was done by Pope or Byron or Tennyson or Longfellow or Poe, and the result can be only a weak imitation. They are re-echoing thoughts and following forms and employing phrases which have already been done to perfection, or, still worse, done to death. What the contributors of this class need to do is to get into touch with life, and to write of the things and employ the forms that are now vital.

Now for a suggestion or two. Those who have poetic talent and ideas, but only a slight mastery of the English language and no knowledge of the mechanism of verse, should have a good dictionary and a book of synonyms; and, in addition, some such book as "A Study of Versification" by Brander Matthews, published by Houghton-Mifflin and Co. of Boston, price $1.25. They should, of course, read the great masters of English poetry, but should not attempt to copy them.

To those who possess some mastery of English, know something about the mechanism of verse and have read good poetry, but who are not in touch with the living and vital thoughts and forms of poetry, we say you can do nothing better than secure a copy of Braithewaite's "Anthology of Magazine Verse for 1915" published by Gomme and Marshall, New York, price $1.50. In the "Anthology" Mr. Braithewaite has gathered together what he considers to be the one hundred best poems appearing during the year 1915 in the United States; and there is no one in the country whose judgment is more final than Mr. Braithewaite's. A perusal of the "Anthology" will put your finger on the pulse of American poets of today. You will

257

be able to see what the best American poets are now writing about and how they are doing it. You will find poetry in all forms, from concrete thoughts in regular lyrics to the most tenuous imagisms in the freest of free verse. But it is all vital and will enable you to know what the living forces are which are at work in present day poetry.

Stranger than Fiction

December 23, 1915

A couple of years ago the writer of these columns wrote and published anonymously a novel entitled, "The Autobiography of an Ex-Colored Man." The book aroused considerable comment and produced a wide difference of critical opinion between reviewers on Northern and Southern publications. Northern reviewers generally accepted the book as a human document, while Southern viewers pronounced the theme of the story utterly impossible. A few of the Northern reviewers were in doubt as to whether the book was fact or fiction.

Here are extracts from the reviews in three newspapers which illustrate the three sorts of opinion expressed by the critics:

> Naturally the name of the writer of "The Autobiography of an Ex-Colored Man" can never be divulged by the publishers of this most remarkable human document. That it is not fiction we are prepared to believe from the sincerity and directness of the work as well as from the fact that it would be impossible for any one to portray such a character without making a hero of the subject if he were a colored man, and it is unthinkable and impossible that a white man could ever gain such an interior view of the life of a person of colored blood. As a dispassionate self analysis it would rank with the confessions of St. Augustine, and, of Marie Bashkirtseff which electrified the world some years ago.
> Portland (Me.) Express.

Here is an extract from the review of one of the undecided critics:

> It is a remarkable human document, being the story of a colored man who was sufficiently light in color to pass as a white man. . . . If the story be a true one, it is more remarkable than any piece of fiction ever written of the colored race. . . . That is just the puzzling thing about the book. It reads more like fiction than fact, yet there is a semblance of truth in it. . . . It is an

X-ray portraiture of the soul of a Negro. . . . The most wonderful story of self-revelation, either in fact or fiction, that has been published in many years. Springfield (Mass.) Union.

Here is a representative opinion of the Southern reviews, which pronounced the idea around which the story was built to be absurd and impossible:

The publishers' note stating that the book gives "a glimpse behind the scenes of the race drama" is not borne out. The publishers' assertion that the mistreatment of the Negroes by white persons in America is "actually and constantly forcing an unascertainable number of fair complexioned people over into the white race" is based upon ignorance of the fact that it is not by complexion alone that race is ascertainable. Only ignorance can see any possibility of a mixture of Anglo-Saxons to distinguish between a North American mixed blood and a white person.
Louisville Courier-Journal.

We reproduced the opinion from the Maine and Massachusetts papers only to throw into stronger relief the opinion from the Courier-Journal. Here is a writer calmly asserting that the slightest ting of African blood is discernable, if not in the complexion, then in some trait or characteristic betraying inferiority. This is, of course, laughable. Seven-tenths of those who read these lines know of one or more persons of colored blood who are "passing."

But the cause of our digging through our files of clippings about "The Autobiography of an Ex-Colored Man" was the recent news in the New York dailies concerning the sensational developments in the proceedings to break the will of Mrs. Frank Leslie, widow of Frank Leslie, the great magazine publisher, in which it was alleged that she was a daughter of Charles Follin, of Louisiana, and that her mother was a Negro slave.

Mrs. Leslie was one of the remarkable women of this city. On the death of her husband, the various Leslie publications were in a precarious condition. She took them in hand and, by energy and intelligence, placed them on a paying basis. When she died she left an estate of almost two million dollars.

If Mrs. Leslie was a colored woman, and there is reason to believe the allegations to be true—a large sum was spent by those who make the allegation in an investigation of Mrs. Leslie's history and pedigree, and in "Who's Who" no mention is made of Mrs. Leslie's mother—we say, if she was a colored woman, her case is stranger than any fiction.

Inside Measurement

March 2, 1916

There are various methods of measurement for ascertaining the progress of the American Negro; for instance, the growth in population and the increase in wealth. These are outside measurements. They indicate progress and give a loose approximation of how much has been made, but they are not an absolute test. A people may increase both in numbers and wealth, and yet not make real progress.

A true and exact estimate cannot be made, except by taking inside measurements. One of the simplest and surest methods of inside measurement would be to keep a record of the number of intelligently written books bought and read each year by the colored people. Increase in population is a measure of procreative power. Increase in wealth is, with us, largely a measure of muscular power. Increase in the reading of good books is a measure of thought power.

Now, numbers-power and wealth-power are essentials of greatness in any people; but they are powers which, by themselves, merely enable a people to spread out; it is thought power which enables a people to rise up. When the millions of Negroes in this country really begin to develop thought-power, they will not only spread out, but they will rise up. Nothing will be able to hold them down.

There is little doubt that a measurement of the race made by the inside method indicated above would show that its progress in thought-power is not commensurate with its progress in numbers-power and wealth-power. We are notoriously a non-reading people. For example, when a great and important book is published which pleads our peculiar cause, out of the ten or twelve million of us in this country, do 100,000 buy and read it? Do 50,000 buy and read it? No. Do 10,000 buy and read it? No. Even 5,000? No.

These figures show that not only the masses but also the intelligent classes of the race are non-readers. And these figures are true both of important books concerning the Negro and important books on all other subjects. Of course, a person may be a deep thinker and never look in a book; but the rule is that thinking people read, and reading makes them think more deeply and more quickly.

The race should correct this serious fault. We must become greater readers. We should not limit our reading to books written about our condition; we should make our reading general, so as to broaden our view of life and the world, and thus be able to better understand our own problem. But regardless of what books he may read, every colored man who makes any pretension to intelligence and progress should possess a "Race Library" of the best ten, twenty, thirty, forty or fifty books that have been written, according to his means will allow.

The editor of any one of the foremost Negro publications would furnish such a list to those who sought the information. Or a post card sent to Young's Book Exchange, No. 135 West 135th Street, New York City, will bring a complete catalogue of such literature.

The following is a list of more or less recently published books which are well worth reading:

"Samuel Coleridge Taylor Musician," a life of the greatest colored composer, by W.C. Berwick Sayer.

"American Civilization and the Negro," by Dr. C.V. Roman, a book of four hundred pages in which the author shows that all "humanity is one in its vices and virtues as well as blood."

"Folk Song of the American Negro," a study and an exposition of American Negro folk-song traced from Africa by Prof. John Wesley Work of Fisk University.

"Phillis Wheatley, Poems and Letters," a complete collection of the poems and letters of the first poet of the race, together with an appreciation by Arthur Schomburg.

"Prince Hall and His Followers," a history of Freemasonry among colored men in America, by George W. Crawford.

"Hazel," a story for colored children, by Mary White Ovington.

The Negro in American Art

March 16, 1916

Whenever a man makes a statement which he knows to be radical, he is always pleased to have it corroborated. Everybody feels safe in stating old truths that are accepted without question, but when you make a statement which on its face sounds false, you always welcome corroboration.

When the writer was in South America he [use] to sling a gun across his shoulder and tramp through the woods; this he did quite often for exercise—how much game he killed is another story. One day he was out hunting with his colleague, the Cuban Consul. In our tramp we ran across the most novel exhibition of fishing that we have ever seen. We saw a native lying stretched out in his canoe puffing on his cigarette, while the fish jumped into his boat. When, in this manner, he had caught as many fish as he wanted, he paddled off. As my friend and I looked on, we both related this incident to friends, and they have smiled and considered it a good South American "fish story." I have explained just how it was done, but they have only smiled the more. I finally had to give up trying to convince anybody of the truth of the story. I could tell my readers the very logical method used by the lazy fisherman to do the trick; but you, too, would smile. The trouble is, I didn't have a kodak to furnish the proper corroboration.

Over and over again, we have made the statement that there is nothing of artistic value belonging to America which has not been originated by the Negro. The statement sounds absurd to most people, even to many colored people. We have cited the Negro folk-stories, Negro folk-music, Negro popular music and Negro dances, and tried to show that they are the source of everything artistic which is native to this country; everything else is borrowed from the old world.

From time to time we have run across bits of partial corroboration. For example, Mr. Vernon Castle publicly admits that the modern dances, of which he is the foremost exponent, are of Negro origin. But, as unqualified testimony, let us reproduce the following striking paragraphs from a full page interview in "The Morning Telegraph" given by Robert J. Coady, a New York artist:

> The Negro is better fitted for a service to art than is the white.
>
> Jack Johnson's shadow dancing is the most beautiful dancing of modern times, and when he strikes a fighting pose we are carried back to the days of Greek bronzes.
>
> Nearly everything that is a contribution to art which is typically American to-day has been produced by the Negro. For example—ragtime, back and wing, the cakewalk, and even the modern forms of dancing—which are decidedly of Negro origin. The sense of rhythm, the sportive faculty, abandon, spirit of play, athletic activities—have their beginnings somewhere in the almost primitive depths of Africa.
>
> The Negro lives a life, even in this age of cold commercialism, that is full of poetry.

Mr. Coady in his interview goes on to state that Cezanne, the father of modern painting, though born in France, had a creole mother, and that this Negro-Spanish influence is what is felt in his work. He also says that Picasso, as master of the "new art," is of Spanish and Negro ancestry. His intimation is that if America contributes anything original to painting, it will be due to Negro influence.

Prejudice and Art

May 11, 1916

We have said several times in this column that in art the Negro encounters less prejudice than in any other field of endeavor. If a Negro writes a great poem or a great book, or paints a wonderful picture or composes real music, his color is little or no hindrance to his gaining recognition and appreciation of his work. This is one of the paradoxes of American prejudice. It is more difficult for a strong, able-bodied colored man to break through the New York labor union, and get a job to carry a hod than it is for a talented colored composer to get a hearing for his music in Carnegie Hall or Aeolian Hall.

There has just been completed at Jacksonville, Fla., a new armory for the First Regiment of the National Guard of that state. This armory was opened last week. It was christened by a musical festival given under the auspices of the Ladies' Friday Musicale, and the work that was rendered was "Hiawatha's Wedding Feast" by Coleridge-Taylor. A well known Southern tenor of Atlanta, Ga., was engaged to sing the famous "Onaway, Awake, Beloved." Does it not seem more than strange that the opening of an armory in a city of the far South should be celebrated with the rendition of a musical work which was created by a Negro brain?

The Jacksonville papers extolled Coleridge-Taylor's music before and after the performance. Jacksonville society turned out and made the event a gala one. Those who took part and those who listened were enraptured by the divine art of a black man. Yet, colored citizens were denied admission. Denied admission to a building paid for out of the public funds. Such are the inconsistencies of prejudice.

Mock Culture

March 22, 1917

There is something prevalent among us as a race for which no better term than mock culture can be found. It is the tendency to assume a veneered imitation of white culture and to disdain anything in literature, music or art that is fundamentally Negro. There are colored people who would be ashamed to have their children read the Uncle Remus stories, the only folk-lore this country has produced. There are those who would be ashamed to sing one of the old jubilee songs and who through ignorance speak disparagingly of this body of most beautiful and noble music. There are those who feel that there is something degrading about a poem or song written in Negro dialect, forgetting that Bobby Burns made the Scotch dialect an immortal classic, and not knowing that, for singing, Negro dialect is superior to straight English.

This class of colored people always wait to take their tip from the white people. They are unable to recognize artistic merit in anything that is purely Negro, unless they are first told by the white people that it is great. There were colored people, and perhaps there are still some left, who as recently as fifteen years ago thought that a poem written in Negro dialect was a reflection on the race; after the white people pointed out that the dialect poems written by Paul Dunbar were works of art, there sprung up all over the country literary societies, and schools, and babies, and various other institutions named in honor of Dunbar.

We intend to follow up this subject of mock culture.

A Real Achievement

May 31, 1917

Perhaps there is not in the City of New York a more discriminating dramatic critic than George Jean Nathan of "Smart Set." Mr. Nathan is not only a dramatic critic but he is an authority on the drama; being the author of many books and articles on that branch of art. Each year Mr. Nathan gives a survey of the New York theatrical season. In the current number of "Smart Set" he gives the best plays, the ten best performances by actors and the ten best performances by actresses.

In the list of the ten actors giving the best performances in New York during the past season, Mr. Nathan names two as tied for seventh place; they are Fritz Leiber in the "Merchant of Venice" and Opal Cooper in "The Rider of Dreams." In the list of the ten actresses giving the best performances, Mr. Nathan names for ninth place Inez Clough in "Simon the Cyrenian." For those who may not know, we say that Opal Cooper and Inez Clough are both colored performers who took part in the production recently given by the Colored Players.

Of course, the order of merit that Mr. Nathan awards to the performances of these various actors and actresses is entirely arbitrary; some other critic would probably arrange them differently; in fact, might omit several of the names which Mr. Nathan has included; but the mere fact that George Jean Nathan, who by the way is one of the most "cruel critics" in New

York, does include Mr. Cooper and Miss Clough in his lists is proof beyond doubt that the work of these two colored performers reached an exceptionally high level measured by the soundest standards of criticism.

The great satisfaction comes from the fact that the work of these artists was not measured by an intermediate standard, but by the highest standard of criticism. Mr. Nathan did not say that they did well for colored performers, but he gauged them in comparison with all the best performers on the New York stage. It is comparatively easy to be a "Black Shakespeare" or a "Black Booth" or a "Black Paderewski," because, in nearly every instance, that sort of modified reputation is gained by a modified standard of measurement; and these modified standards of measurement for our artistic efforts have been a great drawback to our development. So we consider that the places accorded Mr. Cooper and Miss Clough by a competent critic who compared their work with that of all the best performers on the New York stage, mark a real artistic achievement for the race.

Superior Races

September 27, 1917

Every once in a while somebody puts out a play that has for its object the fostering of race prejudice. The Negro has been the chief victim of that sort of propaganda in this country. We have had "The Clansman," "The Birth of a Nation" and other such productions. Next to the Negro, in this respect, have been the Japanese. The Chinese and the Hindus have also suffered in the same manner.

The latest effort in this direction was a play called "The Pawn" produced in one of the local theatres. It was anti-Japanese, and had a run of about two consecutive weeks which, in New York City, means that it was a failure. I did not see the play, but was much interested in reading Louis Sherwin's scathing review of it. It was splendid to see a critic of Mr. Sherwin's importance rise up in his wrath and smite the venture hip and thigh. He not only smote "The Pawn" in particular, but dealt a stinging blow to the ignorance and arrogance that prompts such exhibitions. In one of the paragraphs of his review, Mr. Sherwin said:

> For my part I must admit an overwhelming contempt for all these addle-pated cacklings about the superiority of the white race. The more I see of some white people the more highly I esteem Asiatics. But why do I waste good, healthy scorn on such rubbish as "The Pawn"? It can safely be left to sink of its own soggy stupidity.

265

This was not only correct criticism, but true prophecy, for "The Pawn" closed five days after the above quoted lines were published. And not only does the paragraph contain true prophecy, but sound philosophy.

It shows, at least, poor taste to cackle about the superiority of the white race at the present time. The modern civilization built up by the white race is falling. It is falling just as surely as civilizations that went before it have fallen.

European civilization, as we know it, began less than five hundred years ago. It was largely founded on force and nourished by robbery. At the beginning of the Fifteenth Century, what we call modern Europe, was very low in the scale of civilization. It could not be compared to India and was below China. At that time the old Roman civilization was flickering out in Constantinople. Europe might have remained in ignorance and poverty had it not been for three things that happened almost simultaneously. Those three things were the fall of Constantinople, the discovery of America and the invention of the gun.

When the Turks captured Constantinople, the Greeks, who had kept Greek and Latin learning alive there all through the dark ages, made their escape and fled to Western Europe. They carried with them the science, philosophy, literature and art of the classic age. The result was the spread of knowledge among peoples who, up to that time, had known almost nothing of the higher and finer things of life. The discovery of America stirred the imaginations of the people of Spain, England, France, Portugal and Holland, and started those nations on a course of discovery and exploration. The invention of the gun gave them an implement which enabled a few daring men to conquer and dominate the new lands which they discovered.

So far as the wealth and power of modern Europe is concerned, it may be accredited to the gun more than to anything else. This weapon that made a hundred white men equal in battle to a thousand men of the so-called weaker races placed the riches of America, of Africa, of India and the isles of the sea entirely at the mercy of Europe. And so all the rest of the world was robbed of its wealth in order to make Europe rich and powerful and cultured. And not only was the wealth of all the rest of the world taken, but the people of all the rest of the world had a yoke placed on their necks which they have not yet been able to throw off. The Chinese invented gunpowder; if they had also invented the gun and used it as Europe did, China would to-day be the ruler of the world.

And so, I say again that the civilization of modern Europe was largely built on force and robbery. Its surpassing wealth and power are due almost entirely to the gun. We see the little island of England with forty million people, people who a thousand years ago had not reached the level that had long been attained by many of the tribes of Africa, dominating the more than three hundred million people of India, people whose civilization, philosophy, literature and industries go back five thousand years.

And as this modern European civilization was built up by the gun, it is being destroyed by the gun. Gun power is the thing by which it is measured. For instance, Japan has had government and industries and art—an art which has recently wrought a revolution in the art of Europe—for thousands of years, but it was only when she showed gun power that she was given a place among civilized nations according to the European standard.

It would be interesting to make here a comparison between so-called white civilization and the civilizations of darker races in the light of absolute fulfillment of human happiness; but that is another story, one that we shall take up at another time.

When Is a Race Great?

March 11, 1918

One of the deepest desires of the human heart is to find a panacea. For his physical ills man is constantly hoping to find a "cure all," a single remedy which will free him from all bodily ailments. For his moral ills he is constantly hoping to find some single religious or ethical doctrine which will soothe his conscience and calm the fears of his immortal soul. In somewhat like manner, the American Negro has sought for a panacea for his ills as a race. And at times he has thought that the panacea had been found; for many have been offered. Some have cried, "Let us but get education!" Some have cried, "Let us but get land and money!" And others have cried, "Let us but get political power!"

But there is no such thing as a panacea. We cannot be made and kept busy well by a dose of some magic herb or drug, but we must observe and keep all of the laws of health and hygiene. We cannot be saved by repeating some prayer or confessing some single creed; we must strive to apply to our daily lives all of the principles of Christianity and ethics. Neither is there any panacea for our ills as a race. Not alone by large or small doses of this or that kind of education, not alone by the possession of land and money, not alone by having political influence and power shall we be made whole. There is no magic method. There is no short cut. We must develop and practice all the common virtues and become the possessors of all the common powers that go to make a people great.

And yet, although there is no single recipe to be followed for making a race great, there is a single standard by which the greatness of a race can be measured. The greatness of a race may be measured by the literature it has produced.

To substantiate this assertion there is first of all the uncontrovertible fact that every race or people which is acknowledged as great has produced a literature which is great in more or less direct proportion to the acknowledged greatness of that race or people. But there is something deeper than this mere fact. There is a psychological reason underlying it. A great literature is both the result and the cause of greatness in a people. Let me make that clearer; noble actions give birth to great literature, and great literature stimulates to noble actions. The explanation is simple; human actions are never entirely disinterested, the doer is always actuated by some motive. Noble actions always entail hard work or sacrifice or heroism, and the doer is sustained, if not actuated, by the hope of reward of some kind. The doer of noble things regards no reward for his hard work or his sacrifice or his heroism so high as that of being held permanently in the memory of his fellows. He cannot achieve that reward if he belongs to a people, which does not or cannot make literature. If he belongs to a people that can and does make literature, not only does the doer of noble things gain his reward, but others are inspired to like noble actions.

For example, a soldier on the battle field is chiefly sustained and moved to heroic action by this double inspiration which literature gives; he has the inspiration from the written record of glorious deeds by men of his race, and he has the inspiration of the hope that he may become a part of that record; this accounts for many brave deeds done by men of small physical strength and timid natures. In fact, it is difficult to conceive of men fighting bravely without being actuated by this motive in some degree. Even among people where the record is not a written one, the motive is fundamentally the same. And as with the deeds of the soldier, so with the other noble achievements of life.

I have been prompted to this somewhat philosophical discussion by a book which recently came from the press. The book is, "The Negro in Literature and Art in the United States," by Benjamin Brawley, Dean of Morehouse College, Atlanta. Mr. Brawley is also the author of "A Short History of the American Negro," of various essays and articles, and is a poet of fine feeling. In this latest publication he has given a history and to some extent a compilation of what the Negro has accomplished in literature and art in this country. It opens with a chapter on Negro genius, and then, beginning with Phillis Wheatley, treats of Negro writers down to the present day. There are also chapters on the orators, the stage, painters, sculptors and music. The appendix contains a useful bibliography.

This book has real value; and its value consists not only in the material which it includes; but in what it omits. Mr. Brawley is a man with the intelligence and training which enable him to employ the discriminating judgment necessary for such work; and in this the race and public are fortunate. So many compilations of race achievements have been gotten out by men who were not fitted for the work; they lacked the intelligence and training, and some of them lacked honesty of purpose. Books of great Negroes have been published in which the "greatness" of many of the characters included consisted in their ability to furnish a biographical sketch, a photograph and five dollars in cash.

Mr. Brawley's book is scholarly and sincere. His estimates of the work done by those of whom he writes are not arrived at by piling superlative adjectives on top of each other. He does not make any undue allowances for that work on account of color, but measures it by the literary standards of the world. So his estimates are not relative, but absolute.

"The Negro in Literature and Art" ought to be widely read. If it is it will do much to encourage the production of that literature through which races and peoples attain a place in the esteem of the world. For, as I have said, no matter how many things go to make a people great, it is acknowledged as great only when it has produced great literature.

American Genius and It's Local

July 20, 1918

We have often referred to the writings of H.L. Mencken. His English is a mental cocktail, an intellectual electric shock. Anybody who habitually dozes over conventional English ought to take Mencken at least once a week in order to keep the moss and cobwebs out of their brains. Mr. Mencken writes excellently on a wider range of subjects than any other one writer in the United States, and whatever his topic may be, he is always interesting. But he is at his best when he is talking about the theatre or literature or music or philosophy or feminism or criticism. On these subjects he is an authority.

The chief charm of Mencken is that he always has a fresh point of view on even the oldest subject. If the subject is one that does not admit of a fresh point of view, Mencken does not touch it, he considers it as already finished, exhausted; as a subject to be left in an embalmed state in the tomb of literature. It is into this very pit that Mencken always avoids that so many writers fall; they do not even know when a subject is exhausted. For that reason so many fledgling poets attempt to write odes to birds and flowers (skylarks, nightingales, daisies and roses), not realizing that Keats and Shelley and Burns and a host of others have done the job to a finish.

Mencken's style is all his own; nobody in the country writes like him. Sometimes we know that he is laughing at his readers, and sometimes we suspect that he is laughing at himself. We might call him a humorous cynic; and when he is most cynical, he is most enjoyable. He is the cleverest writer in America to-day.

But those who look merely for cleverness in Mencken are missing the best part of him; the best part of Mencken is truth. He gets at truth because he is devoid of the sentimental and mawkish morality which seems to be the curse of nearly everybody who writes in the English language. In other words, he is free and is therefore not afraid to write the truth. Many a writer is sincere enough, but bound by so many traditions and conventions that he cannot write the truth. Mencken pays no regard to traditions and conventions as such; he has absolutely no respect for them merely on account of their age.

The other day we picked up an article headed, "Mr. Cabell of Virginia." The article was by H.L. Mencken. Of course we were at once interested in Mr. Cabell because Mr. Mencken was talking about him. The article was a critical estimate of Mr. Cabell's work as a novelist. We know very little about that work, never having read any of Mr. Cabell's books; but Mr. Mencken puts high value on him; and we have made up our mind to read at least one of those books at the first opportunity. The critic gives as one of the reasons why Cabell should be read the following: "he is the only indubitably literate man left in the late Confederate States of America." Then he goes on to say:

> Let the last consideration engage us first. What I mean to say is that Cabell is the only first-rate literary craftsman that the whole South can show. In all that vast region with its 30,000,000 or 40,000,000 people and its territory as large as half a dozen Frances or Germanys, he is the only author worth a damn—almost the only one who can write at all. The spectacle is so strange that I can't keep my eyes from it. Imagine an empire as huge as the Holy Roman, and with no more literature than Pottstown, Pa., or Summit, N.J.— not a poet, not a serious historian, not a critic good or bad, not a dramatist dead or alive, and but one novelist!

Then Mr. Mencken takes up the question of the lack or rather the absence of literary men and women in the South, and says:

> The causes of this paucity I have hitherto discussed and guessed at. Perhaps the soundest theory is that which holds that the civil war destroyed the whole civilization of the region and well nigh exterminated the civilized Southerner. The few who survived came North, leaving the soil to the Ethiop and the poor white trash. The latter now struggle for possession in the manner of dogs and cats, with the odds increasingly in favor of the black. Of the two, he alone shows any cultural advance; he begins to produce artists, and even sages. But the poor white trash, now politically dominant in all the southern states, produce only traders, schemers, politicians and reformers—in brief bounders.

There is an interesting question raised here. Why is it that the South produces no first-rate literature? As Mr. Mencken says, this whole wide region with "not a poet, not a serious historian, not a critic good or bad, not a dramatist dead or alive." We think we can shed a little light on this question. Mr. Mencken thinks the condition may be due to the fact that "the Civil War destroyed the whole civilization of the region and well nigh exterminated the civilized Southerner." But why should not the poor white trash produce something? Is it possible that they can be so innately inferior to the Southern aristocracy? Were they any more handicapped than the "Ethiop," who, Mr. Mencken says, "alone shows any cultural advance"?

We do not think that the destruction of the old Southern civilization or any innate inferiority of the poor white trash is the reason; the real reason is that the white South of to-day is using up every bit of its mental energy in this terrible race struggle. All of the mental efforts of the white South run through one narrow channel; the life of every Southern white man as a man and a citizen, most of his financial activities and all of his political activities are impassably limited by the ever present "Negro problem." All of the mental power of the white South is being used up in holding the Negro back, and that is the reason why it does not produce either great literature or great statesmen or great wealth. That is, the white South is less intensely interested in forging ahead than it is in keeping the Negro from forging ahead. Witness: In Alabama there is opposition to a compulsory education law because under it Negro children would be compelled to go to school.

On the other hand, the Negro is not using up any of his strength in trying to hold anybody back, he is using every ounce of it to move forward himself. His face is front and toward the light; when the white man tries to force him back he, the white man, turns from the light and faces backward. Unless the white people of the South [are] right about this question, the Negro will in the long run distance them in all the higher and finer achievements.

Some New Books of Poetry and Their Makers

September 7, 1918

It is a great relief to get away occasionally from discussion of injustices and lynchings and discriminations and talk about something else. So every once in a while this writer takes his readers on a little excursion through other subjects.

This time we are going to talk about three new books of poetry by colored authors. But even so, there is nothing that has a more direct bearing on what we call the Negro problem than the production of literature by colored writers. Some time ago we said in this column that there is no one means through which a race may become great, but that there is only one measure by which its greatness is recognized and acknowledged.

Not by the possession of wealth alone or the holding of political power alone or the acquiring of this or that sort of education alone can a race become great; it must possess and exercise all of the virtues and powers that go to make a great race. On the other hand, when a race has become great the common measure of its greatness is the amount and standard of the literature it had produced.

Let us state this proposition in several other ways: The world does not know that a race is great until that race produces great literature. The production of great literature is proof that a race is great. There never has been a great race that did not produce a great literature. No race that produced a great literature has ever been looked upon by the world as distinctly inferior.

The application to the colored people of America can be made direct. To become a great people they will need wealth, they will need all of the political power and privileges that go with American citizenship, they will need all kinds of education; in a word, they will need all the virtues and powers that have made the white people great. And still, the American Negro will not be recognized and acknowledged as great until he has produced great literature, but the production of literature will be the proof of that greatness and a guarantee of its recognition.

The American Negro has done very little so far in literature; that is, very little in pure literature. Colored writers have written a great many pamphlets and books, but the great majority of these writings have been entirely polemical. The majority of them have been written for the direct purpose of proving the equality of the black man. Now the truth is that one piece of pure literature is worth one hundred or one thousand pieces of that sort of writing. One thin volume of poetry by Paul Dunbar goes farther to prove the intellectual equality of the black man than nine-tenths of all the controversial literature written by American Negroes in the past seventy-five years.

Let us suppose that Pushkin, the national poet of Russia, and Dumas, the greatest romantic novelist of France and of the world, for that matter, instead of being respectively a colored Russian and a colored Frenchman, had been colored Americans, can anyone estimate the influence they would have had on opinion regarding the race in this country? It is harder to convince a Russian or a Frenchman of the colored man's inferiority from the mere fact that Pushkin wrote in Russia and Dumas in France. If they had written in America, the proof of the colored man's equality would be easier.

People are often misled into thinking the man of money is the man who is looked up to. Well, he is while he is alive; that is, while people who "look up to him" think they can get something out of him. But the real pride of a people is not in its men of wealth but in its men of letters. Who knows the names of the wealthy men of Greece? Nobody. But every school boy knows Homer and Aeschylus and Aristotle. There is only one name in Roman history that can be placed alongside Virgil and Cicero, and that is Julius Caesar; and it must be remembered that a good part of Caesar's fame rests upon his authorship of one of the best histories ever written. What is the deepest pride that an Englishman has in his race? Is it that he belongs to a race that manufactures and exports more cotton goods than any other in the world? No, his deepest pride lies in the fact that he belongs to a race that produced Shakespeare.

It is no exaggeration to say that one colored American poet or dramatist or novelist of the first magnitude; that is, one that would command the attention and recognition of the world, would do more to batter down prejudice against the race than ten colored American millionaries. It may be that the stage of development that will produce the millionaire must come before the stage that will produce the men of letters of the first magnitude, but that does not alter the truth of the above statement.

*　*　*　*

But we started out to talk about some new books of poetry by colored writers. We have three volumes on our desk, and each of them is a promise of the racial greatness that is developing, because each of them is an example of creative art.

We have "From the Heart of a Folk" by Waverly Turner Carmichael. In the introduction to this book, written by Prof. James Holly Hanford of Harvard University, we are told that Mr. Carmichael is a full-blooded Negro who up to a year ago was never out of his native state of Alabama. Mr. Carmichael is evidently quite young, but he shows promise as a poet. He is spontaneous and has a keen sense of humor. Most of his verses are written in dialect and reveal a strong influence of Dunbar; and it is by inviting this direct comparison with Dunbar that Mr. Carmichael suffers most; for Mr. Carmichael's dialect is still crude, while Dunbar made dialect poetry as finished as it is possible to make it. No colored poet can write Negro dialect poetry without inviting comparison with Dunbar, and he is almost certain to suffer by the comparison with Dunbar. This comparison is made still more perilous if the younger poet chooses any of the subjects already written on by Dunbar.

For instance, it is impossible not to draw a comparison between the following from Mr. Carmichael:

> I went home wid me gal las' night,
> Dat darlin' little miss,
> An' time we started off from church
> I ask'd hur fur a kiss;
> She drapped'd hur head an' kind o' blush

273

Den say, "I recon so";
I kis'd hur 'bout a dozen times
An' den she ask'd fur mo'.

With the following from Dunbar:

Seen my lady home las' night,
Jump back, honey, jump back.
Hyeahd huh sigh a little sigh,
Seen alight gleam from huh eye,
An' a smile go flittin' by—

Nor can we escape the following comparison; this from Carmichael:

I don' ker 'bout yo' cake an' pie,
An' neither 'bout yo' chicken;
I wouldn't give a dime fur all
Dat you have in yo' kitchen;
W'en I come doun to visit you,
I'll eat what please the masses;
Make t'ings as common as you kin,
An' gea me bread an' lasses.

And this from Dunbar:

When you set down at de table,
Kin' o' weary like an' sad,
An' youse jes' a little tiahed
An' purhaps a little mad;
How yo' gloom tu'uns into gladness,
How yo' joy drives out de doubt
When de oven do' is opened,
An' de smell comes po' in' out;
Why, de 'lectric light o' heaven
Seems to settle on de spot,
When yo' mammy says de blessin'
An' de con'n pone's hot.

There are other instances in Mr. Carmichael's book in which this comparison with Dunbar cannot be avoided. Yet Carmichael has done some very good things. He has imagination and humor and a fine sense of rhythms. There is no doubt that he will be heard from.

Another book is "The Heart of a Woman" by Georgia Douglas Johnson. Mrs. Johnson is already well known as a writer of verse; she has contributed for a number of years to various magazines. Her collection of poems prove her to be a true lyric singer. The strength and light that so often flash out of these delicate verses are amazing. Take for instance the following little mother's croon which starts so lightly and see how it grows in strength:

> Sweeter far than lyric tune
> Is my baby's cooing tune;
> Brighter than the butterflies
> Are the gleams within her eyes;
> Firmer than an iron band
> Serves the zephyr of her hand;
> Deeper than the ocean's roll
> Sounds her heart-beat in my soul.

Mrs. Johnson's volume is well named; see how much of a woman's heart is revealed, and yet hid, in the following:

> Winter-aback sweeps the inward eye,
> Fleet o'er the trail to a rose-wreathed sky,
> Girt by a cordon of dreams I dwell
> Deep in the heart of the old-time spell
> Almost, the tones of your whispered word,
> Almost! the thrill that your dear lips stirred,
> Almost!! that wild pulsing throb again—
> Almost !!! ('Tis winter, the falling rain.)

There are many other things in Mrs. Johnson's volume worth quoting. Many more that prove her to be a true lyric poet. And we might say just here that we hope Mrs. Johnson will not yield to the temptation of letting her mere gift run away with her. It may be well for her to roughen her art a bit.

The other book is "The Band of Gideon" by Joseph S. Cotter, Jr. Mr. Cotter is a young colored man of Louisville, Ky. His father before him did a good deal of literary work, and perhaps continues to do it. Young Cotter suffers from ill health, and nearly all of the poems in his little volume were written on a sick bed. Cotter's book is the thinnest of the three before me, it contains only 29 pages, but in those few pages he shows the greatest promise. Carmichael goes back to traditional dialect—and at some time the writer will say something about the relation of Negro dialect to present-day Negro poetry. Mrs. Johnson confines herself entirely to conventional lyric forms. But Cotter is free and bold. He has imagination and fine poetic sense, and besides a splendid mastery of the tools that every poet must know how to use—words. He has no use for the worn out rhym(e)s; he achieves rhythms without them.

Listen to this "Prayer" from a poet who writes on a sick bed:

275

As I lie in bed,
Flat on my back;
There passes across my ceiling
An endless panorama of things—
Quick steps of gay-voiced children,
Adolescence in its wondering silences,
maid and man on moonlit summer's eve,
Women in the holy glow of Motherhood,
Old men gazing silently thru the twilight
Into the beyond.
O God give me words to make my dream-children live.

Or read the whole race question put into thirteen lines, and short ones at that:

Brother, come!
And let us go unto our God.
And when we stand before Him
I shall say—
Lord, I do not hate,
I am hated.
I scourge no one,
I am scourged.
I covet no lands,
My lands are coveted.
I mock no peoples,
My people are mocked.
And, brother, what will you say?

But Cotter can be not only free and bold and able to throw off his old chains of the art, he can be tender and lyrical. Listen to the following form of an invalid poet:

I am so tired and weary,
So tired of the endless fight,
So tired of waiting the dawn
And finding endless night.

That I ask but rest and quiet—
Rest for the days that are gone,
And quiet for the little space
That I must journey on.

We repeat that in these poets there is promise of the racial greatness that is developing. The racial greatness that will be witnessed by a great literature, and which the world will thereby be forced to acknowledge.

Resurgence of the Negro in Literature

April 22, 1922

A half dozen years ago it was next to impossible to get anything at all published about the Negro. Neither newspapers nor magazines nor book publishers cared for the Negro as a subject. Of course, there always has been in newspapers current news of Negro crimes, etc. but we are speaking of the Negro as a subject for discussion pro and con.

The last twelve months has witnessed a resurgence of the Negro in literature and collaterally on the stage. All of this indicates a stirring which has been going on in the subconscious mind of the public ever since the War and is now working out consciously.

The "come back" of the Negro to the New York stage is a sure indication of this. Within the last five years there have been five plays with colored actors produced on Broadway. (It may be necessary to say to those not familiar with New York City that "Broadway" means the first class theatres devoted to dramatic and musical productions in the theatrical district of the Borough of Manhattan.) Three of these were serious plays and two were musical comedies. Of the serious plays, one, "The Emperor Jones," was one of the outstanding theatrical successes of the season, and of the musical plays, "Shuffle Along," is one of the greatest musical hits that New York has ever known. It has been running for a solid year in the same theatre.

This festival is merely a more obvious demonstration of what is going on in books. The last twelve months have seen the great publishing houses of New York turn out a half dozen important books by or about the Negroes. This marks a great change when we consider that only a few years ago none of the leading publishers in New York were in the least interested in anything touching upon the Negro. Publishers of books have changed because they have sensed and realized the fact that there is a reading and purchasing public for the kind of book about the Negro now being published. I believe that his reading and publishing public has been greatly increased by the colored people themselves. The fact that for so many years colored people were not book buyers is one of the chief reasons why so few good books about the Negro were published, and even now the number of colored people who regularly buy books is infinitesimally small. If there were

277

twenty thousand, or even ten thousand, colored people in the United States who could be depended upon to purchase worth while books about the Negro, any publisher in the country would be glad to publish such books.

This resurgence of the Negro literature is remarkable not so much because books about the Negro are again being published but because the books are so different. This difference is strikingly illustrated in two novels, both written by Southern white men, one of them "Birthright" (Century Company), and the other "White and Black" (Harcourt, Brace and Company).

Both of these books are destined to be widely read and much discussed.

In fiction heretofore written by Southern white authors there has been only one kind of Negro treated with any consideration and that was the Negro of the old Mammy and Uncle class. But in "Birthright" and "White and Black" we have two Southern white authors making an honest attempt to exhibit a slice of life in the South. It is true that both these authors have their shortcomings and neither of them is entirely free from the limitations of prejudice, but there is no doubt that both of them have striven to be sincere and honest.

Perhaps a number of colored people have already read "Birthright" as it ran as a serial in the "Century" magazine, and no doubt most of those who have read it were disappointed in the way the story was finally worked out and concluded. There are grounds in the story for such disappointment. But even so we should remember how far in advance it is of the traditional fiction about the races that has come out of the South. Whatever deficiencies of knowledge regarding the black South the author of "Birthright" shows he makes up for (them) by his full and absolute knowledge of the white South, and that white South he does not spare. He holds it up as it is—provincial, ignorant and prejudiced.

I think, however, that "White and Black," is a better story and stronger. The author of "White and Black" knows his white South fully as well as does the author of "Birthright" and he knows his black South better. "White and Black" takes in a wider range of race relations in the South than does "Birthright." It considers these relations not only in the conventional light of race prejudice but also in the light of economics. Neither is the author afraid to speak out plainly on that element in the problem which is almost absolutely taboo, the sex element.

Neither of these books will prove entirely satisfactory to colored readers but because they are by Southern white writers who have broken entirely from the old traditional school of Southern fiction and have striven to present the truth about race conditions in the South, they are important enough to be widely read by colored people.

A Real Poet

May 20, 1922

For years the great poet has been regarded as the highest manifestation of the intellectual, esthetic, and in many cases spiritual, powers of a race. In the names that have come down through history it is those of the great poets that blaze out brightness. It is chiefly upon the achievements of such poets that races and peoples claim greatness for themselves.

There are of course four names which in their influence and appeal stand on a level with or even above the greatest poets. They are Budda, Confucious, Christ and Mohammed. But these four great religious teachers were after all great ethical poets. Judged in every light they do represent the highest peaks of the genius of the races that produced them. But these names are limited to oriental races. No occidental race has yet produced a great religious teacher. Among the occidental peoples the great poet still stands almost unrivaled. There are other lists, of course, that contain names of wide influence and appeal. For example, the soldiers' list can show Alexander, Caesar and Napoleon. But there is not an occidental people in which the final test would not put its greatest poet above its greatest soldier.

The times are slightly changed and the glamour about the poet may be somewhat dimmed. We are living in a very material age, and the man of science, the man who is able to bend the force of nature to the well being of humanity is coming into ascendency. There may come a time when from achievements in science there will spring names that will shed a luster as bright and enduring as names of Homer, Shakespeare, Dante, Moliere, and Goethe.

However, to my mind, this is improbable. The materialism of the present age may be but a transitory state. Moreover, although the scientist may contribute what in the utilitarian sense is far more important to humanity, he can never take hold of the imaginations of men and stir their souls like the poet. It therefore seems that as long as man loves the beautiful the great poet will hold his supreme place.

I have indulged in this rather weighty sounding introduction simply to induce a train of thought. I wish my readers to think of the production of poets by a race as a vital thing. It is vital not only as an indication of the development of the race but it is vital as to the place and recognition which that race is given by the world at large.

In accordance with the temper of the age, and more particularly, in accordance with false ideas with which the mind of the Negro in America has been impregnated, we Aframericans are prone to think of one of our number who conducts a successful corner grocery store as being far more vital and important as a factor in our progress than one who turns out a sheaf of poems, even though the poems are real poetry. We are prone to think of the grocer as one who is laying foundation stones in our racial greatness and of the poet as doing little more than wasting his time.

Without disparaging the successful grocer, I must say that this evaluation is all wrong. It would be interesting, if it were possible to calculate how many successful Negro grocers it would take to equal the force of Paul Laurence Dunbar as a factor in the progress of the race and in having the progress recognized by the world. I am now driving at the truth contained in the words of Jesus Christ when He said, "Man shall not live by bread alone." If the race would develop its greatness and highest possibilities it needs not only to support its grocers but also to appreciate its poets.

All of this is merely introductory to a few words to call attention to a Negro poet who has risen like a new and flaming star on the horizon. The poet is Claude McKay.

Mr. McKay deserves a full and prompt appreciation. We should not do in his case what we were guilty of in the case of Dunbar, that was, not to recognize or not even to know his greatness until it was acclaimed by the whites.

Mr. McKay is a real poet and a great poet. I mean by this that he has both the poetic endowment and the ability to make that endowment articulate; and he is yet far from his full growth. He is still a young man. He is a poet of beauty and a poet of power. No Negro poet has sung more beautifully of his own race than McKay and no Negro poet has equalled the power with which he expresses the bitterness that so often rises in the heart of the race. As an example of that power we quote his sonnet, "If We Must Die," written after the terrible riots in the summer of 1919:

> If we must die, let it not be like hogs
> Hunted and penned in an inglorious spot,
> While round us bark the mad and hungry dogs,
> Making their mock a tour accursed lot.
> If we must die, O let us nobly die,
> So that our precious blood may not be shed
> In vain then even the monsters we defy
> Shall be constrained to honor us though dead!
> O kingsmen! we must meet the common foe!
> Though far outnumbered let us show us brave,
> And for their thousand blows deal one deathblow!
> What though before us lies the open grave?
> Like men we'll face the murderous, cowardly pack
> Pressed to the wall, dying, but fighting back!

The race ought to be proud of a poet capable of voicing it so fully. Such a voice is not found every day.

Mr. McKay's volume, "Harlem Shadows," published by Harcourt, Brace & Company, New York, is already attracting the attention of the critics of the country. What he has achieved in this little volume sheds honor upon the whole race.

Negro Theatrical Invasion of Europe

May 19, 1923

The invasion of the theatrical stage by colored performers, which began with the production of "Shuffle Along," has been extended from New York to London and over to Paris. After dissolving of the Williams & Walker and the Cole and Johnson Companies there followed a period of about ten years in which the Negro was almost completely kept off the stage, except in vaudeville houses. In the meantime Negro theatres sprang up all over the country and colored theatrical talent was generally employed in furnishing entertainment for only colored audiences. These Negro theatres raised up a new group of colored performers.

No colored company was given a chance on "Broadway" until the appearance of "Shuffle Along." The "Shuffle Along" people had to stoop to conquer, but they were confident that they had a great entertainment and if given a chance could make good. They did have a great entertainment and New York immediately recognized it, with the result that the play ran for more than a solid year on "Broadway," and that is a record equalled by very few white shows.

Since the success of "Shuffle Along" Broadway has not been without a colored show. There are now two in the city, one musical comedy and the other a company of serious actors. A colored show now seems to be one of the necessary features of Broadway night life.

And now the invasion has reached over to London and Paris. Florence Mills, who made herself famous overnight with "Shuffle Along," has gone to London with the "Plantation Revue." The London manager who took her and her company over stated that he considered Miss Mills one of the finest musical comedy artists in the world; that she could be mentioned in the same breath with Yvette Guilbert and Marie Lloyd.

Some dispatches from London indicate that there will be the same sort of opposition to colored theatrical performers as there has been to the colored musicians. One dispatch stated that English actors out of work will protest against the importation of Negro performers.

A dispatch from Paris states that "The Emperor Jones" will be produced on June 3. A colored actor named Bengelia will play the part which was made famous by Mr. Charles Gilpin in this country. Mr. Bengelia is said to be the only serious Negro actor in Europe. He is a native of Africa but is reported as having a good education and speaking refined French. He has played with great success a number of parts in productions under the manager of the famous Odeon Theatre.

We hope that this invasion of Europe will be as successful as it has been in New York.

14 Music

When he refers to the colored players as "so-called musicians" he may think he is slurring them, but, instead, he is slurring the white society people, and hotel and cafe proprietors who prefer Negro musicians.

James Weldon Johnson, "The Poor White Musician"
(September 23, 1915)

In the following editorials Johnson emphasized the three main artistic achievements made by the race—"folk-stories, the cake-walk, and Negro music." These three achievements, he contended, discount any charge of inferiority because they represent the work of the race as a whole. He considered "Negro music" the highest artistic contribution made by the race.

Believing that blacks possessed a natural ability, Johnson told his readers that nothing of original artistic value had come out of the United States which had "the power of universal appeal," except what had been created by the American "Negro."

"The Poor White Musician"

September 23, 1915

Perhaps nothing should astonish us during these days of war, when the world seems to be up side down; but the following letter written to The Globe is in a tone so unusual and unexpected that we reproduce it in full:

> Editor of the Globe, Sir—Why does society prefer the Negro musician? is a question which is not infrequently discussed by white musicians; yes, I dare say, by artists. The Negro musician is to-day engaged at most of the functions given by society, especially its dances. Why this preference should be given to the Negro "so-called" musician, who hasn't the slightest conception of music, rather than to the Caucasian musician, who has spent well nigh a fortune—aside from numerous years of painstaking study—is incomprehensible.
>
> Surely it isn't because of the oft-refuted contention that ragtime music demands the Negro musician, for the white musician has proven time and again that he can render a ragtime selection better than the Negro. Why should a famous dancing couple prefer a Negro orchestra for their dancing exhibitions? Even the New York hotels are now beginning to discard the white musician for the Negro. It will not be long before the poor white musician will be obliged to blacken his face to make a livelihood or starve.
>
> EUGENE DE BUERIS
> New York, September 8.

Was a more pitiful wail ever uttered? And is it not difficult to grasp that fact that it is a white man and not a Negro who is uttering the wail?

The writer is evidently a New York musician, and he cannot understand why the Negro musicians of this city are making competition so strong for their white professional brothers. Some persons not acquainted with the facts might jump to the conclusion that the colored men worked cheaper than the whites, but it is certain that Mr. De Bueris would have been glad to make that charge in his letter, if such were the case.

On this point let us relate an amusing incident which happened a few days ago. A society lady called up on the telephone a man who makes a business of supplying musicians, and asked the price for a band of ten men. The man she called up is a colored man and supplies colored musicians, but as his office is on Broadway, such a thought seems not to have been anywhere near the lady's mind. He told her what ten men would cost for an evening. She was amazed and said to him, "Why I can get colored musicians for that price!"

The fact is, colored musicians charge more than white musicians; so we can see that after all there is some excuse for the bewilderment of Mr. De Bueris. Let us see if we can't enlighten him a bit.

When he refers to the colored players as "so-called musicians" he may think he is slurring them, but, instead, he is slurring the white society people, and hotel and cafe proprietors who prefer Negro musicians. But Mr. De Bueris is all wrong in belittleing the musical ability of these men. They may not have spent "as many fortunes or as many years of painstaking study" as the white musicians, but what has that to do with natural musical ability? Nothing. It only goes to show that white men need to spend fortunes and years of study in order to play music as well, or almost as well, as Negroes do naturally. Let Mr. De Bueris think of what would happen to the white musicians if the colored men spent fortunes and years in study, and let him be thankful.

There are good and sufficient reasons why Negro musicians are preferred at social affairs. Modern music and modern dancing are both Negro creations.

Since ragtime has swept the world and become universally known as American music, there have been attempts to rob the Negro of the credit of originating it; but this is in accord with an old habit of the white race; as soon as anything is recognized as great, they set about to claim credit for it. In this manner they have attempted to rob the Negro of the credit of originating the plantation stories and songs. We all remember how after the Russo-Japanese war attempts were made to classify the Japanese as white. In the same way, scholars have "doubted" that the Zulus are real Negroes. Had Jack Johnson continued as champion, somebody would have tried to prove that he was not a real Negro. By this method, the white race has gathered to itself credit for originating nearly all the great and good things in the world. It has taken credit for what has been accomplished by the ancient Egyptians, the East Indians and the Arabs, by the simple process of declaring those black people to be white.

The truth is, the pure white race has not originated a single one of the great, fundamental intellectual achievements which have raised man in the scale of civilization.

The alphabet, the art of letters, of poetry, of music, of sculpture, of painting, of the drama, of architecture; numbers, the science of mathematics, of astronomy, of philosophy, of logic, of physics, of chemistry; the use of metals and the principles of mechanics were all invented or discovered by darker and, what are, in many cases, considered inferior races. The pure white race did not originate even the religion it uses.

But all of this is another story; let us get back to the "poor white musician."

Not only is modern American music a Negro creation but the modern dances are also. The dance steps which society debutantes are now learning and those which are the latest thing on the stage have been known among

Negroes for years. Then it is only natural that when it comes for modern dancing, the Negro musician should be the real thing.

In a way, Mr. De Bueris is right when he says that white musicians can play ragtime as well as Negro musicians; that is, white musicians can play exactly what is put down on the paper. But Negro musicians are able to put into the music something that can't be put on the paper; a certain abandon which seems to enter in the blood of the dancers, and that is the answer to Mr. De Bueris' question, that is the secret, that is why Negro musicians are preferred.

And let us add a word to the Negro musician upon efficiency in his work. He cannot afford to run along merely upon his great natural gift.

This letter written to The Globe shows that the white musicians feel his competition, and that means that they will stop at nothing to put him out of business. Let the Negro musician improve and develop himself. He may not be able to spend a fortune, but he can, by some slight sacrifices, put in his spare time on painstaking study. It is only in this way that he can continue to hold his own.

American Music

January 13, 1916

Mme. Yvette Guilbert, one of the greatest artists on the French stage, in an interview which she gave after her recent arrival in the United States, had the following to say concerning American music:

> In America, apart from a few ditties like "Suwanee River," the only beautiful folk-songs I have found are Negro melodies. I don't know why Americans have done so little in the folk-song field. Perhaps they have been too busy to concern themselves with such things.

This statement will pain many white, and surprise a great many colored people, because there are so many white people who dislike to admit it is true, and there are so many colored people who don't know it.

Mme. Guilbert, with true artistic and critical sense, goes to the root of the matter, but she makes a mistake, perhaps an excusable one, when she makes an exception of "a few ditties like 'Suwanee River.'" The fact is, "Suwanee River," "Kentucky Home" and most of the Foster songs are founded in Negro melodies. Stephen Foster was simply the first white man to see the artistic value of these melodies and harmonies and to make use of them. Foster, in his most widely known songs, not only used Negro melodies but also Negro sentiments.

For years white American musicians have been writing the things which have been better written by the musicians of Europe, as a result, they have created nothing which has made an impression on the world. In the meantime, the only contribution to music which this country has made that has received universal acknowledgement owes its creation to Negroes. While American composers have been making fair and mediocre copies of German, Italian and French compositions, American Negro music in its triumphant march has swept the world.

Skilled musicians in the United States have largely ignored this Negro music. When they have striven to be original they have gone to Indian themes and legends, but here they have worked sterile soil. But there is no way around it; if a great American music is to be built, it must be built out of what the Negro has created or not at all. Perhaps, this work is being providentially left for the great Negro composers who are certain to come.

We are here reminded of the fact that so many colored people are yet unable to properly estimate the value of the three artistic creations made by the race in this country; in fact, a great many are still somewhat or somehow ashamed of them. We refer to the folk-stories, which were collected by Joel Chandler Harris under the title of "Uncle Remus"; the cake-walk, from which was developed nearly all of the modern dances now so popular; and Negro music. These three achievements are the greatest proof which the race has yet brought against the common charge of inferiority, because they are not the work of one or two gifted individuals but of the race as a whole. They are a demonstration that the Negro is a creator, a creator of that which has the power of universal appeal. They show that from his own inner consciousness the Negro can evolve that which will move and influence the world. And that is proof of inherent power.

Of the three, the cake-walk stands on the lowest grade; however, dancing is one of the recognized arts, and the cake-walk captured two continents as the greatest American dance. The French people called it "the poetry of motion." Even the royalty of Europe practiced its intricate steps. In the modern dances, the cake-walk has, perhaps, reached its highest artistic developments. The folk-stories have already been given fixed place in literature by "Uncle Remus." What a lasting pity that this work was not done by some colored man! The highest contribution made by the race to art is Negro music, and that still remains almost wholly undeveloped. And what a mine of material it is!

To sum up the whole matter, nothing of artistic value has come out of the United States which has made a universal appeal to the world, except what has been created by the American Negro.

Writers of Words and Music

March 2, 1918

My colleague, Lester A. Walton, expressed mild indignation last week over the manner in which lyricists are generally ignored on concert programs. Writing of a concert recently given in Boston Mr. Walton said:

> In glancing over the program I note that the usual policy of completely ignoring the lyricist was consistently followed out. For what reason the writer of the words to a song is always kept in the background on high-class musical programs has always been a source of wonderment to me. When I ask those who should know, for instance the publisher, I am repeatedly told, "Merely a matter of custom!"

For every custom there is some sort of a reason. Then if it is the custom generally to ignore or not to accord recognition to the writer of the words to a musical composition on what reason is the custom founded?

To get at the reason we must go back a little into the history of words wedded to music. The first phase of what is known as the modern song was the songs of the troubadours. The troubadours flourished from the 10th to the 14th centuries. In these songs the words were the chief feature, the music was merely incidental. The poets told in these songs wonderful and beautiful stories of war and adventure and love, and the listeners hung upon each word that fell from the singer's lips. With the development of the vocal art there came a change; the listener gradually became more interested in the sound than in the story. Early in the 18th century the concert aria was well established, and the music was filled with runs and trills and other florid decorations. People were astonished and then delighted by these vocal pyrotechnics, words to a song took not only second, but a very insignificant place. In fact, the greater portion of many of the songs required nothing more than the syllable "Ah." As a natural consequence the words fell off in quality.

The same thing was true in opera. The Italian school was then in undisputed ascendancy, and vocalization was carried to such a high pitch of perfection that libretto writers had to make their words fit the notes as best they could. As a result, the words to the opera of the period were often little more than doggerel. Sopranos simply tra-la-la-ed. That was opera.

But even with the change wrought in song writing by Schumann and Brahms and in opera writing by Wagner, a chance which made it the business of the composer to interpret the words of the text and to emphasize the emotional situations of the story, words remained an unimportant part of musical compositions. Take what is, perhaps, Verdi's greatest opera, "Aida," an opera in which he followed the Wagnerian principle of making the music support and develop a tragic story; how many even of the people who are well versed in music know who wrote the words of "Aida"? The man who wrote the words of this immortal work was Antonio Ghislanzoni. Be honest and admit that you never heard of him.

But let us come down from opera. If a vote should be taken on the most famous song written in America in the last twenty years, I have no doubt that the vote would go to "The Rosary." It is a beautiful song, a song that everybody knows, and stranger still, a song to which everybody knows the words. When a person hums "The Rosary," he also hums the words. Most people who know anything about composers know that Nevin wrote the music, but not one person out of a hundred knows or cares who wrote the words.

The writers of words have just grievance. Nevin could never have written such a song as "The Rosary" if the poem had not given him the idea and the inspiration. As Mr. Walton says, Alex Rogers wrote the words for "The Rain Song" and "Exhortation," two of Will Cook's most famous songs, songs that could not have been written had Rogers not first furnished the idea and inspiration. Mr. Walton himself wrote the words that gave birth to the beautiful little plantation ballad, "Mammy." But what can Rogers and Walton and the rest of us expect when nobody is even bothered about who wrote the words to "The Rosary?"

There is, of course, an explanation to the whole thing and it is this. Sound has a wider appeal than sense. That is a truth not applicable merely to ignorant people, but people of intelligence and good taste. Most people who go to the opera go there not to be stirred by the story and music of a great tragedy, they go to hear a Galli Curci warble like a bird or to hear a Caruso hit a high C.

Naturally, I stand with the word writers and say that something ought to be done. At the recitals given in Aeolian Hall and Carnegie Hall a "book of words" is folded in each program, so the listener can see who is the author of the text of the song and at the same time find out what the singer is singing about—a more or less necessary arrangement—since most singers do not sing words. But such a method would be too expensive for the average concert; nevertheless, it would be a simple matter to print the name of the lyrist in italics directly under that of the composer and so give him the credit that is due him without taking away any of the honor belonging to the musician.

Yet, I fear, Brother Walton, that you and I and all the rest of the word writers are up against it. I guess these composer fellows feel that we ought to be happy because they allow our names to be printed on the music.

Classic Music in New York

March 25, 1922

Undoubtedly New York is thought of by the rest of the country as the exclusive home of jazz music. There are good reasons for this opinion. It is New York that ninety-nine per cent of the writers of jazz music live and do their work. It is in this city that the greater part of the musical performances that make a specialty of jazz music are produced. Many of these shows are never seen in any other city but New York. It is also in New York that there are a large number of restaurants and cafes and caberets where popular music is played. But the idea that New York is exclusively the home of jazz music is a great error.

New York is also the home of classic music, despite the traditional claims of Boston. This is especially true of symphonic music. New York is the only city in the country that supports more than one great symphony orchestra. Some one may ask how many people after all of the population of New York go to Carnegie Hall to hear the Philharmonic or the New York Symphony Orchestra or to the Metropolitan Opera House to hear the Metropolitan Orchestra? It may be said that only the musical highbrows do so. That, however, does not take away from New York's claim to musical culture. The fact remains, nevertheless, that it has a large enough number of musical highbrows to keep these several institutions going.

But that is not the end of the matter. New York carries the best orchestra music to the musical low-brows and makes them listen to it, and what is better, the musical low-brows are showing more and more that they appreciate and enjoy it. This is done through the super motion pictures of New York.

An article by Deems Taylor, the music critic of the "World," in that paper for last Sunday, gives a survey of music in those motion picture theatres which is astonishing to anyone who is not familiar with them. He points out that the five super motion picture theatres of New York—the Capitol, the Criterion, the Rialto, the Rivoli and the Strand—each maintains a high class symphony orchestra with a library of standard orchestra music, librarians, copyists and all the other personnel of the symphony orchestra including high priced conductors and assistant conductors.

The Capitol Theatre employs an orchestra of seventy-one men and two organists. The conductor is a gold medal graduate of the Budapest Conservatory and a former assistant conductor of the Dresden Opera House. The Criterion employs an orchestra of thirty-eight men and two organists. The conductor is a graduate of the Vienna Conservatory and a musician of note. The Rialto has an orchestra of forty-one men and two organists. The conductor is a graduate of the Vienna Conservatory and was concertmaster at the Vienna Opera House under Gustave Mahler. The Rivoli maintains an orchestra of thirty-eight men and two organists. The conductor is a former concertmaster and assistant conductor of the Philharmonic Orchestra and is a well known composer. The Strand Theatre mains an orchestra of forty-nine men and two organists. The conductor is a graduate of the Leipsic Conservatory and was for some time professor of harmony and composition at the Cleveland Conservatory.

As Mr. Taylor points out, these orchestras do not indulge in operatic potpourris and so-called "popular classics." Their performances consist of the same pieces that appear upon the programs of the best symphony orchestras of the country, the Boston Symphony, the Philharmonic, the New York Symphony, the Philadelphia Symphony.

These five orchestras play to thousands where the symphony orchestras play to hundreds and the people prove that they enjoy the music, for they continue to pack these great theatres. Never have any of these orchestras found it necessary to lower the standard of their performances. It is difficult to estimate how much they are doing to educate the taste and the appreciation of the average New Yorker for first class orchestral music.

It is true that New York is the home of jazz, but the question may well be asked, how many other cities in the United States are supporting five, four, three, two or even one first class symphony orchestra in motion picture theatres?

Notes

Introduction

1. Roy Wilkins, *Standing Fast* (New York: The Viking Press, 1981), p. 53.
2. Nathan Irvin Huggins, *Black Odyssey: The Afro-American Ordeal in Slavery* (New York: Vintage Books, 1977), p. xii.
3. August Meier and Elliott Rudwick, "The Rise of the Black Secretariat in the NAACP, 1909–1935," *The Crisis* (February 1977): 65.
4. Arthenia Bates Millican, "James Weldon Johnson: In Quest of an Afrocentric Tradition for Black American Literature" (Ph.D. diss. Louisiana State University at Baton Rouge, 1972), p. 224.
5. Ibid.
6. James Weldon Johnson, *New York Age* editorial "Do You Read Negro Newspapers?" October 22, 1914.

Chapter 1

1. Johnson, *New York Age* editorial "How Opinion is Created," March 4, 1922.

Chapter 2

1. Robert L. Zangrando, "James Weldon Johnson and the Dyer Anti-Lynching Bill," *Langston Hughes Review* 8. nos. 1 and 2 (1989): 76–79.
2. Howard Reed Barksdale, "James Weldon Johnson, Man of Letters" (master's thesis, Fisk University, 1936), p. 45.
3. Ibid., p. 56.
4. Eugene Levy, *James Weldon Johnson: Black Leader, Black Voice* (Chicago: University of Chicago Press, 1973), p. 232.
5. See James Weldon Johnson's *Along This Way* (New York: Viking Press, 1933), p. 373.
6. Zangrando, "James Weldon Johnson and the Dyer Lynching Bill," p. 78.

Chapter 3

1. Johnson, *New York Age* editorial "Woman Suffrage," October 21, 1915.
2. Ibid.
3. Anna Julia Cooper's quote in Page Smith's *The Rise of Industrial America* (New York: McGraw-Hill, 1984), p. 657.

Chapter 5

1. John Hope Franklin, *From Slavery to Freedom* (New York: Vintage Books, 1969), p. 547.
2. James Weldon Johnson, *Negro Americans, What Now?* (New York: Viking Press, 1934), p. 43.
3. Franklin, *From Slavery to Freedom,* p. 549.
4. Ibid.

Chapter 6

1. Johnson, *Negro Americans, What Now?,* p. 86.
2. Ibid., p. 8

Chapter 7

1. Johnson, *New York Age* editorial "Responsibilities and Opportunities of the Colored Ministry," February 8, 1917.
2. Ibid.

Chapter 8

1. Johnson, *Negro Americans, What Now?* p. 29.
2. Rayford Logan, *The Betrayal of the Negro* (New York, Collier Books, 1969), p. 392.

Chapter 10

1. Johnson, *New York Age* editorial "The Candidate Who Squares Up to Requirements," October 15, 1914.

Chapter 11

1. Johnson, *New York Age* editorial "Under the Dome of the Capitol," May 3, 1917.

2. Johnson, *New York Age* editorial "Vote the Republican State Ticket," October 12, 1916.

3. Memorandum from James Weldon Johnson to Dr. W.E.B. Du Bois, December 8, 1922, James Weldon Johnson Papers in the James Weldon Johnson Memorial Collection of Negro Arts and Letters, Beinecke Library, Yale University.

4. Johnson, *New York Age* editorial "A New Third Party," March 25, 1922.

Chapter 12

1. Levy, *James Weldon Johnson,* p. 205.

Chapter 13

1. Johnson, *New York Age* editorial "When Is a Race Great?" March 11, 1918, and *The Book of American Negro Poetry,* ed. James Weldon Johnson (New York: Harcourt Brace Jovanovich, 1922; reprinted, 1969) p. 9.

2. Franklin, *From Slavery To Freedom,* p. 503.

Bibliography

Works By James Weldon Johnson

Along This Way: The Autobiography of James Weldon Johnson. New York: Viking Press, 1933. Reprinted, with an introduction by Sondra Kathryn Wilson, New York: Penguin Classics, 1990.

The Autobiography of an Ex-Colored Man. Boston: Sherman, French & Co., 1912. Reprinted, New York: Penguin Classics, 1990. Reprinted, with an introduction by Henry Louis Gates, Jr., New York: Alfred A. Knopf, 1990.

Black Manhattan. New York: Alfred A. Knopf, 1930. Reprinted, with an introduction by Sondra Kathryn Wilson, New York: Da Capo Press, 1991.

Fifty Years and Other Poems. Boston: Cornhill Publishers, 1917.

God's Trombones: Seven Negro Sermons in Verse. New York: Viking Press, 1927. Reprinted, New York: Penguin Classics, 1990. Produced on audio by Sondra Kathryn Wilson for Penguin-Highbridge, 1993.

Negro Americans, What Now? New York: Viking Press, 1934.

Saint Peter Relates an Incident: Selected Poems. New York: Viking Press, 1935. Reprinted, with a preface by Sondra Kathryn Wilson, New York: Penguin Classics, 1992.

The Book of American Negro Poetry, edited by James Weldon Johnson. New York: Harcourt Brace and World, 1922. Reprinted, New York: Harcourt Brace Jovanovich, 1969.

The Books of American Negro Spirituals, edited by James Weldon Johnson with J. Rosamond Johnson. New York: Viking Press, 1925–1926. Reprinted, New York: Da Capo Press, 1989.

Secondary Sources

Adelman, Lynn. "A Study of James Weldon Johnson." *Journal of Negro History* 52 (April 1967): 128–45.

Akar, John J. "An African View of Black Studies with International Dimensions." *CLA Journal* 14 (1970): 7–18.

Aptheker, Herbert. "Du Bois on James Weldon Johnson." *Journal of Negro History* 52 (1967): 224–27.

Bacote, Clarence A. "James Weldon Johnson and Atlanta University." *Phylon* 32 (1971): 333–43.

Baker, Houston. "A Forgotten Prototype: *The Autobiography of an Ex-Colored Man* and Invisible Man." In *Singers of Daybreak,* edited by Houston Baker. Washington, D.C.: Howard University Press, 1974.

Barksdale, Howard Reed. "James Weldon Johnson as a Man of Letters." Master's thesis, Fisk University, 1936.

Bone, Robert. *The Negro Novel in America.* New Haven: Yale University Press, 1965.

Braithewaite, William Stanley. "A Review of the *Autobiography of James Weldon Johnson.*" *Opportunity* 11 (1933): 376–78.

Bronz, Stephen H. *Roots of Negro Racial Consciousness, the 1920's: Three Harlem Renaissance Authors.* New York: Libra Publishers, 1964.

Canady, Nicholas. "*The Autobiograpy of an Ex-Colored Man* and the Traditions of Black Biography." *Obsidian* 6 (Spring–Summer 1980): 76–80.

Carroll, Richard A. "Black Racial Spirit: An Analysis of James Weldon Johnson's Critical Perspective." *Phylon* 32 (Winter 1971): 344–64.

Clark, Peter W. "A Study of the Poetry of James Weldon Johnson." Master's thesis, Xavier University, 1942.

Collier, Eugenia. "The Endless Journey of an Ex-Colored Man." *Phylon* 32 (Winter 1971): 365–73.

———. "James Weldon Johnson: Mirror of Change." *Phylon* 21 (Fourth Quarter, 1960): 351–59.

Copans, Sim J. "James Weldon Johnson et le patrimonie cultural des noirs africains." Cahiers de la compagnie Madeleine Renaud-Jean Louis Barrault 61 (1967): 42–48.

Davis, Arthur P. *From the Dark Tower: Afro-American Writers 1900 to 1960.* Washington, D.C.: Howard University Press, 1974.

Davis, Charles T. "The Heavenly Voice of the Black American." In *Anagogic Qualities of Literature,* edited by Joseph P. Strelka, 107–19. University Park: Pennsylvania State University Press, 1971.

Fleming, Robert E. "Contemporary Themes in Johnson's *Autobiography of an Ex-Colored Man.*" *Negro American Literature Forum* 4 (Winter 1970): 120–24, 141.

———. "Irony as a Key to Johnson's *The Autobiography of an Ex-Colored Man.*" *American Literature* 43 (March 1971): 83–96.

Gallagher, Buell G. "James Weldon Johnson: Man of Letters." *Crisis* 78 (Winter 682) (June 1971): 119–22.

Garrett, Marvin P. "Early Recollections and Structural Irony in *The Autobiography of an Ex-Colored Man.*" *Critique* 13 (1971): 5–14.

Huggins, Nathan Irvin. *Harlem Renaissance.* New York: Oxford University Press, 1971.

Jackson, Miles, Jr. "James Weldon Johnson." *Black World* 19 (June 1970): 32–34.

———. "Literary History: Documentary Sidelights: James Weldon Johnson and Claude McKay." *Negro Digest* 17 (June 1968): 25–29.

Kostelanetz, Richard. "The Politics of Passing: The Fiction of James Weldon Johnson." *Negro American Literature Forum* 3 (March 1969): 22–24, 29.

Levy, Eugene. *James Weldon Johnson: Black Leader, Black Voice.* Chicago: University of Chicago Press, 1973.

———. "James Weldon Johnson." In *Black Leaders of the Twentieth Century,* edited by John Hope Franklin and August Meir. Chicago: University of Chicago Press, 1980.

Lewis, David Levering. *When Harlem Was in Vogue*. New York: Oxford University Press, 1989.

————. *The Portable Harlem Renaissance Reader*. New York: Viking Penguin, 1994.

Logan, Rayford W. and Michael R. Winston. "James Weldon Johnson," *Dictionary of Negro Biography*. New York: W.W. Norton, 1981, 353–57.

Long, Richard A. "A Weapon of My Song: The Poetry of James Weldon Johnson." *Phylon* 32 (Winter 1971): 374–82.

Mason, Julian. "James Weldon Johnson." *In Fifty Southern Writers After 1900*, edited by Joseph M. Flora and Robert Bain, 280–89. New York: Greenwood Press, 1987.

Miller, Ruth, and Peter J. Katopes. "The Harlem Renaissance: Arna Bontemps, Countee Cullen, James Weldon Johnson, Claude McKay, and Jean Toomer." In *Black American Writers: Bibliographical Essays. Vol. 1, The Beginnings Through the Harlem Renaissance and Langston Hughes,* edited by Thomas Inge, et al., 161–206. New York: St. Martin's Press, 1978.

Millican, Arthenia Bates. "James Weldon Johnson: In Quest of an Afrocentric Tradition for Black American Literature." Ph.D. diss., Louisiana State University, 1972.

O'Sullivan, Maurice J. "Of Souls and Pottage: James Weldon Johnson's *The Autobiography of an Ex-Colored Man*." *CLA Journal* 23 (September 1979): 60–70.

Ovington, Mary White. *The Walls Came Tumbling Down: The Autobiography of Mary White Ovington, a Founder of the NAACP*. New York: Schocken Books, 1947.

Redding, J. Saunders. *To Make A Poet Black*. Chapel Hill: University of North Carolina Press, 1939. Reprinted, College Park, Md.: McGrath Publishing Co., 1968.

Rosenblatt, Roger. "*The Autobiography of an Ex-Colored Man*." In *Black Fiction*, Cambridge: Harvard University Press, 1974. 173–84.

Skerret, Joseph T., Jr. "Irony and Symbolic Action in James Weldon Johnson's *The Autobiography of an Ex-Colored Man*." *American Quarterly* 32 (Winter 1980): 540–48.

Starke, Catherine Juanita. *Black Portraiture in American Fiction: Stock Characters, Archetypes, and Individuals*. New York: Basic Books, 1971.

Whitlow, Roger. *Black American Literature: A Critical History*. Chicago: Nelson-Hall, 1973.

Wilson, Sondra Kathryn, guest editor. "Collected Writings of James Weldon Johnson." *Langston Hughes Review* 7 (Spring/Fall 1989).

————. "James Weldon Johnson." *Crisis* Winter (January 1989): 48–51, 117, 118.

———— with Warren Marr. *Paying For Freedom: The Story of the NAACP Life Membership Program*. New York: NAACP Press, 1988.

Wohlforth, Robert. "Dark Leader: James Weldon Johnson." *New Yorker,* September 30, 1933, 20–24.

Young, James O. *Black Writers of the Thirties*. Baton Rouge: Louisiana State University Press, 1973.

Index